Hypatia's Heritage

MARGARET ALIC

Hypatia's Heritage

A History of Women in Science from Antiquity
through the Nineteenth Century

Beacon Press   Boston

Beacon Press
25 Beacon Street
Boston, Massachusetts 02108

Beacon Press books are published under the auspices
of the Unitarian Universalist Association
of Congregations in North America.

First published by The Women's Press Limited in 1986

Printed in the United States of America

92 91 90 89 88 87 86   8 7 6 5 4 3 2 1

Library of Congress Cataloging-in-Publication Data

Alic, Margaret.
  Hypatia's heritage.

  Bibliography: p.
  Includes index.
  1. Women in science—History.   I. Title.
Q130.A48   1986b   509.2'2   86-47510
ISBN 0-8070-6730-X
ISBN 0-8070-6731-8 (pbk.)

Contents

Acknowledgments

Over the years many people have contributed their talents to the researching and writing of this book.

Debbie Lev has been a part of the project from its inception. Together we began to research the history of women in science. And together we taught the women's studies class that was the seed for this book. My discussions with her have been of the greatest value. Debbie has also read and criticised portions of the manuscript and she contributed the illustrations of Maria's apparatus and the astrolabe.

John Alic, Nick Allen, Howard Cutler, Esther Lev, Deb Simes, Lillie Wilson and Anndy Wiselogle read various chapters and offered many helpful suggestions and ideas. Lembi Kongas provided guidance when I found myself lost in a maze of anthropological theories. Jim and Anita Alic, Bella Brodzki, Shirley Lev, Jonathan Potkin, Marjorie Speirs, Noam Stampfer and Jeff Zucker all contributed in other ways to the completion of this book. I am grateful to each of them for their ongoing encouragement.

In addition to reading the manuscript and suggesting a number of improvements, Dale Spender has devoted herself to seeing the work through to publication.

I am grateful to Ros de Lanerolle and Jen Green, the editors at The Women's Press, and to the Women's Studies Program of Portland State University for believing in this project. And it could never have been completed without the valuable assistance of the interlibrary loan librarians at the Multnomah County Library, Portland State University and the Oregon Graduate Center.

Michael R. Smith spent countless days and weeks editing drafts of all but the last few chapters of the manuscript. Whatever merits this book may possess are, in large part, due to Michael. He was the perfect editor.

I am grateful to all of these people for their contributions and encouragement. However, I alone am responsible for whatever errors appear here. Some errors are, unfortunately, inevitable in a field of history as new as this one. Research on the history of women in science has barely begun.

Margaret Alic, Portland, Oregon, July 1985

Illustrations

Grateful acknowledgement is made for permission to reprint:

Hypatia. From Elbert Hubbard, *Little Journeys to the Homes of Great Teachers* (New York: William Wise & Co., 1928).

The Pythagorean Universe. From Gerald Tauber, *Man's View Of The Universe* (New York: Crown Publishers, Inc., 1979).

The *Tribikos*. From a drawing by Debbie Lev, after F. Sherwood Taylor's reconstruction, 'The Evolution of the Still', *Annals of Science* 5 (1945).

The *Kerotakis*. From a drawing by Debbie Lev, Ibid.

The Gold-Making of Cleopatra. From C.A. Burland, *The Arts of The Alchemists* (London: Weidenfeld, 1967).

The components of a plane astrolabe. From a drawing by Debbie Lev.

Hildegard's first scheme of the universe. From Charles Singer, *From Magic to Science: Essays on the Scientific Twilight* (New York: Dover Books, 1958).

Hildegard's later scheme of the universe. Ibid.

Elisabeth and Johannes Hevelius. From P.V. Rizzo, 'Early Daughters of Urania', *Sky & Telescope* 14.

Title page to Emilie du Châtelet's translation of Newton's *Principia*. Courtesy of I. Bernard Cohen.

From Mary Somerville's *The Connexion of the Physical Sciences*, revd., *The Athenaeum* 221 (1832).

Margaret Cavendish by Abraham van Diepenbeke. Courtesy of the Mansell Collection.

Marie Lavoisier's illustration of the 'gazometer'. From *Traité elementaire de chemie* (Paris: Couchet, 1789).

Anna Morandi Manzolini. From Geoffrey Marks and William K. Beatty, *Women in White* (New York: The Scribner's Book Companies, Inc., 1972).

The Herschel's house at Datchet. From Fred Hoyle, *Astronomy* (New York: Doubleday & Co, Inc., 1962).

Herschel's 40-foot telescope. Ibid.

Caroline Herschel. From J.B. Sidgwick, *William Herschel: Explorer of the Heavens* (London: Faber & Faber, 1953). Courtesy of the History Museum of Hanover.

Emilie du Châtelet. From Andre Maurel, *The Romance of Mme du Châtelet & Voltaire* (D. Appleton, 1931).

Ada Lovelace. From Doris Langley Moore, *Ada: Countess of Lovelace* (New York: Harper & Row, Publishers, Inc., 1977).

Sóphia Kovalévsky. From Sofya Kovalevskaya, *A Russian Childhood* (Berlin: Springer-Verlag, 1978).

Mary Somerville. From Teri Pearl, *Math Equals: Biographies of Women Mathematicians + Related Activities* (Menlo Park, Ca: Addison Wesley, 1978). Courtesy of Culver Pictures.

1 Hypatia

Introduction

Science is that body of knowledge that describes, defines and, where possible, explains the universe – the matter that constitutes it, the organisms that inhabit it, the physical laws that govern it. This knowledge accumulates by a slow, arduous process of speculation, experimentation and discovery that has been an integral part of human activity since the dawn of the race. Women have always played an essential role in this process.

Yet we think of the history of science as a history of men. More than that, we think of the history of science as the story of a very few men – Aristotle, Copernicus, Newton, Einstein – men who drastically altered our view of the universe. But the history of science is much more than that. It is the story of the thousands of people who contributed to the knowledge and theories that constituted the science of their eras and made the 'great leaps' possible. Many of these people were women. Yet their story remains virtually unknown.

This is a history of women in science that begins in prehistoric times and ends with the last decade of the nineteenth century – just as Marie Curie began to uncover the mysteries of radioactivity. Her work would change forever, not only our understanding of the physical universe, but the structure of scientific research and the position of women scientists.

This book covers the work of women in the physical and natural sciences and mathematics. (It should be noted that by the nineteenth century mathematics had advanced to the point where the contributions of women would be accessible only to students of mathematics – therefore it has not been possible here to explain the details of their work.) It will be left to others to document the immense contributions of women to the development of the social sciences. The practice of medicine is both a natural science and a social science. The position of women in the medical profession has always been closely linked to the position of women in other sciences and a history of women in science cannot neglect the story of women physicians. However the emphasis here is on women's contributions to medical science rather than their work as medical practitioners. Likewise, the distinction between science and technology is often a fine line. Here the emphasis is on those technological developments by women that were either based on their own scientific work or that directly benefited scientific research.

Unfortunately, the history of science as we know it is primarily a history of western science. Woman's role in the independent and advanced scientific tradition of China is just beginning to be revealed. Other societies and cultures throughout the world developed their own science and women most certainly made important contributions to those traditions. Such work, however, is beyond the scope of this book.

The rich and significant heritage of American women in science will not be considered here. Although the first important American woman scientist – the astronomer Maria Mitchell – flourished in the mid-nineteenth century, she was the originator of a long and branching lineage of distinguished American women scientists working within the confines of the women's colleges. It was a tradition that continued well into the twentieth century. To tell the story of Maria Mitchell and other American women scientists of the late nineteenth century would take us far beyond the time frame of this book. Their exciting story will have to wait.

Scientific work requires intelligence, creativity, education and determination. As a result, the history of science is always the history of a select group of individuals. The history of women in science is, unfortunately, even more selective. For the most part, it is the story of privileged women in a position to attain an education and pursue scientific interests despite their exclusion from educational facilities and the formal and informal fraternities of male scientists. With a few important exceptions these women, like their male counterparts, came from the upper classes and had the resources that enabled them to pursue their studies.

Just as the woman scientist's position in society was fundamentally different from that of the male scientist, much of her scientific work was also fundamentally different. Women overcame major obstacles to become scientists, often at the expense of their personal lives. Their priorities were their own. Yet these women made substantial contributions to science. We have to recognise the existence of their work before its significance can be fairly assessed.

At times the woman scientist was a truly rare phenomenon – a cultural curiosity. At other times it was common for women to pursue scientific endeavours although their contributions are not generally recognised. Those women of whom we have record almost certainly represent only a small minority of female scientists. The story of one woman may suggest the existence of an unrecognised sub-culture within a community. For this reason it is important to consider, not only those women who made documented contributions to science, but also women who devoted themselves to scientific interests. They reflect the historical reality of women's continuing interest in and aptitude for science. It is in societies where an interest in science was widespread among women that historians should begin to search for lost women scientists of the past.

For most of recorded history western societies have been dominated by men. History books reflect this male bias. They have ignored the history of women. As science and technology became increasingly valued by patriarchal societies, the scientific work of women was increasingly devalued. As more people, women and men alike, became interested in science, the assertions that women were incapable of scientific work became more vehement. Today, science and technology have come to dominate our society. And once again we are hearing that women are incapable of scientific creativity.

But women are fighting back. They are speaking out against such patriarchal attitudes. They are asserting that women, including women scientists, can change the world. And one step toward such change is to rediscover the history of women in science.

Prologue

In March 1696 the alchemist, philosopher and 'scholar gypsy' Francis Mercury van Helmont arrived in Hanover. There he met with the founder of modern German science, Gottfried Wilhelm von Leibniz, and Leibniz's closest colleague, the Electress Sophia of Hanover. Van Helmont had brought with him a recently published book, *The Principles of the Most Ancient and Modern Philosophy*, which was to become a cornerstone of Leibniz's new philosophy of nature. As such, it profoundly influenced the development of eighteenth-century natural philosophy and the rise of modern science. Although no author's name appeared on the title page of *The Principles*, the preface attributed the work to 'a certain English Countess, a Woman learn'd beyond her sex, being very well skill'd in the Latin and Greek tongues, and exceedingly well vers'd in all kinds of Philosophy.' The English Countess was the Lady Anne Finch Conway, a 'forgotten' woman from the history of science.

Anne Conway was not unique. Hundreds of women scientists have been excluded from our history books. In every society and in every historical era women participated in the development of science and technology. They observed nature, experimented in laboratories, developed techniques, designed apparatus and speculated about the structure of the universe. Like Anne Conway, these women devised philosophical systems to explain the world around them and reconcile their empirical observations of nature with the dictates of moral philosophy and religion. And, like Anne Conway, they have been lost to history.

The story of Lady Conway is a fitting introduction to the history of women in science. She was in some respects the archetypal woman scientist: a member of the aristocracy, she embarked on a rigorous course of self-education, made her contributions to science, and was forgotten. Her philosophy of nature represented one of the last attempts to cement together the spiritual and material worlds into an organic whole. Indeed, for a time Conway's 'vitalistic' natural philosophy – encompassing a universe made up of basic indivisible particles called 'monads', each endowed with a vital life force – stood in lone opposition to the mechanistic universe based on mathematical law as devised by René Descartes and Sir Isaac Newton.

Yet today, despite a renewed interest in vitalistic philosophy amongst some of the scientific community, Anne Conway remains virtually unknown. For reasons of propriety her name was omitted from the title page of her most important treatise, and her work attributed to its editor, Francis van Helmont. Anne Conway was thus robbed of the credit she deserved because of her sex, just as so many other women have had their work attributed to male scientists, been demoted posthumously to the position of assistant or 'help-mate', or had their very existence denied by historians. It is these women who are the subject of this chronicle. And Anne Conway seems a good place to begin.

Anne (née Finch) was born in December 1631 in London's Kensington House, now Kensington Palace. At the age of 12 she was taken ill with a fever, which precipitated the migraine attacks that were to recur with increasing frequency and severity for the rest of her life. In typical seventeenth-century fashion, her family attributed her headaches to over-zealous study, for at an early age Anne had mastered several languages and had developed a serious interest in science and philosophy.

Very few seventeenth-century women had the advantage of a formal education, but Anne was more fortunate than most. She had an older brother, John, who provided her with books and directed her studies. And it was her brother who first introduced her to the ideas of Descartes, the French natural philosopher whose work became a central focus of the scientific revolution. Descartes was just becoming known in England through the efforts of John's teacher, the Cambridge platonist, Henry More. About 1650, shortly before John left for Italy, Anne wrote to More herself requesting assistance with her studies. At a time when women were expected to confine their interests to the domestic arts, this was an extraordinary step, but it proved to be the beginning of a relationship that was to provide both her – and Henry More – with intellectual and emotional sustenance for nearly 30 years. More began to translate Descartes for Anne's personal use and his earliest letters to her, evolving into a voluminous correspondence, were treatises on the Cartesian philosophy that they would both eventually come to challenge.

At the age of 19, Anne married Edward, Viscount Killultagh, first Earl of Conway. With her new husband frequently away on business, the young countess found herself with ample time for scholarly pursuits. She taught herself mathematics and astronomy, and studied the ancient Greek geometry of Euclid with a tutor.

Anne Conway's friendship with Henry More grew. After the Conways moved from London to Ragley Hall in Warwickshire, More was a frequent visitor, later becoming a more or less permanent resident. In July 1653 Conway and More began to study the *Kabbala*, the traditional mediaeval mystical text derived from the Hebrew scriptures and an important source for the theories of alchemy. It was no coincidence that in her search for the organic unity of nature, Anne based her philosophy on the ancient alchemical and Kabbalist traditions that maintained the equality of male and female principles.

But Anne's health was deteriorating. After a bout of smallpox that claimed the life of her two-year-old son in 1660, she was never again free of the debilitating pain that frequently interfered with her work. Her numerous physicians were of little use: twice she nearly died as a result of their mercury treatments. The great doctor William Harvey pronounced her incurable, as did the famous faith-healer Valentine Greatrakes. After 1664 Anne Conway never again left Ragley Hall.

In 1654 the romantic and already legendary figure of Francis Mercury van Helmont, an editor of the *Kabbala Denudata*, the largest collection of Latin Kabbalist treatises, first appeared in John Finch's letters to his sister from Italy. The son of a famous iatrochemist (one of those who envisioned the human body as a chemical system and who began to apply alchemical principles to medicine), van Helmont was thought to be in possession of a universal panacea, and Finch hoped his remedy could cure Anne's migraines.

In 1670 van Helmont arrived in England bearing letters to Henry More from another woman scholar, Elizabeth of Bohemia. His intended one-month's stay in England was to last nearly ten years, most of it spent at Ragley Hall where he set up a chemistry laboratory with More. Like others before him, van Helmont was unsuccessful in his attempts to cure the Countess's headaches, but despite her chronic illness, Ragley Hall became an intellectual centre and Anne Conway was its centrepiece.[1]

Although she lived in the shadow of two of the most learned men of her generation, Anne remained an independent thinker. She went far beyond the work of More and van Helmont in creating an original and complete philosophical synthesis. Seventeenth-century science was beginning to challenge the old Christian precepts and Anne Conway hoped to reconcile her religion with the new scientific theories: and she was one of the first publicly to dispute the philosophy of Descartes. Descartes had formulated a mechanistic universe of matter in motion in which all living organisms were reduced to mere machines. Human beings alone possessed a soul – and this was altogether separate from the world of matter. Conway denied this distinction between matter and spirit, viewing them as inextricably entwined. To her, nature was not a cosmic machine but a living entity, made up of individual monads endowed with a vital force and organised and integrated by the Cosmic Order. Matter and spirit were interchangeable.

Like many seventeenth- and eighteenth-century naturalists, Anne Conway believed that the different species of plants and animals were organised in a continuous Great Chain of Being: a hierarchy of nature increasing in complexity and culminating, on earth, with humans. The self-educated philosopher and feminist Lady Mary Lee Chudleigh (1656-1710) wrote:

> we have reason to believe, that as we see an innumerable Company of Beings below us, and each Species to be less perfect in its kind, till they end in a Point, an indivisible Solid: so there are almost an infinite Number of Beings above us, who as much exceed us, as we do the minutest Insect, or the smallest Plant.[2]

Conway's insistence that matter could undergo monadic transformation into higher forms paved the way for the development of modern evolutionary theories.

After Anne Conway's death in 1679, van Helmont returned to continental Europe taking with him a number of her papers. Among them was her notebook written between 1671 and 1675 and containing her philosophical system. Believing her work to be of lasting importance, van Helmont arranged for its publication in

Holland in 1690 in Latin translation. Two years later it was
translated back into English and published in London as *The
Principles of the Most Ancient and Modern Philosophy, Concerning
God, Christ, and the Creature; that is, concerning Spirit, and Matter
in General.* It was to have a significance far beyond its small size and
readership.

Prior to van Helmont's arrival in Hanover with Conway's book,
Leibniz had carried out a lengthy correspondence on van Helmont's
philosophical writings with his pupil and friend, the Electress Sophia
of Hanover, from whom he had obtained two of van Helmont's books.
In long discussions with Leibniz and Sophia, van Helmont now
carefully explained the ideas contained in Conway's work. It was the
formative period of Leibniz's philosophy and within a few months he
was using the term 'monad' to describe elemental matter. Conway's
concept of the monad as the indivisible basis of all matter and life
eventually coalesced into Leibniz's philosophical system – the
'monadology.'

By the time Leibniz read the work of Anne Conway, Sir Isaac
Newton's *Principia* had already been published, replacing Descartes's
arbitrary mechanistic hypotheses with a mechanistic cosmology
based on mathematical law. In opposition to both the Cartesian
mechanistic universe and the Newtonian universe of elemental
particles possessing gravity, Leibniz proposed a universe consisting
of monads endowed with life force – a concept derived from Anne
Conway.

Although the scientific revolution finally culminated in the
triumph of the Newtonian world view, controversy over the
mechanistic versus vitalistic hypotheses continued to rage for years.
In the 1730s, when Emilie du Châtelet introduced the works of
Newton to the French scientific community, she presented the
forces vives (the vital monads of Conway and Leibniz) as the
metaphysical basis for Newtonian physics. The *forces vives* remained
a subject of debate in France until late in the eighteenth century and
the vitalists had a major influence on the German natural philosophers and the development of modern biology. Yet Anne Conway's
contributions to vitalism went unrecognised. Although Leibniz
himself repeatedly acknowledged the 'Countess of Kennaway' as the
source for his ideas, her work continued to be attributed to van
Helmont.

At a crucial time in the history of science – the early days of the scientific revolution – Anne Conway was a natural philosopher of the first rank. But she was by no means alone. Her work influenced, and was influenced by, that of other women philosophers.

Ironically these women are remembered today for their social and political positions rather than their science. But just as Anne Conway supplied More and van Helmont with new ideas and subjects for study, so Elizabeth of Bohemia, the Princess Palatine (1618–1680), influenced her teacher Descartes, and Elizabeth's sister, the Electress Sophia of Hanover, inspired Leibniz. Elizabeth of Bohemia later studied with Leibniz and corresponded with van Helmont, but it was to Descartes that she owed her allegiance. She was the philosopher's closest friend and colleague, and many of their letters concern the duality of matter and spirit. Elizabeth lectured on Cartesian philosophy at the University of Heidelberg and Descartes dedicated his *Principles of Philosophy* (1644) to her. Their extensive correspondence evolved into his *Treatise on the Passions*, dedicated to Queen Christine of Sweden.[3]

The Electress Sophia (1630–1714) was Leibniz's closest associate, both politically and intellectually, from the 1670s until her death, in the year her son became King George I of Great Britain, and she also carried on an extensive philosophical correspondence with van Helmont. Her daughter Sophia Charlotte (1668–1705) studied with Leibniz as well, and in 1700 persuaded her husband, Frederick I of Prussia, to establish the Berlin Academy with Leibniz as its perpetual president.

Sophia Charlotte's ward, Caroline of Brandenburg-Ansbach (1683–1737), first studied with Leibniz in 1696, shortly before she became the Princess of Wales. Later, as Queen, her court included Newton, Samuel Clarke and Lady Mary Montagu among the frequent visitors. It was Queen Caroline who mediated the famous 1716 correspondence between Leibniz and Clarke, a disciple of Newton, on the conflict between the mechanistic and vitalistic philosophies.

Leibniz also carried on a scientific and philosophical correspondence with Lady Damaris Masham (1658–1708), daughter of Anne Conway's friend Ralph Cudworth and a student of John Locke.

But within this impressive circle of women philosophers, it was Anne Conway who made the greatest contribution to the history of science. Above all else the scientific revolution concerned the nature and relationship of matter and motion – the life work of Anne Conway – and she should not be forgotten.

Throughout history women scientists have been ignored, robbed of credit and forgotten. Their scientific work has been suppressed or expropriated in a variety of ways. Often women were recognised and respected as scientists in their own day, but were ignored or discredited by later historians who refused to acknowledge that women had been important scientists. Although there were probably female scientists in virtually every culture and era, most of the truly successful women scientists flourished in societies that were receptive, at least in part, to the female scholar. Yet the more serious a woman was about her science, the more difficult her situation became. Thus, although amateur science was generally looked upon as an acceptable preoccupation for the English lady of the eighteenth and nineteenth centuries, Lady Mary Montagu and Mary Somerville both chose to settle in Italy with its thousand-year tradition of respected women scholars.

Since very few women had access to formal education many women scientists were dependent on their fathers, brothers or husbands for their training. This meant they were in constant danger of having their work attributed to their male colleagues. Many of these men were careful to give the women proper credit. It was usually other scientists and later historians who robbed them of their due, since every major accomplishment by a woman scientist spoke out strongly for the equality of women. Other women had the significance of their scientific work undercut both by their contemporaries and by later historians who cast aspersions on their personal lives.

Women scientists often chose to publish under a male pseudonym to ensure that their work would be taken seriously. Problems of identifying authorship were further compounded by a woman's loss of her name upon marriage. Sometimes, as with the early alchemists, women were forced to disguise their identities for political and religious reasons. As a result these are the least known of women scientists.

Several of the women in this book were outspoken feminists but most women scientists were neither revolutionaries nor champions of women's rights. They were too busy conducting scientific research. Some of them, like the astronomer Caroline Herschel, suffered from very low self-esteem fostered by a lifetime of sexual oppression. They frequently devalued their own contributions to science. Very few women scientists were willing to jeopardise their social position or go against the dictates of propriety in order to receive credit for their work. Thus, like Anne Conway, their publications were anonymous or appeared under a pseudonym.

There is an important and neglected aspect of the history of science. It is the story of the women who have carried on the tradition of scientific and technological advance from prehistoric times up to the present day. My heroine is Woman the Discoverer.

1
Goddesses and Gatherers: Women in Prehistory

[Women] have been essential to the making of history. Thus, all history as we know it, is merely pre-history. (Gerda Lerner, p. 366)

I. The First Women Scientists

Even the simplest tool made out of a broken bough or a chipped stone is the fruit of long experience ... The skill to make it has been acquired by observation, by recollection, and by experiment. It may seem an exaggeration, but it is yet true to say that any tool is an embodiment of *science*. For it is a practical application of remembered, compared, and collected experiences of the same kind as are systematized and summarized in scientific formulas, descriptions, and prescriptions.(V. Gordon Childe, 1964, p. 15)

The systematic development of knowledge and technology that we call 'science' originated in the millennia of prehistory, and early women were among these first 'scientists'. They invented tools, accumulated knowledge about edible and medicinal plants, and probably discovered 'the chemistry of pot-making, the physics of spinning, the mechanics of the loom, and the botany of flax and cotton'.[1] These developments occurred over long periods of time, arising independently in different parts of the world. Progress resulted from the activities of many individuals, both male and female, for most early societies were probably egalitarian, with women involved in every aspect of subsistence and therefore in every aspect of developing science and technology.

Traditionally anthropologists have emphasised the skills and tools (or weapons) of 'Man the Hunter'; but until recently they have ignored the knowledge and tools acquired by 'Woman the Food Gatherer'. Gathering, rather than hunting, was the primary subsistence activity of our early ancestors, and women gatherers were the first 'botanists'. Through a process of experimentation they learned to distinguish between hundreds of plants at various stages of growth; they identified locations and habitats; named species and varieties; and discovered methods for neutralising or removing poisons from otherwise edible vegetation. Food-gathering requires a concept of time, and prehistoric women learned to relate astronomical events, such as the phases of the moon or the rising of a star, to seasons and the availability of plant products. Their ability to exploit new sources of vegetable sustenance improved steadily over thousands of years, each generation passing on its cumulative knowledge.

Early women developed the tools and technology they needed to gather, prepare and preserve food. Carriers for food and infants – slings woven from plant fibres – 'may have been one of the most fundamental advances in human evolution.'[2] Women used sticks, levers, hand axes and simple flints for digging roots and scraping and pulverising plant material. Later, they invented the mortar and pestle, and a primitive mill for grinding grain and seeds. (The tools developed by prehistoric women for preparing and cooking food are still in evidence in modern-day chemistry laboratories.) As hunting became more important, women learned to butcher and process animal products and how to tan and convert leather to a variety of uses. They invented needles and discovered natural dyes and colour fixatives.

Women have always been healers, surgeons and midwives. As gatherers they discovered the medicinal properties of plants and learned how to dry, store and mix botanicals. Through experimentation and careful observation they discovered which herbs provided effective treatment for various ailments. It can be argued that there was little improvement in medical science from the prehistoric woman botanist experimenting with roots and herbs, until the discovery of sulpha drugs and antibiotics in the twentieth century.

Our early ancestors learned to prepare clay and fire pottery and they discovered the chemistry of glazes. The kilns of early women potters eventually evolved into the forges of the Metal Ages. By

Cro-Magnon times women were manufacturing jewellery and mixing cosmetics – the origins of the science of chemistry.

The most important revolution in human history took place about 14,000 years ago with the beginnings of crop cultivation and the domestication of animals. No one knows exactly how it came about, but during the small-scale horticultural stage intermediate between a gathering–hunting and an agricultural way of life, women selected wild plants for cultivation and developed new edible varieties. In the 'Fertile Crescent' – from the Mesopotamian valleys of the Tigris and Euphrates to the Nile Valley of Egypt – women domesticated barley, flax, millet and wheat from wild grasses; in China they domesticated rice, and in North America, potatoes and maize. Altogether some 250 species of plants were cultivated in prehistoric times. This selective breeding of useful plants and animals marks the beginnings of the science of genetics.

In horticultural societies cultivation was usually the work of women. But their technological advances in tool-making, crafts and agriculture, including the invention of the hoe and a primitive plough, freed men from the rigours of hunting. Thus, with the shift to the ploughing and irrigation of permanent fields, agriculture became the domain of men.[3] Likewise, as the importance of animal-herding increased, the role of women in caring for livestock diminished. In the Fertile Crescent this change occurred about 10,000 BC.

With the development of agriculture, the rate of technological advance accelerated dramatically. By 6000 BC the peoples of the Fertile Crescent, the Indus Valley and China were reshaping the face of the earth for the first time. Planned cultivation required systematic astronomical observations and calendars. The wheel was invented and wheeled carts moved goods and people. The potter's wheel transformed the manufacture of household utensils into a specialised craft. Textile industries flourished, and cloth became a major trading commodity of the Phoenicians, who sailed the Mediterranean establishing contact and trade among the peoples of the Fertile Crescent. By 1100 BC metal weapons and tools became widely available and civilisations entered the Iron Age.

Agricultural surpluses supported the new urban populations of specialised craftspeople, merchants, clerks and priests. Larger and more complex social organisation, and the requirements of planned agriculture, industry and trade led to the development of sophisticated number notations, systems of weights and measures, and, finally, to written language.

Agriculture and pottery were now firmly in the hands of men. With the loss of her primary role in food production and manufacture, woman's opportunities and her economic and political status diminished. As we enter the era of recorded history, we find that the role of women in developing science and technology, while still important, had already begun to decline.

Nevertheless the contributions of those early women were not forgotten. The oral histories of early societies form the basis of the myths and religions of the Bronze Age in which women had a prominent place. Goddesses and heroines invent tools, develop agriculture and study astronomy and medicine. Thus, evidence for the early scientific work of women can be traced in these oral traditions.

2. Goddesses and Heroines

The Mother Goddess religions, so widespread during the Bronze Age, are usually dismissed as fertility cults. While it is true that male deities were often more important in early religions, the powers and attributes of the goddesses should not be underestimated. Female deities, such as the pre-Olympian Gaia and her daughter Themis, created the earth and its inhabitants, establishing order from chaos. Later goddesses contributed the tools essential for the development of civilisation. Neolithic women were often thought to be possessed of magical powers, not only because of their ability to give birth, but also because of their skills in the domestic sciences – manufacturing, pottery, agriculture, the domestication of animals and healing. It was these achievements that early cultures personified in their goddesses.

The most important of all the goddesses of antiquity was Isis, the Mother Goddess of the early Egyptians. Women retained a prominent place in Egyptian civilisation longer than in neighbouring Neolithic societies and Isis was often represented as promoting equality for all people. Perhaps this was why Isis cults were particularly attractive to women, commoners and slaves. These cults flourished in Rome and throughout the Mediterranean well into the Christian era.

The attributes of Isis and the rituals associated with her worship were typical of goddesses world-wide. Isis gave the indigenous people of the Nile their laws, religion, writing and medicine (as did Ishtar for the Assyrians); she invented the embalming process and the science of alchemy; most importantly, she taught the Egyptians agriculture and how to make food from grain. In port-cities she became the patroness of navigation and commerce, perhaps because she was credited with inventing the sailing boat. As her cult spread, she became identified with innumerable other Mediterranean goddesses.

In contrast to the Egyptians, Greek mythology contained very little magic. This may be one reason why Greek society was so conducive to the early development of natural philosophy – the study of nature and the physical universe – for despite their home high on Mount Olympus, the Greek deities were essentially down-to-earth. Not only did they resemble humans physically, but they embodied human virtues and vices, achievements and failures. Only their immortality distinguished them from their human prototypes. The Etruscans and their Roman successors lifted a large part of their mythology from the Greeks.

While lacking the supreme power of Isis, Pallas Athena, the patroness of Athens (Roman Minerva) was another all-purpose goddess, and one of the most important Greek deities. She symbolised wisdom (her symbol was the owl) and purity, and like Isis, Athena–Minerva was credited with many of the major advances made by women during the long millennia of prehistory. As the goddess of agriculture she invented the plough and bridle, and taught the Greeks to yoke oxen and tame horses. She created the olive tree and first pressed olive oil. She also presided over crafts, and thus invented the cart, iron weapons and armour (as goddess of war, she symbolised strategy). She invented numbers and made the first flute, although she never learned to play it.

The Greek Demeter (Sumerian Nisaba), who with Dionysos ruled supreme on earth, was the goddess of corn and grain. Ceres, the Roman goddess of grain and fertility, childbirth and death, was eventually assimilated into Demeter. The later Christian historians were reluctant to ascribe much credit to these goddesses: Boccaccio identified Ceres as a mortal Queen of Sicily who invented agriculture, the plough and ploughshare, domesticated oxen, and first made grain into leavened bread.

Women were usually credited with the invention of spinning and weaving. Isis, Athena and Minerva all taught their peoples to spin and weave linen. The Egyptian Neith, like Athena, ruled over the unlikely combination of war and the domestic sciences, including weaving. But Pliny's *Natural History* credited a mortal woman, Pamphile of Cea in Greece, with first picking cotton and learning to comb it, spin it into thread on a distaff and weave it into cloth.[4] The story is also told of Arachne of Colophon, an Asian peasant woman who discovered the uses of woven cloth and invented nets for catching fish or birds. But she was a foolhardy woman who boasted that she was a better weaver than Minerva. The goddess, hearing of this conceit, challenged her to a weaving contest. Some say that Arachne lost to Minerva, others that the two were judged to be equal. Either way Minerva was furious. In a rage she slit Arachne's net and beat her with a shuttle. Then, overcome with shame, Arachne hanged herself and Minerva turned her into a spider so that she could continue to weave. (Whether Minerva acted out of anger or remorse presumably depends on how one feels about spiders.)

Women were also credited with less traditional accomplishments. The Egyptian Seshat was patroness of writing, literature and history (the female Greek muses had the same functions). She was also the goddess of the stars and aided builders in the stellar alignment of temples and other structures. Isis was sometimes identified as the patroness of astronomy. Urania, the Greek muse of astronomy, was pictured holding a celestial globe in her left hand, to which she pointed with a small staff.

That women were acquainted with mathematical principles is illustrated by the story of Dido (whose name means heroic). When her brother, King Pygmalion of the Phoenician centre of Tyre, murdered her husband, Dido fled the city, pausing just long enough to seize her husband's money. While sailing away, she pretended to throw the money overboard, thus successfully sidetracking her pursuers. Eventually she landed on the coast of North Africa where she founded the great city of Carthage. A clever businesswoman, she offered to buy the land for her city from the natives, and to pay a specified price for as much land as could be enclosed by a bull's hide. She then proceeded to solve the mathematical problem of enclosing a maximum area within a fixed perimeter. She cut the hide into very thin strips and tied them end to end, enclosing a semi-circle bounded on one side by the sea. She had solved a problem whose mathematical proof was finally achieved in the nineteenth century.

Since women were the healers of the ancient world, it followed that goddesses would have jurisdiction over sickness and health. Most deities had some healing powers, for in a world of disease the need to pray to a goddess of medicine arose more frequently than the occasion to call on the goddess of astronomy or the alphabet, say. Even cultures which worshipped medical gods, including the Greeks, always had female deities presiding over childbirth and diseases specific to women. The Romans took the cult of medical deities to extremes – they seem to have had a god or goddess for nearly every symptom of disease; some of these goddesses probably represented the deification of early women physicians.

Foremost among the medical goddesses were Isis, Artemis and Minerva. The Greek goddess Ilithyia presided over childbirth. Hygeia (from which the English 'hygene' is derived) (Roman Salus) was the Greek goddess of health. She was the daughter of the god Asclepius (a deified Thessalian physician?) and sister of Panacea (the origin of our word for 'universal cure') who restored health. The temples of Hygeia and Panacea functioned as early hospitals and employed women doctors.

The eighth-century BC epics of Homer were Greek legends dating from the late Bronze Age. Homer modelled the stories into poems and they were passed on orally until the sixth century BC, when they were written down. In the *Iliad*, Agamede, daughter of the King of the Epei, acted as a battlefield doctor on the Plain of Troy and 'knew of all the medicines that are grown in the broad earth'(XI, 740). In the *Odyssey*, Homer reported that Helen of Troy, an excellent physician, had studied medicine in Egypt with the woman doctor Polydamna whose name means 'subduer of many diseases'. Polydamna gave Helen nepenthes, an opiate which wrought the 'mild magic of forgetfulness' (IV, 221). The writings of the later Roman poets Virgil and Ovid also illustrate that medical science was in the hands of women as well as deities.

The chief goddess of the ancient Persians was Immortality who taught medicine to her people. Her treatments utilised words (the law), surgery, plants, texts and righteousness (not a bad combination). She was helped by her sisters, Adisina, the wind goddess who blew away disease, and Agastya who treated illness with medicines.

The Assyrian goddess of medicine was Ishtar. (The Sumerians called her Inanna and the Phoenicians, Astarte.) The Assyrian goddess Gula who presided over death and resurrection, like the Greek Persephone, was called the Chief Physician and Nin-Karrak was the goddess of health. The priestesses of Assyria also acted as physicians.

Some of these goddesses were probably mortal women whose accomplishments originally earned them renown among their own people. Their fame then provided the germ for the stories that grew into legends. An exceptional woman might thus be deified, or incorporated into an existing immortal. Once she had entered the mythology of the local people, she would be adopted by neighbouring cultures. Other goddesses walked the earth only in the fertile imagination of the ancient mind. Whatever the source, mythology illustrated that those early scientific advances were credited to women. This tradition of women scientists was to continue into the era of written history.

2
Women and Science in the Ancient World

One would naturally expect that, in the pruning of our historical traditions which is proceeding so briskly, the fame of the great women of the past is peculiarly doomed to suffer curtailment. (Joseph McCabe, p. 267)

1. The First Written Records

The written history of science begins in Egypt during the Old Kingdom (c. 2778–2263 BC), the age of the pyramids. The Egyptians were interested in the practical aspects of science. Priests and priestesses developed such mathematics and astronomy as were applicable to the problem at hand: wheat stores for trade, or blocks of stone to be cut for the giant edifices. Early Egyptian women owned property, supervised the state-managed textile and perfume industries, and worked as scribes.

Calculating time was the initial impetus for systematic astronomical observation, but soon the Egyptians became interested in Babylonian astrology. Aganice (or Athyrta), daughter or sister of the legendary King Sesostris, used celestial globes and the study of constellations to attempt to predict the future.

Medicine was an established profession in Egypt prior to 3000 BC and educated women worked as doctors and surgeons. The medical schools at Sais and Heliopolis attracted women students and teachers from throughout the ancient world. At the Temple of Sais north of Memphis an inscription reads: 'I have come from the school of medicine at Heliopolis, and have studied at the woman's school at

Sais where the divine mothers have taught me how to cure disease.'[1]
Moses and his wife Zipporah probably studied medicine at Heliopolis
about 1500 BC and Zipporah may also have attended the school at
Sais. During this era, the physician-queen Hatshepsut of the
eighteenth dynasty despatched a botanical expedition to search for
new medicinal plants.

The medical papyri discuss gynaecology, the speciality of women
physicians. The Kahun medical papyrus (c. 2500 BC) may have been
written for the Sais students. It indicates that women specialists
diagnosed pregnancy, guessed at the sex of the unborn child (if the
mother's face was green it would be a boy), tested for sterility and
treated dysmenorrhoea (irregular menstruation). Women surgeons
performed caesarian sections, removed cancerous breasts and set
bones with splints. 'Physician' was often synonymous with 'priestess',
for in the earliest records it was the goddess Isis who prescribed the
cure.

It was not the Egyptians but rather the peoples of Mesopotamia –
the Sumerians, Babylonians and Assyrians – who made the greatest
advances in science though, particularly in observational astronomy.
They charted the motions of the planets and mapped the constellations of the zodiac – and in the process, invented the quasi-science of
astrology. By the seventh century BC the Chaldean astronomers of
Babylon had discovered the saronic eclipse cycle of 6585 days and
could therefore predict if an eclipse was at least theoretically
possible at a given time and place. Learning was in the hands of
priestesses and priests who left great libraries of clay tablets.
Medicine was less sophisticated than in Egypt, but employed
effective remedies in addition to magic, and women healers had a
prominent role.

The Sumerian culture, adopted by the successive invaders of the
region, accorded women relatively high status and autonomy. Under
the Code of Hammurabi (the Babylonian laws) women could engage
in business and own property; they could also become judges and
elders. The perfume industry was very important in ancient Babylon
since aromatic substances were used in medicines and religion as
well as for cosmetics. The apparatus and recipes of perfumery were
similar to those used in cooking. Women perfumers developed the
chemical techniques of distillation, extraction and sublimation, and
cuneiform tablets from the second millenium BC name two of these
early women chemists, Tappûti-Bēlatēkallim and [. . .] ninu (the title

'Bēlatēkallim' indicates female overseer of the palace). This tradition of women chemists was to culminate with the Alexandrian alchemists of the first century AD.

2. The Women Pythagoreans

Greek science began with the Pythagoreans and it was this movement that brought women into the mainstream of developing natural philosophy and mathematics. Pythagoras of Samos (c. 582–500 BC) had travelled throughout the Mediterranean world, studying with many teachers. According to the Greek philosopher Aristoxenus, he obtained most of his moral doctrines from Themistoclea, a Delphic priestess.[2] Pythagoras finally settled in the Greek colony of Croton in southern Italy, between 540 and 520 BC. There he founded a quasi-religious, quasi-political community devoted to mathematical and philosophical speculation. The Pythagorean Community is often referred to as a 'Brotherhood', obscuring the fact that the Order included men and women on equal terms. There were at least 28 women teachers and students in the School. Pythagoras was known as the 'Feminist Philosopher'.[3]

The Pythagorean cosmology (as adapted by Plato, modified by Eudoxus and Aristotle, and further elaborated by Ptolemy) was to form the basis of natural philosophy throughout the Middle Ages, and will be encountered again in the work of Hildegard in the twelfth century (see pp. 62-76). The speculations and discoveries of the Pythagoreans were the common property of the membership, and kept within the Order as mystical secrets.[4] All members wrote under the name of Pythagoras, making it impossible to attribute contributions to individuals; but since women were an integral part of the School, it is reasonable to assume that they were involved in the articulation of this mathematical cosmology that so directly influenced the future course of science.

The Pythagoreans were the first to postulate that matter was discontinuous. They believed that the universe was constructed of numbers and simple ratios, with number units forming the basic elements. Since they were concerned with aesthetics, and since the sphere was the 'perfect geometric shape', it followed that the earth and planets were all spherical and the universe itself consisted of ten concentric spheres. There was one sphere for the fixed stars and one for each of the seven planets (Saturn, Jupiter, Mars, Venus and

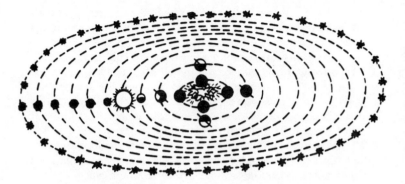

2 *The Pythagorean Universe. The 'counter-earth', the earth, the moon, the sun and the planets revolve through their spheres around the central fire. (The earth and 'counter-earth' are each shown in 4 positions.) The stars remain stationary in the outermost sphere.*

Mercury, the sun and the moon). The ninth sphere belonged to earth and, to reach the magic number 10, they introduced a 'counter-earth'. Each of these bodies moved with uniform motion through its sphere in a circular path from west to east around a central fire. (The fire couldn't be seen from Greece since it was on the opposite side of the earth – and there it was obscured from view by the counter-earth.) The period of rotation increased with the 'nobility' of each heavenly body. The earth, the basest body in the universe, completed its circle in one day. The moon took a month, the sun a year, and the other planets longer still. The fixed stars remained stationary in their sphere. The Pythagoreans believed that the distances between the concentric spheres and the central fire were in the same numerical ratio as the intervals of the musical scale, hence the 'music of the spheres'.[5]

The most famous female cosmologist, Theano, a native of Croton, married Pythagoras when he was an old man. She was his student and disciple and later a teacher in the School. She was credited with having written treatises on mathematics, physics and medicine and on the Pythagorean precept of the 'golden mean' (moderation). Only a few of her letters are extant. Theano and her daughters were reputed to be excellent healers. They were said to have won a debate with the physician Euryphon on the age-old question of foetal development, the women arguing that the foetus was viable before the seventh month. They believed that the human body was a microcosmic copy of the macrocosm – the universe as a whole. This concept reappears often in ancient and mediaeval physiology, and will be encountered in a more sophisticated form in the writings of Hildegard.

Eventually the Pythagorean Community included some 300 members in Croton where they gained control of the local government, but the democratic populace of Croton rebelled against this aristocracy, the School was destroyed, and its members killed or exiled. Supposedly, Pythagoras was killed during the uprising and Theano succeeded him as head of the now-dispersed Community. With the help of two of her daughters, she spread the religious and philosophical system throughout Greece and into Egypt.[6]

The offshoots of the Pythagorean School continued to include women. The names of a few of these fifth-century BC women have survived: Phintys, Melissa, who wrote on the obligations of women, and Tymicha, a Spartan, born in Croton. Legend has it that she and her husband were taken before Dionysius, the tyrant of Syracuse, who demanded to be told the mysteries of Pythagorean science. Though he offered a large reward, they refused to reveal the secrets. Instead, Tymicha bit off her tongue and spat it in the tyrant's face.[7]

3. Women Philosophers of the Golden Age of Greece

Outside of the Pythagorean Community, there were few opportunities for women scientists in Greek society. In general, the Greeks were a patriarchal people and it was only in the small militaristic city-state of Sparta that women had any degree of power.[8] Athenian women – at least the wives of wealthy citizens – were as secluded as the later women of Islam. In a society that venerated learning most women remained illiterate. However, even in Athens and the other male-dominated city-states, a few individuals were able to overcome the cultural impediment of their sex and contribute to the development of natural philosophy.[9]

Aglaonice of Thessaly became famous in the fifth century BC for her ability to predict eclipses of both the sun and moon. Although she must have used the saronic eclipse cycle discovered by the Chaldean astronomers, she was widely regarded as a sorceress. She flaunted her reputation, bragging that she could make the sun and moon disappear at will. In AD 77 Pliny wrote:

Long ago was discovered a method of predicting eclipses of the sun and moon – not the day or night merely but the very hour. Yet there still exist among a great number of the common people an established conviction that these phenomena are due to the compelling power of charms and magic herbs, and that the science of them is the one outstanding province of women. (25,10)

It was in classical Athens that the foundations for the natural philosophy, metaphysics and political ideology of western civilisation were first established. In the fifth century BC, encouraged by political and military successes, the city-state entered a period of prosperity and intellectual greatness. The citizens of Athens (about 10 per cent of the population) were freed for political and cultural activities by a labour force of women, and male foreigners and slaves. The growth of a democratic form of government in Athens attracted philosophers and mathematicians from throughout the Mediterranean world, many of whom were Pythagoreans. They were called sophists, since they claimed to teach knowledge. In actuality they taught their students rhetoric and how to win arguments using mathematical logic, a useful skill in a 'democratic society'. With the Athenian philosophers, science became more empirical. They were the first to distinguish clearly between science and religion. They encouraged the direct and careful observation of nature, the use of deductive logic, and the maxim that observed phenomena were due to natural rather than supernatural causes.

Prostitution was a flourishing profession in classical Athens. The high-class prostitutes, the *hetairai* ('companions to men') were usually foreign-born women barred by law from marrying Athenian citizens. These *hetairai* were often educated, artistic and intellectual, forming a class in their own right, for they were free from the restrictions imposed on the wives of Athenian citizens.

The most famous of these *hetairai* was Aspasia (470–410 BC), who was born in Miletus in Ionia, the daughter of Axiochus, a learned man who had given her a fine education. She came to Athens to engage in the intellectual life of the city but on arrival found herself, as a foreigner, classified as a courtesan.

After about 445 BC Aspasia lived with Pericles, the military and political leader of Athens. She was said to have written his famous funeral oration of 430 BC and she appears in Plato's *Dialogues* as a teacher of Socrates. Æschines, in his Socratic Dialogue 'Aspasia', identified her as a sophist instructor. Plutarch said she taught rhetoric to many noble Athenians: 'Socrates himself would sometimes go to visit her, and some of his acquaintance with him; and those who frequented her company would carry their wives with them to listen to her.' This was despite her occupation being 'anything but creditable', for Aspasia kept a salon – or as Plutarch called it, 'a home for young courtesans'[10] – where the leaders of classical Athens gathered to discuss questions of politics and science. Included in her salon was Anaxagoras, the important Ionian philosopher who first suggested that the moon and planets were similar to the earth and that the moon shone by reflected light. Anaxagoras and Aspasia were both prosecuted for impiety and were spared only through the intervention of Pericles.

In Plato's *Symposium* Socrates referred to his teacher Diotima, priestess of Mantineia who was probably a Pythagorean. Plato's mother, Perictione, was also well versed in Pythagorean mathematics and philosophy. Alone among the Athenian philosophers, Socrates and Plato spoke out for the education of women.

It was usually foreign women who studied at Plato's Academy. Because of laws barring women from public meetings, they may have dressed as men in order to attend lectures unnoticed. Lasthenia and Axiothea had read the works of Plato and came to the Academy to study natural philosophy. Axiothea, of the Peloponnesian city of Phlius, was particularly interested in physics. After Plato's death she studied with his nephew Speusippus and eventually became a teacher herself. Lasthenia, from Arcady, became a philosopher and the 'companion' of Speusippus.

With them at the Academy was Arete of Cyrene (fl. 370–40 BC). She was the daughter of Aristippus, founder of the Cyrenaic School of philosophy. Arete was elected to succeed her father as head of the School. She is said to have taught natural science, moral philosophy and ethics in Attica for 35 years, and to have written at least 40 books, including treatises on Socrates, agriculture and education. Her pupils included some 110 philosophers. The epitaph on her tomb called her 'the splendour of Greece' with 'the beauty of Helen, the virtue of Thirma, the pen of Aristippus, the soul of Socrates, and the tongue of Homer'.[11]

The influence of Aristotle on the history of science far surpassed that of all other Greek philosophers. In Aristotle's cosmology, the mathematical spheres of the universe were replaced by physical, crystalline ones, and he added spheres to help explain the 'irregular' movements of the planets. His later biological works, based on original observation, were his greatest achievement. He classified and dissected hundreds of animal species, noting important similarities and differences between them. In Athens he established his Lyceum and was succeeded there by his pupil Theophrastus who continued the observations and classifications within the plant kingdom. Aristotle believed women to be definitely inferior to men. In this, he was more representative of Greek thought than was his teacher Plato. In his very influential work on embryology, *De Generatione Animalium*, he argued that the female was 'a male deformed' and that the male's semen was the source of the soul (II, 737[a]). Aristotle's opinions on this subject, as on others, were to prevail for the next 2000 years. This bias against women was incorporated into most systems of natural philosophy and contributed to the widespread belief, among both women and men, that science was the domain of the male.

Epicurus settled in Athens about 300 BC where he taught that the world was governed by chance, and revived the 'atomism' of Democritus and Leucippus. As in the Academy, women were admitted to the Epicurean School on an equal basis with men. Epicurus carried on a correspondence with Themista, who was referred to as 'a sort of female Solon'.[12] Leontium was a disciple and probably the 'companion' of Epicurus. She wrote a criticism of Theophrastus that was praised by Cicero.[13] While admitting that she was a recognised scholar, Boccaccio claimed that Leontium's critique was obviously instigated by jealousy. Obviously. 'If she had preserved womanly honour,' wrote Boccaccio, 'her name would have been much more splendid and glorious, for she had great intellectual powers.' He spoke of her as having dragged down the study of philosophy. Women such as Leontium 'smear it [philosophy] with shameful stains, trample it with unchaste feet, and plunge it into filthy sewers' (p. 132). With men like Boccaccio 'Praising Famous Women,' it is no wonder so few female philosophers have appeared in our history books.

Ancient and mediaeval historians were more often concerned with the chastity or licentiousness of their female subjects than with their intellectual achievements. The sexual histories of Theano, Aspasia, Lasthenia and Leontium were considered of greater importance than their scholarship. The works of Roman women such as Lais, Elephantis and Salpe were discounted because of their purported immorality. These women may have found it necessary to remain outside the accepted confines of married life in order to educate themselves and pursue scientific interests; or perhaps the attacks on their characters were thinly-disguised attempts to discredit their accomplishments and to discourage others. In spite of this, the women of the Athenian Schools were part of the Platonic tradition that influenced science into the Christian era.

4. The Medical Women of Classical Greece

The relative lack of superstition among the Greeks pushed their medical science to new heights of sophistication. The Hippocratic doctrine stated that the human body contained four humours – the sanguineous, choleric, melancholic and phlegmatic – corresponding to blood, yellow and black bile, and phlegm. The concept that good health required a balance of the four humours had a profound effect on medicine for nearly 2000 years.

In most Grecian cities there were women physicians and surgeons who benefited from the theoretical advances being made at the medical schools of the Aegean. But as time went on women found themselves increasingly restricted to the practice of midwifery, a pattern that is repeated throughout history until finally, in the nineteenth century, women lost even that foothold. Although Hippocrates was credited with founding schools of gynaecology and obstetrics with women students, his school on the island of Cos, the centre of empirical medicine, was closed to women. In contrast, its rival school at Cnidos on the coast of Asia Minor, though less scientifically innovative, encouraged women students.

Hippocrates recognised the value of folk medicine – the herbal remedies discovered by women healers. One of these early herbalists was Artemisia, a powerful ruler, Queen of Caria in Asia Minor. Artemisia was said to be familiar with every herb used in medical treatment and Theophrastus, Strabo and Pliny all praised her skill.[14]

Practising medicine was rarely as easy for common women as it was for queens. In Athens in the fourth century BC women doctors were accused of performing abortions and were barred from the profession. (Abortion was common among the ancients but was periodically declared illegal, especially during outbreaks of misogynist sentiment.) The story of Agnodice provides an example from classical Athens of the power of women united in a common cause, even in the most patriarchal of societies. Hyginus, the Roman historian and librarian to the Emperor Augustus, was the authority for this tale, recounted in a letter published in 1687 by Mrs Celleor, a prominent English midwife:

> Among the subtle Athenians a law at one time forbade women to study or practise medicine or physick on pain of death, which law continued some time, during which many women perished, both in child-bearing and by private diseases, their modesty not permitting them to admit of men either to deliver or cure them.[15]

Over 2000 years later feminists were still arguing that women doctors were essential to protect the modesty of female patients. Agnodice dressed as a man and went to Alexandria in about 300 BC to study medicine and midwifery with the famous physician and anatomist, Herophilus. She could not have chosen a better teacher, for Herophilus had made important contributions to medical science: he was the first to perform anatomical dissections in public; he identified the brain as the seat of intelligence and recognised the function of nerves; and he was the first to distinguish between veins and arteries.

Returning to Athens still disguised as a man, Agnodice set up a successful practice among the women of the aristocracy. In an amusing version of the story, the Athenian physicians who from their earliest days were adept at protecting their professional interests, became very jealous at the success of this new doctor. They denounced Agnodice 'as one that does corrupt men's wives.'[16] To their embarrassment, Agnodice then revealed herself to be a woman; but in so doing, she opened herself up to prosecution both as a woman physician and for practising under false pretences:

> she was like to be condemned to death for transgressing the law ... which, coming to the ears of the noble women, they ran before the Areopagites, and the house being encompassed by most women of the city, the ladies entered before the judges, and told them they would no longer account them for husbands and friends, but for cruel enemies that condemned her to death who restored to them their health, protesting they would all die with her if she were put to death.[17]

The organised resistance worked. Agnodice went free and was allowed to continue to practise and to wear her hair and clothes as she chose. The law was subsequently changed: henceforth, freeborn women were permitted to study and practise medicine, as long as they treated only women. Upper-class Greek women took up the study of medicine and their influence was to spread throughout the Roman Empire.

5. The Roman Matrons

The Romans were less interested in science than the Greeks, and their culture never supported the development of mathematics. Instead of promoting their own arts and sciences, the Romans attempted to assimilate those of the Greeks, and since the Roman intellectuals were fluent in Greek as well as Latin, there were few translations of Greek texts. Thus, with the fall of the Western Roman Empire and the isolation of the Eastern Byzantine Empire, the Latin-speaking world was eventually cut off from Greek knowledge.

Women were all but enslaved under Roman law; yet their social position was far better than in classical Athens and continued to improve over the five centuries of the Empire. Roman women learned to read and write, and upper-class matrons were educated by tutors. Plutarch, in his life of Pompey, spoke of the Roman general's child-bride, Cornelia Scipio, as having been well educated, particularly in geometry and philosophy.

Julia Domna, wife of the Emperor Septimus Severus, was well versed in philosophy, geometry and the other sciences. She shared in her husband's rule, and was famed for her salon which included such notables as the historian Diogenes Laertius and the physician Galen.

During its early centuries Rome had no professional doctors. When the Romans conquered Greece in the second century BC, medical women were brought to Rome as slaves and the Romans began to adopt, organise and compile Greek medicine as they had the other sciences. By the first two centuries AD, medicine was a flourishing profession in the Empire. The Romans were leaders in the establishment of medical schools (with state-paid teachers) and in the founding of public hospitals in Rome and its provinces. The hospitals were often staffed by educated noble women. Female physicians were numerous and there were more opportunities for common women to enter the profession. Their status approached that of the male physician and they treated men as well as women and children.

Soranus of Ephesus (98-138 AD) wrote a Greek text on obstetrics and gynaecology for his women students. He believed that women should be treated only by other women and that these 'medica' should have a sound knowledge of anatomy:

> we call her the best midwife if she ... in addition to her management of cases is well versed in theory. And ... if she is trained in all branches of therapy (for some cases must be treated by diet, others by surgery, while still others must be cured by drugs).(I, 4)

He wrote in an easy-to-memorise style and for hundreds of years his remained an important text for doctors and midwives alike.

References to many Roman medical women appear in the work of Soranus, Galen (the most influential of the medical writers), and in Pliny's *Natural History*. Despite the lack of advances in medical science generally, numerous women were writing treatises and making contributions in the fields of obstetrics and gynaecology. Unfortunately, most of their works have been lost. Amongst the earliest of these women were the obstetricians Elephantis (or Philista) and Lais. Elephantis wrote medical books and was a professor in Rome. According to Soranus, she was so beautiful that she was forced to lecture from behind a curtain so as not to distract her students.[18]

Pliny treated both women harshly:

> Lais and Elephantis do not agree in their statements about abortives . . . or in their other portentous or contradictory pronouncements, one saying that fertility, the other that barren-ness is caused by the same measures. It is better not to believe them. (28, 81)

He might have added that it was better not to believe any of the medical writers, male or female. Pliny also quoted Salpe and Olympias. Salpe of Lemnos, whom he referred to as a courtesan, was fond of animal remedies such as toasted earthworms and dung. She wrote on the diseases of the eye, a medical speciality that often fell within the province of the woman physician. She instructed her patients to 'foment the eyes with urine to strengthen them' (28, 66). Olympias the Theban, who probably lived during the reign of Tiberius (14–37 AD), wrote a book of prescriptions, including chapters on women's diseases, preventing miscarriage and inducing abortion by an application of mallow and goose grease. Pliny quoted a number of her remedies for female ailments (20, 226).

Scribonius Largus was physician to the Emperor Claudius. Travelling with the Emperor through Western Europe in AD 43, he made lists of remedies found in the foreign colonies as well as those treatments already in use in Rome. With an eye to royal patronage, Scribonius quoted from the prescription books of contemporary ladies of nobility. These women enjoyed experimenting with drug compounds and trying out their remedies on unsuspecting members of their households. Among them were Messalina, the notorious third wife of Claudius; Livia, the wife of Emperor Augustus; his sister Octavia; his daughter Julia, and Antonia, the daughter of Octavia and Mark Antony. Livia, who died in AD 29 at the age of 86 had a better education than either of her husbands and studied philosophy with foreigners at court. Ruellius, who published the treatise of Scribonius Largus in 1529, claimed that these women were as famous for their medicine in their own age as Galen.[19]

There is also a grisly Rabbinical tale concerning Queen Cleopatra VII (69–30 BC), consort of Julius Caesar and Mark Antony. Supposedly an interest in foetal development inspired her to order the dissection of female slaves at various stages following conception. A later authority, claiming that the male foetus was fully formed in 41 days and the female in 81, cited these experiments as evidence. This was countered with the argument that the subjects may have been pregnant before the experiment was begun, the abortive drugs used at the outset proving ineffective.[20]

Galen's friend Antiochis worked with him at the medical school on Esquiline Hill in Rome. She specialised in arthritis and diseases of the spleen, and Galen probably copied some of her prescriptions. Her home town in Asia Minor erected a monument to her which read:

Antiochis, daughter of Diodotos of Tlos; the council and the commune of the city of Tlos, in appreciation of her medical ability, erected at their own expense this statue in her honour.[21]

Metrodora was a contemporary of Soranus and wrote a treatise on diseases of the uterus, stomach and kidneys. There is a twelfth-century manuscript of this treatise in the Laurentian Library in Florence, consisting of 263 parchment pages divided into 108 chapters.

Of the many women writing on gynaecology and obstetrics, the most important were Cleopatra and Aspasia. Cleopatra lived in Rome in the second century. Her treatise *De Geneticis* was widely used until at least the sixth century when it became confused with the work of 'Muscio' (a Latin paraphraser of Soranus). Much of it was copied by other writers as well, but during the Renaissance her extant work was collected and reprinted. She may be the same Cleopatra who wrote on cosmetics and skin diseases, since these subjects were almost invariably included in early gynaecological treatises. Aspasia was a second-century Greco-Roman physician who specialised in obstetrics, gynaecology and surgery. Aetios of Amida, court physician to a sixth-century Byzantine emperor, quoted Aspasia extensively in his medical encyclopaedia. Eleven chapters of his book on gynaecology and obstetrics were attributed to her. The works of Cleopatra and Aspasia constituted the major medical writings of women until Trotula in the eleventh century.[22]

Medicine was the only scientific pursuit encouraged by the Romans and it was perhaps the only profession consistently open to women. Although women had always been – and would continue to be – herbalists and healers as well as midwives, they would never again achieve the professional status of the Roman woman physician. Increasingly their work would be restricted, first to the treatment of other women and then to the practice of midwifery. And while the woman medical writers of the Empire understandably emphasised pregnancy, childbirth, abortion and diseases specific to women, their descriptions and prescriptions went far beyond these, covering the whole range of human ailments. In this they represented the end of an era. The women medical writers who followed in later centuries were, with a few important exceptions, far more restricted in their subject-matter.

The rise of Christianity did little for the advancement of science. The Church was anti-intellectual: faith was all-important; there could be no such thing as 'proof'; scientific research was superfluous since the Second Coming was imminent. Tertullian the Carthaginian, a third-century Church father, vented his wrath on women physicians and midwives, accusing them all of being abortionists.

Despite these reactionary tendencies many early Christians supported equality for women. There is evidence that third- and fourth-century female physicians, particularly Christian women devoting themselves to medical charity, had access to libraries, and the works of Galen and Soranus and the treatises by women. When these Christian women were thrown to the lions – as they so often were – their martyrdom inevitably augmented their reputations as healers.

'Zenobia, in her oasis at Palmyra, dared defy the Roman legions for years, for "she knew all science, history, and military art".'[23] Queen of Palmyra in Asia Minor, Zenobia's studies were directed by her chief adviser for state affairs, the famous Greek scholar Longinus. After her husband King Odenathus was assassinated in 267, Zenobia continued his military exploits, proclaiming herself Queen of the East and thereby provoking the Roman Emperor Aurelian to make war on her. After years of siege, she was finally defeated and taken captive to Rome in 273. There she was pardoned and proceeded to lead the life of a Roman matron. Her scholarly daughter thus became Aurelian's Empress, and her grand-daughter the Queen of Persia. It was this regal descendant who introduced Greek medicine into Persia and protected the doctors and teachers of the new medical school at Edessa. During the fifth century the Edessa school was superseded by the important medical school at Jundishapur where women studied alongside men. This school, with its excellent library and famous teachers and scholars, became a major Arab centre for the preservation of Greek learning during the Dark Ages.

3
From the Alexandrians to the Arabs

In 332 BC Alexander the Great entered Egypt where he founded the marble city of Alexandria at the mouth of the Nile. Within a century Alexandria had grown into a cosmopolitan metropolis of a million people and had replaced Athens as the centre of Greek science.

In 306 BC Alexander's general, Ptolemy, took over the rule of Egypt, establishing the Ptolemaic dynasty. Like Alexander, Ptolemy had been a student of Aristotle. Arriving in Egypt, he was distressed to find that scientific investigation there was hopelessly entangled with established religion. He set about changing this situation, bringing scientific study firmly under the auspices of the state; he founded the Museum, a large institute devoted to research and teaching. (Though allied with Aristotle's Lyceum, it bore a closer resemblance to a modern Institute for Advanced Studies.) All the major philosophical schools of antiquity were represented there; the government employed over 100 professors and built the Great Library, a zoo, botanical gardens, an observatory and dissecting rooms. Alexandria soon became home to some of the greatest scientists of the ancient world. When in 30 BC Egypt became a Roman colony, Rome remained the seat of political power, but Alexandria became the intellectual hub of the Empire.

1. The Alexandrian Alchemists

By the time of Claudius Ptolemy (AD 85–165), the Greco-Roman world had already entered a scientific decline. There was a widespread belief that all important knowledge resided in the works of the 'ancients' (the classical Greeks) – even Ptolemy, one of the most important observational astronomers of antiquity, could barely conceive of himself or his contemporaries formulating new ideas or making discoveries unknown to their predecessors.

Alchemy was the one science that flourished in Alexandria during these barren times. This strange and secret study involved the search for the process of transmuting common metals into silver and gold (the alchemist's penchant for secrecy may have served as protection from official persecution or arisen from the traditional secrecy of the craft fraternities and mystical cults). At any rate, the literature of alchemy is allegorical and obscure, and has often been dismissed as incomprehensible sorcery. But the true alchemists of antiquity were physicists seeking to understand the nature of process and of life. Grounded in Aristotelian science, they were the first to combine theory with experimentation. With the methods and utensils of the household kitchen, they invented the techniques and apparatus that still serve as basic laboratory tools. Despite the mystical basis of alchemy, early practitioners clearly distinguished between the simulation of gold and silver, by gilding or preparing alloys of base metals, and their ultimate goal of the transmutation of metals, finally achieved by physicists in the twentieth century. Metals were thought to be living organisms in the process of evolving toward the perfection of gold; the alchemist was encouraging this natural process by transferring the 'spirit' or vapour of gold to a base metal, as manifested by the transfer of colour.

Alchemy drew on several sources: the formulation and manufacture of cosmetics, perfumes and imitation jewellery – major Egyptian industries; the artistic tradition – the mixing of dyes and the theories of colour; and Gnosticism, an esoteric mixture of Jewish, Chaldean and Egyptian mysticism, neo-platonism and Christianity, centred in Alexandria. In the Gnostic tradition, as in ancient Taoism, the male and female were equal – a precept which became a cornerstone of alchemical theory.

Egyptian alchemy probably originated in ancient Mesopotamia where women chemists developed the techniques used in the formulation of perfumes and cosmetics. The chemistry of the Babylonians reached Alexandria, via the oral craft tradition, in which the woman chemist took a leading role. (For this reason the work of the early alchemists was sometimes called *opus mulierum* – 'women's work'.) The goddess Isis was identified as the founder of the arcane science and *Isis the Prophetess to her Son Horos* was one of the earliest alchemical treatises. In order to publish with impunity, alchemists often wrote under the name of an ancient deity or celebrity.

The theoretical and practical bases of western alchemy, and therefore of modern chemistry, were laid down by Maria the Jewess.[1] Maria wrote under the name of Miriam the Prophetess, sister of Moses, causing some historians mistakenly to identify the biblical Miriam as an alchemist. Maria is thought to have lived in Alexandria in the first century AD. She wrote many treatises which were later expanded, corrupted and confused with other works. Fragments of her writings, including the *Maria Practica*, exist in collections of ancient alchemy.

While her theories were to prove influential, above all else she was an inventor of sophisticated laboratory apparatus for distillation and sublimation. She described her constructions in great detail. Her *balneum mariae* (water bath) has remained an essential piece of laboratory equipment for nearly 2000 years. 'Maria's bath' resembled a double-boiler and was used, as is a modern water bath, to heat a substance slowly or to maintain it at a constant temperature. In modern French a double-boiler is still referred to as a *bain-marie*.

Maria also invented a still, called the *tribikos* (see Figure 3). It consisted of an earthenware vessel for holding the liquid to be distilled, a still-head for condensing the vapour (the *ambix* or *alembic*), three copper delivery spouts fitted into the still-head, and glass receiving flasks. A gutter or rim on the inside of the still-head collected the distillate and carried it to the delivery spouts. Cold sponges were used to cool the still-head and receivers. Maria's description included instructions for making the copper tubing from sheet metal and she compared the thickness of the metal to that of a 'pastry-cook's copper frying-pan'.[2] Flour paste was recommended for sealing the joints.

Isis had been concerned primarily with the superficial colouration of metals and fusing them to obtain alloys. In contrast, Maria was interested in the prolonged action of the vapours of arsenic, mercury and sulphur on metals. For this purpose she developed the *kerotakis* process – her most significant contribution to alchemy. The *kerotakis* (see Figure 4) was the triangular palette used by artists to keep their mixtures of wax and pigment hot. Maria used the same palette for softening metals and impregnating them with colour. *Kerotakis* came to signify her entire 'reflux' apparatus, consisting of a sphere or cylinder with a hemispherical cover, set over a fire.

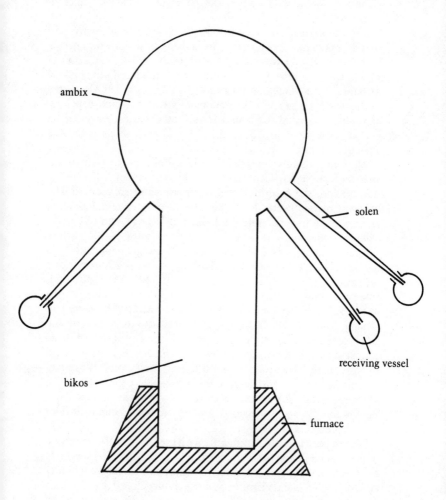

ambix

solen

bikos

receiving vessel

furnace

3 F. Sherwood.Taylor's reconstruction of the Tribikos or three-armed still.

Sulphur, mercury or arsenic sulphide solutions were heated in a pan near the bottom. Near the top of the cylinder, suspended from the cover, was the palette containing a copper–lead alloy (or other metal) to be treated. As the sulphur or mercury boiled, the vapour condensed at the top of the cylinder and the liquid flowed back down, thus establishing a continuous reflux. The sulphur vapours or the condensate attacked the metal alloy yielding a black sulphide – 'Mary's Black' – thought to represent the first stage of transmutation. Impurities collected on a sieve while the 'scoria' (the black sulphide) flowed back down. Continued heating eventually yielded a gold-like alloy, the exact products depending on the metals and mercury or sulphur compounds used. The *kerotakis* was also used for the extraction of plant oils such as attar of roses.

Maria was the most practical of all early alchemists and she described her apparatus in a clear expository style; but her theories were typical alchemical aphorisms of the 'One is All and All is One' variety. She believed that metals were living beings, male or female, and laboratory products the result of sexual generation: 'Unite the male with the female, and you will find what you seek.' She said that silver thus combined easily, but copper coupled 'as the horse with the ass, and the dog with the wolf'.[3] But Maria also formulated theories in accord with laboratory inventions. She adopted the concept of the macrocosm–microcosm, and applied it to the 'above-below' arrangement in distillation and reflux.

Little is known of Cleopatra the alchemist, despite an extant discourse and a single surviving papyrus sheet with symbols and diagrams.[4] She was associated with Maria's School and may have been her contemporary in Alexandria. Lindsay calls Cleopatra's discourse 'the most imaginative and deeply-felt document left by the alchemists' (p. 260). She placed the imagery of conception and birth, the renewal and transformation of life, firmly into the literature of alchemy. The papyrus, the *Chrysopoeia* ('Gold-making') of Cleopatra (see Figure 5), pictured the archetypal symbol of the serpent eating its tail (the *Ouroboros*) and an inscribed double ring:

One is the Serpent which has its poison according to two compositions, and One is All and through it is All, and by it is All, and if you have not All, All is Nothing.[5]

Within the ring were the symbols for gold, silver and mercury. Also

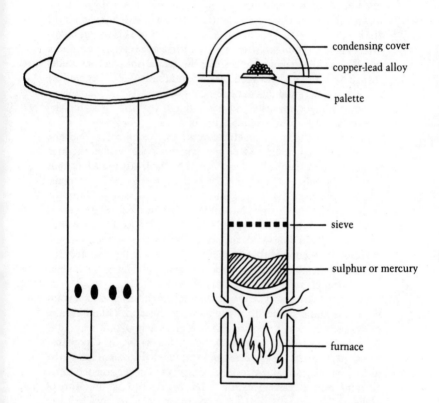

4 F. Sherwood Taylor's reconstruction of the Kerotakis.

illustrated was a *dibikos* (a two-armed still) and a *kerotakis*-type apparatus. In the laboratory, Cleopatra investigated weights and measures, attempting to quantify the experimental side of alchemy. Her procedures were similar to Maria's and she used the sun and fermenting horse-dung as laboratory heat sources.

Zosimus of Panopolis and his sister (or friend) Theosebeia (*soror mystica*, 'mystical sister') collaborated on *Cheirokmeta*, a 28-book encyclopaedia of chemistry (c. AD 300). *Cheirokmeta* was based on the ideas and techniques of Maria and Cleopatra. Sections of this work are extant in Greek and Syriac translations, as are long letters on alchemy written by Zosimus to Theosebeia. One of these contains a diatribe against the teachings of another female alchemist, Paphnoutia.

Maria and Cleopatra mark both the beginning and the end of alchemy as a true experimental science. The third-century Roman Emperor Diocletian initiated the systematic persecution of the Alexandrian alchemists and burned their texts. The Arabs rescued the science and ancient alchemy reached Europe during the Middle Ages, but by that time it had degenerated into mystical mumbo-jumbo. There were very few advances in laboratory chemistry from the fall of Alexandria until the middle of the seventeenth century.

2. Hypatia of Alexandria

She was a person who divided society into two parts: those who regarded her as an oracle of light, and those who looked upon her as an emissary of darkness. (Elbert Hubbard, p. 280)

A slight scientific renaissance occurred in fourth-century Alexandria, illuminated by the most famous of all women scientists until Marie Curie. For fifteen centuries Hypatia was often considered to be the *only* female scientist in history. Even today, for reasons that have more to do with the romanticising of her life and death than with her accomplishments, she is frequently the only woman mentioned in histories of mathematics and astronomy.[6]

Hypatia is the earliest woman scientist whose life is well documented. Although most of her writings have been lost, numerous references to them exist. Furthermore, she died at a convenient time for historians. The last pagan scientist in the western world, her violent death coincided with the last years of the Roman Empire.

Since there were to be no significant advances in mathematics, astronomy or physics anywhere in the West for another 1000 years, Hypatia has come to symbolise the end of ancient science. Though the decline had already been in progress for several centuries, after Hypatia came only the chaos and barbarism of the Dark Ages.

When Hypatia was born in AD 370, the intellectual life of Alexandria was in a state of dangerous confusion. The Roman Empire was converting to Christianity and more often than not the Christian zealot saw only heresy and evil in mathematics and science: ' "mathematicians" were to be torn by beasts or else burned alive.'[7] Some of the Christian fathers revived the theories that the earth was flat and the universe shaped like a tabernacle. Violent conflicts among pagans, Jews and Christians were spurred on by Theophilos, Patriarch of Alexandria. It was not a propitious era in which to become a scientist, or a philosopher.

Hypatia's father, Theon, was a mathematician and astronomer at the Museum. He closely supervised every aspect of his daughter's education. According to legend, he was determined that she develop into a 'perfect human being' – this in an age when females were often considered to be less than human! Hypatia was indeed an exceptional young woman. She travelled to Athens and Italy, impressing all she met with her intellect and beauty. Upon her return to Alexandria, Hypatia became a teacher of mathematics and philosophy. The Museum had lost its pre-eminence and Alexandria now had separate schools for pagans, Jews and Christians; however, Hypatia taught people of all religions and she may have held a municipal Chair of Philosophy. According to the Byzantine encyclopaedist Suidas, 'she was officially appointed to expound the doctrines of Plato, Aristotle, &c.'[8] Students converged on Alexandria to attend her lectures on mathematics, astronomy, philosophy and mechanics. Her home became an intellectual centre, where scholars gathered to discuss scientific and philosophical questions.

Most of Hypatia's writing originated as texts for her students. None has survived intact, although it is likely that parts of her work are incorporated in the extant treatises of Theon. Some information on her accomplishments comes from the surviving letters of her pupil and disciple Synesius of Cyrene, who became the wealthy and powerful Bishop of Ptolemais.

Hypatia's most significant work was in algebra. She wrote a commentary on the *Arithmetica* of Diophantus in 13 books. Diophantus

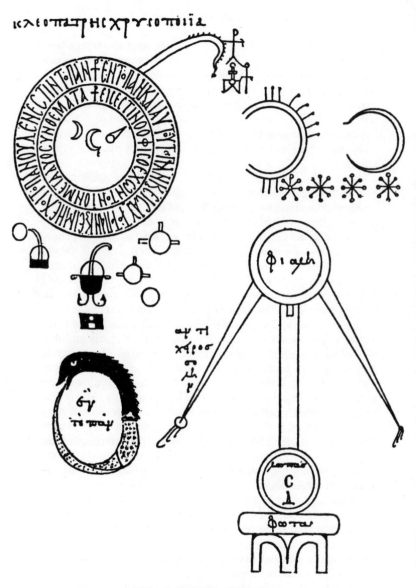

5 The Gold-Making of Cleopatra

lived and worked in Alexandria in the third century and has been called the 'father of algebra'. He developed indeterminate (Diophantine) equations, that is, equations with multiple solutions. (A common example of this type of problem is the variety of ways of changing a pound using different denominations of pence – 50p, 20p, etc.). He also worked with quadratic equations. Hypatia's commentaries included some alternative solutions and many new problems subsequently incorporated into the Diophantus manuscripts.

Hypatia also authored a treatise *On the Conics of Apollonius* in eight books. Apollonius of Perga was a third-century-BC Alexandrian geometer, the originator of epicycles and deferents to explain the irregular orbits of the planets. Hypatia's text was a popularisation of his work. Like her Greek ancestors, Hypatia was fascinated by conic sections(the geometric figures formed when a plane is passed through a cone). After her death, conic sections were neglected until the beginning of the seventeenth century when scientists realised that many natural phenomena, such as orbitals, were best described by the curves formed by conic sections.

Theon revised and improved upon Euclid's *Elements* of geometry and it is his edition that is still in use today. Hypatia probably worked with him on this revision. Later she co-authored with him at least one treatise on Euclid. Hypatia also wrote at least one book of Theon's work on Ptolemy. Ptolemy had systematised all contemporary mathematical and astronomical knowledge in a 13-book text which he modestly called a *Mathematical Treatise*. Mediaeval Arab scholars renamed it the *Almagest* ('Great Book'). Ptolemy's system remained the leading astronomical work until Copernicus in the sixteenth century. Hypatia's tables for the movements of the heavenly bodies, the *Astronomical Canon*, may have been part of Theon's commentary on Ptolemy, or a separate work.

In addition to philosophy and mathematics, Hypatia was interested in mechanics and practical technology. The letters of Synesius contain her designs for several scientific instruments including a plane astrolabe (see Figure 6). The plane astrolabe was used for measuring the positions of the stars, planets and the sun, and to calculate time and the ascendant sign of the zodiac.

Hypatia also developed an apparatus for distilling water, an instrument for measuring the level of water, and a graduated brass hydrometer for determining the specific gravity (density) of a liquid.

Fourth-century Alexandria was a centre for neoplatonic scholars. Although Hypatia may have studied at the neoplatonic school of Plutarch the Younger and his daughter Asclepigenia in Athens, she subscribed to a more tolerant, mathematically-based neoplatonism.[9] There was rivalry between the neoplatonic schools of Alexandria and Athens, with the Athens school emphasising magic and the occult. But to the Christians, all Platonists were dangerous heretics.

That Hypatia became enmeshed in Alexandrian politics is indisputable. Her student Hesychius the Jew wrote:

> Donning the philosopher's cloak, and making her way through the midst of the city, she explained publicly the writings of Plato, or Aristotle, or any other philosopher, to all who wished to hear . . . The magistrates were wont to consult her first in their administration of the affairs of the city.[10]

As a pagan, an espouser of Greek scientific rationalism and an influential political figure, Hypatia thus found herself in a very dangerous position in an increasingly Christian city. In 412 Cyril, a fanatical Christian, became Patriarch of Alexandria, and intense hostility developed between Cyril and Orestes, the Roman Prefect of Egypt, a former student and long-time friend of Hypatia. Soon after taking power, Cyril began persecuting Jews, driving thousands of them from the city. Then, despite the vehement opposition of Orestes, he turned his attention to ridding the city of neoplatonists. Ignoring Orestes' pleadings, Hypatia refused to abandon her ideals and convert to Christianity.

Hypatia's murder is described in the writings of the fifth-century Christian historian, Socrates Scholasticus:

> All men did both reverence and had her in admiration for the singular modesty of her mind. Wherefore she had great spite and envy owed unto her, and because she conferred oft, and had great familiarity with Orestes, the people charged her that she was the cause why the bishop and Orestes were not become friends. To be short, certain heady and rash cockbrains whose guide and captain was Peter, a reader of that Church, watched this woman coming home from some place or other, they pull her out of her chariot: they hail her into the Church called Caesarium: they stripped her stark naked: they raze the skin and rend the flesh of her body with

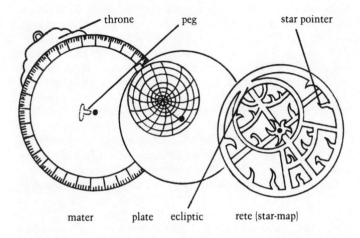

throne   peg   star pointer

mater   plate   ecliptic   rete (star-map)

6 The components of a plane astrolabe

sharp shells, until the breath departed out of her body: they quarter her body: they bring her quarters unto a place called Cinaron and burn them to ashes. (p. 380)

This took place in March 415, just over a century after the pagans had murdered Catherine, a Christian Alexandrian scholar. Hypatia's murderers were Parabolans, fanatical monks of the Church of St Cyril of Jerusalem, possibly aided by Nitrian monks. Whether Cyril directly ordered the murder remains an open question. At the very least he created the political climate that made such an atrocity possible.[11] Cyril was later canonised.

Orestes reported the murder and asked Rome to launch an investigation. He then resigned his office and fled Alexandria. The investigation was repeatedly postponed for 'lack of witnesses' and eventually Cyril proclaimed that Hypatia was alive and living in Athens. Hypatia's brutal murder marked the end of platonic teachings in Alexandria and throughout the Roman Empire.

With the spread of Christianity, the appearance of numerous religious cults and widespread religious chaos, interest in astrology and mysticism replaced scientific investigation. In 640 Alexandria was invaded by the Arabs and what was left of the Museum destroyed. But even though Europe had entered the Dark Ages, Greek science was to survive in Byzantium and flourish in the Arab world.

3. The Survival of Science

The Dark Ages were not as bleak a time for women as one might expect. In the Byzantine Empire a succession of women rulers pursued scientific interests. In China women engineers and Taoist adepts pushed science and technology forward at a steady rate. With the rise of Islam and the subsequent conquest and unification of the Arab regions, translations and elaborations of ancient Greek works formed the basis of Arab science. A diverse and tolerant culture, the early Moslem empire preserved and expanded upon the knowledge of antiquity. Women studied at the medical school in Baghdad and female alchemists followed the teachings of Maria the Jewess. If Moslem women scholars are not recorded in the historical texts, their existence is at least testified to by stories from the *Arabian Nights*.[12]

The compelling legend of the Arab slave-girl Tawaddud reminds us that even the most patriarchal of cultures have recognised the scholarly achievements of women. Her story occupied Shaharazad from the 436th through the 462nd of the Arabian nights. When Abu al-Husn of Baghdad found himself destitute, his beautiful young slave Tawaddud proposed that he offer her to the Caliph Harun al-Rashid for an exorbitant price on account of her exceptional abilities. So the Caliph summoned to his palace Ibrahim, the brilliant rhetorician, who brought along readers of the Koran, doctors of law and medicine, astrologers, scientists, mathematicians and philosophers, all for the purpose of examining the extraordinary claims of the slave girl. First, Tawaddud was tested on every aspect of the Koran and its laws. When she had answered each question correctly, she put to the Koranist a question that he was unable to answer. The unfortunate scholar forfeited his clothes and was sent away humiliated. Next a physician questioned her on physiology. Tawaddud described in detail the veins, bones and internal organs of the body, and the relation of the four elements to the four humours and humoural disease. She elucidated the internal and external symptoms of disease, emphasising the importance of a reasonable and moderate diet and cautioning against the common medical practices of bleeding and cupping. She quoted Galen and answered all questions put to her.Then Tawaddud, in turn, posed a riddle for the physician who replied in frustration: 'O Commander of the Faithful, bear witness against me that this damsel is more learned than I in medicine and what else, and that I cannot cope with her' (Burton p. 227). A philosopher quizzed her on the nature of time and ceded to her when she correctly solved a story problem in arithmetic. Finally she triumphed over Ibrahim himself, despite his elaborate efforts to trap her.

The Caliph paid Abu al-Husn 100,000 gold pieces for Tawaddud and offered to grant her any request – she asked to return to her master and together they joined the court of the Caliph where, presumably, they lived happily ever after.

Today the empresses of Byzantium are remembered primarily for their infamous deeds and scandalous love affairs: less frequently do we hear of their scientific pursuits. But the Greek scientific tradition lived on in the Eastern Empire, albeit in a somewhat degenerate form, and royal women such as Julia Anicia and the Empresses Eudocia and Pulcheria studied medicine and the natural sciences with scholars at court. The Empress Zoe (d. 1050) turned her private apartments into a chemistry laboratory where she spent many years experimenting with perfumes and developing ointments.

The most famous of the Byzantine women scholars was Anna Comnena (1083–1148), daughter of Emperor Alexius. A student of mathematics, astronomy and medicine, she authored The Alexiad, a history of her father's reign. His many wars provided her with the opportunity to dwell on her favourite subject – military technology – and The Alexiad is filled with detailed descriptions of weapons and military tactics. But Anna was also well acquainted with the works of Plato and Aristotle and she included Galenic medical theory and advice in The Alexiad.

Even in Europe, engulfed as it was in political and economic chaos, the position of women could have been worse. The decline of Roman medicine had inadvertently resulted in a de facto expansion of the role of medical women: male physicians had begun to believe themselves above the routine and often unpleasant drudgery of patient care. First in Italy, and later throughout Europe, doctors began assigning the bulk of their practice to female assistants and slaves, turning over the care of the sick to nurses, surgery to the barbers, and prescriptions to apothecaries. This arrangement was to last for hundreds of years: it enabled a few women, especially in Italy, to become medical scientists as well as healers.

At the end of the eighth century, Charlemagne's short-lived Carolingian renaissance promoted the establishment of abbey schools throughout the Holy Roman Empire, and for the first time some girls were afforded a rudimentary formal education. But above all else it was the rapid growth of monastic life that created opportunities for the woman physician and scholar. As we shall see, some of these women even achieved political power. Throughout the Middle Ages, monastic women enjoyed a degree of intellectual freedom and self-sufficiency that they would not experience again until the twentieth century.

4
Medicine and Alchemy: Women and Experimental Science in the Middle Ages

1. Trotula and the 'Ladies of Salerno'

Throughout mediaeval Europe women were practising medicine and surgery with a degree of competence. But it was Trotula and the 'Ladies of Salerno' (the *Mulieres Salernitanae*) who helped to bring about the medical renaissance that signalled the end of the Dark Ages in Europe and a renewed interest in the science of the ancient Greeks. In both popular tradition and in scientific circles, the *Mulieres Salernitanae* were renowned as physicians and medical scholars, and Trotula was pre-eminent amongst them. Indeed, she was one of the most famous of all mediaeval scientists – that is, until the early twentieth century when historians, unable to accept the existence of such a woman in eleventh-century Italy, conveniently wrote her out of the history of medicine.

The school of Salerno in Southern Italy was the first mediaeval medical centre not connected with the Church. By the eleventh century it had gained a reputation for its scientific and practical course of study and qualified as the first European university. Here scholars began translating the ancient Greek medical writings from Arabic into Latin. An original Salernitan collection, the *Regimen Sanitatis Salernitanum*, became one of the most popular medical works of all time. The school was to have a major impact on the development of medical faculties elsewhere.

That women studied and taught medicine at Salerno is less surprising in light of the educational opportunities available to Italian women from the days of the Romans through to the Renaissance period. Although most upper-class Italian women remained illiterate, the universities of Italy were open to them and there existed a tradition of female students and professors.

The details of Trotula's life are little known. The nineteenth-century editor of the Salernitan treatises, Salvatore de Renzi, identified her as the wife of the physician Johannes Platearius and the mother of two medical writers, Matthias and Johannes the Younger. She is probably the same Trotula who died at Salerno c. 1097. A member of the old noble family, the di Ruggiero, Trotula had an extensive medical practice and several treatises to her credit. When the university was reorganised in the mid-eleventh century, she joined her husband and sons on the faculty, and together they worked on a medical encyclopaedia, the *Practica Brevis*. The classic Salernitan text, *De Aegritudinum Curatione*, probably compiled in the twelfth century, included the teachings of the seven chief masters of the school, among them both Johannes Platearius and Trotula.[1]

The most important work credited to Trotula was *Passionibus Mulierum Curandorum* (*The Diseases of Women*), later known as the *Trotula Major*. Another treatise, *Ornatu Mulierum* (the *Trotula Minor*), on cosmetics and skin disease, was eventually incorporated into the first. Despite many later interpolations in the text, most modern medical scholars concur with Dr Hurd-Mead's assessment of *Passionibus Mulierum*:

> It bears the gentle hand of the woman doctor on every page. It is full of common sense, practical, up-to-date for its time, in fact far ahead of the eleventh century in its surgery and analgesics as well as in the care of the mother and infant during the post-partum period. No book so good of its kind had ever been written, and none followed it for centuries. (1930, p. 364)

At times Trotula's advice seems uncannily modern, emphasising the importance of cleanliness, a balanced diet and exercise, and warning against the effects of anxiety and stress. Her cures rarely employ astrology or blatant superstition and, like Hildegard a century later, she prescribed simple, affordable remedies for the poor.

In her prologue to *Passionibus Mulierum* Trotula described her medical calling:

> Since then women are by nature weaker than men it is reasonable that sicknesses more often abound in them especially around the organs involved in the work of nature. Since these organs happen

to be in a retired location, women on account of modesty and the fragility and delicacy of the state of these parts dare not reveal the difficulties of their sicknesses to a male doctor. Wherefore I, pitying their misfortunes and at the instigation of a certain matron, began to study carefully the sicknesses which most frequently trouble the female sex.[2]

Trotula's medical theories belie some of our modern assumptions about mediaeval gynaecology. She referred to menses as 'flowers' and her first chapter dealt with amenorrhoea (failure to menstruate):

For just as trees do not produce fruit without flowers so women without menses are deprived of the function of conception. This purgation occurs in women just as 'pollutio' occurs in men. (p. 2)

She went on to relate irregular menstruation to diet, exercise, disease or 'excessive grief or anger or excitement or fear' (p. 3). She recommended a variety of herbs as well as massage and sexual intercourse as methods of initiating menstruation.

Trotula's explanation of excessive menstrual flow illustrates her understanding of the Galenic and Hippocratic theories:

Yellow bile pouring back from the gall bladder makes the blood feverish to such an extent that it cannot be contained in the veins. Sometimes a salty phlegm is mixed with the blood and thins it and makes it burst forth outside. If the blood which comes becomes yellowish or inclines to a yellow colour, it is due to the bile. If it inclines toward a whitish colour it is due to the phlegm. If to a red colour it is from the blood. (p. 9)

Trotula discussed birth control and the causes and treatments of infertility, pointing out that 'conception is hindered as often by a defect of the man as of the woman' (p. 16). The couple should keep in mind, according to Trotula, that the best time for conception is the last day of menstruation.

Trotula's obstetrics were also advanced. She reintroduced perineal support during labour, to prevent the tissue between the vulva and the anus from tearing, a procedure that had been neglected since ancient times. She also described for the first time how to stitch a torn perineum after childbirth:

There are certain women who, through the severity of childbirth, chance to rupture the private parts . . . Likewise to some women harm occurs in childbirth on account of the mistakes of those attending. There are some for whom vulva and anus become one and the same passage. From these women the womb comes out and grows hard . . . After this [softening and replacing the womb] we sew the break between the anus and the vulva in three or four places with a silk thread. (p. 28)

Trotula suggested how to prevent such tears, as well as methods for managing difficult labour:

If the child does not come forth in the order in which it should, that is, if the legs or arms should come out first, let the midwife with her small and gentle hand moistened with a decoction of flaxseed and chick peas, put the child back in its place in the proper position. (p. 23)

In her chapter on infant care Trotula recommended visual and gentle audible stimulation for the child. She instructed mothers in the choice of a wet-nurse and prescribed soothing lotions for babies cutting teeth.

Trotula (or later copyists of her treatise) also discussed a variety of general medical problem, from lice, worms, toothaches and chapped hands, to eye disease, cancer and deafness; but modern weight-watchers would probably shun her reducing methods: the obese person was to be smeared with cow-dung and wine and placed in a steam cabinet or in heated sand four times per week!

Trotula's famous treatise was a standard medical school text until the sixteenth century. By the thirteenth century she had entered the popular folklore as well. An epic poet of northern France, Rutebeuf (fl. 1250–80), recounted the story of a travelling herbalist (patent medicine hawker) who used the following advertisement to attract the gullible:

My good friends, I am not one of those poor preachers, nor one of those poor herbalists . . . but I belong to a lady who is named Madame Trote of Salerno, who makes a kerchief of her ears, and whose eyebrows hang down as silver chains behind her shoulders; know that she is the wisest lady in all the four quarters of the world.[3]

Thus Trotula the legend became divorced from her scholarly treatises.

The difficulties in tracing the history of *Passionibus Mulierum* are compounded by its popularity. It was copied frequently and copyists took many liberties with the text. It was plagiarised almost as often and appeared under a number of different titles. Sometimes selected chapters were incorporated into other works. *Passionibus Mulierum* seems to have undergone major rewriting in the thirteenth century when a Salernitan woman doctor abridged the manuscript and made substantial revisions in the text and style. It was this edition that was used by the French, German and English translators.

Manuscripts of *Passionibus Mulierum* did not always bear Trotula's name and, when they did, it was often in a corrupted form (Trottola, Tortola, etc.). As early as the twelfth century, manuscript copies were occasionally ascribed to her husband. But the copyist who did the most harm to Trotula's good name was the one who substituted its masculine form – Trottus.

The first printed edition of *Passionibus Mulierum* appeared in Strasbourg in 1544. This large folio volume also included some of the natural science writings of Hildegard of Bingen. Victorius Faventinus published another edition in Venice ten years later. Praising Trotula, he claimed to have personally tested many of her remedies, whilst admitting to having added 'certain inventions of his own for the glory of the Venetian Republic and of the reigning Pope'.[4]

The sixteenth-century printed editions of *Passionibus Mulierum* varied little in the text and not at all on important points. But when Kaspar Wolff of Basle published an edition in 1566, without apparent reason he attributed the work to Eros Juliae and gave it a new title. (Eros was a Greco-Roman freeman, physician to Julia, the daughter of Emperor Augustus. He had authored a book on gynaecology and complexion care that was printed in Strasbourg in 1564.) Some later publishers copied the error, attributing the treatise to Eros or Erotian.[5] Of course, this was absurd. Both Eros and Erotian lived centuries earlier than many of the authorities cited in the text, but later historians used this confusion in the early printed editions to maintain that the work was in fact a compilation by a male Salernitan doctor.

Although the controversy surrounding Trotula had its origins in the sixteenth century, it was the twentieth-century German medical historian Karl Sudhoff and his students who attempted to eliminate the *Mulieres Salernitanae* altogether. According to Sudhoff, the

'Ladies of Salerno' were, by definition, midwives and nurses, not physicians; therefore they could not have authored the obstetrical treatises since these included surgical directions and were far too sophisticated for mere midwives. Furthermore, the theoretical *Passionibus Mulierum* barely discussed the major concern of the midwife – the normal process of childbirth. Thus we have a circular argument: since the women of Salerno could not have been physicians, they could not possibly have known enough medicine and surgery to have written the treatises. Of course, this overlooks the fact that Trotula clearly distinguished herself from the midwives: 'It is to be noted that there are certain physical remedies whose virtues are obscure to us, but which are advanced as done by midwives' (p. 22). Sudhoff claimed that the gynaecological treatise was called 'Trotula' because that was a common Salernitan female name. Charles Singer argued further that the treatise was erotica masquerading as gynaecology and that Trottus named it after a woman to disguise its pornographic nature! Unfortunately, the standing of Sudhoff and Singer as medical historians was such that even feminists were reluctant to dispute them. So the 'Ladies of Salerno' were reduced to midwives, albeit 'the most illustrious of mediaeval midwives.'[6]

Italian medical historians, on the other hand, have steadfastly supported Trotula's authenticity and the existence of Salernitan women physicians in the eleventh and twelfth centuries. Castiglioni asserted that women were definitely among the students at the university and the Salernitan historian Mazza claimed that the most important teachers at the early medical school were women.[7]

Sudhoff, Singer and others argued that the Trotula manuscripts must have been written by a man because no woman could or would have written so explicitly about sexual matters. Trotula's straight-forward descriptions of the diseases of celibacy and sex seem to have offended the Victorian-minded historians of the early twentieth century. (Chapter 35 of the treatise, for example, was entitled 'On the manner of tightening the vulva so that even a women who has been seduced may appear a virgin.') But mediaeval readers had no difficulty with frank discussions of sexuality. In the Middle Ages, at least, a discussion of sexuality was not considered out of place in a gynaecological treatise.

We may never know for certain whether a woman named Trotula was a practising physician and professor at Salerno, or whether she authored the treatises in question. But given the mediaeval Italian acceptance of women scholars, there can be no doubt that eleventh-century Salernitan society could have accommodated such a woman authority. There are countless examples from ancient and mediaeval times of men whose existences are less established than Trotula's and whose writings may not have survived in any form; yet history reveres them. Because historians have been unable to accept the accomplishments of women, feminists are forced to reaffirm repeatedly the historical validity of Trotula and other women scientists.

2. Women and Medicine in the Later Middle Ages

Medicine remained almost the only outlet for the scientific interests of mediaeval women. As the Crusaders spread disease through Europe and the Middle East, the demand for doctors increased and more women entered the profession. Hospitals were built along the routes to the Holy Land – many of them initially staffed almost entirely by women. Although books for the herbalist and midwife became more readily available in the later Middle Ages, most women continued to learn traditional herbal medicine from their mothers. They raised botanicals in their gardens and experimented with remedies and treatments.

The twelfth and thirteenth centuries witnessed the Age of Scholasticism and the rise of the European universities. The nature of scientific investigation was changing. Theology, law and medicine became professions requiring a university education, and everywhere but in Italy the universities were closed to women.

In France early in the twelfth century women studied privately and taught medicine at Montpellier, but in 1220 the University of Paris barred from practice all but bachelors on its own faculty, and by 1239 Montpellier had passed similar laws.

Increasingly, the medical profession was organised into a strict hierarchy, with the doctor at the pinnacle. Beneath him were women apothecaries, barbers and surgeons, usually trained by their husbands or parents, who worked within the guild system, compounding remedies, letting blood and performing operations. At the bottom of the hierarchy were the unlicensed practitioners, 'wise women and folk doctors whose prescriptions were simpler (and cheaper) than those of the physician, and often surprisingly similar.'[8] As competition for patients and the power of the university medical faculties increased, laws against women healers were enforced, and women who had been called physicians in the thirteenth century were branded as charlatans and witches in the fourteenth and fifteenth centuries. The situation was better in countries such as Germany that lacked universities. There medicine remained in the hands of women throughout the Middle Ages.

Most advances in medical science in this period were made by surgeons and ophthalmologists who were able to observe their patients closely. With obstetrics and gynaecology, these were the specialities of the medical woman. Between 1389 and 1497 there were 15 licensed women doctors in Frankfurt, including three Jewish women specialising in Arab ophthalmology. Barbara Weintrauben wrote a medical treatise during the fifteenth century and prestigious German midwives extended their practices to include general medicine. In the late sixteenth century Marie Colinet of Bern (Mme de Hilden), a midwife and surgeon, introduced the use of heat for dilating and stimulating the uterus during labour; performed successful caesarian sections; and first used a magnet to extract a piece of metal from a patient's eye. (This is usually attributed to her husband although he gave her full credit for the procedure.)

3. Women Scientists of the Italian Renaissance

The intellectual traditions of the Roman matron were kept alive in mediaeval and Renaissance Italy. The country boasted a disproportionate number of female scholars, including Olympia Morata and Tarquinia Molza, renowned for their knowledge of classical Greek science. In the fifteenth and sixteenth centuries noble Italian women were educated by the famous humanists. Young girls were then sent to the courts of these scholarly women where they in turn received instruction in the arts and sciences that was equivalent to the education afforded males. In fact, mediaeval Italian schools were often co-educational.

Throughout Italy women physicians practised medicine, surgery and the various specialities. Most obtained a licence by passing an examination after studying at a school or with a private tutor. Less prestigious licences could be obtained on the basis of legally-attested proof of successful treatment. Many women doctors studied with a relative, enabling a practice to be passed on and secret healing methods kept within the family. Others attended medical courses at the Italian universities.

With competition from the universities of Bologna, Padua and Naples, Salerno declined as a medical centre. Nevertheless, more women studied there than elsewhere, several of them producing medical treatises: in the thirteenth century Rebecca Guarna authored *De Febribus, De Urinis* and *De Embryone*; Abella (b. 1380) wrote two treatises in Latin verse, *De Atrabile* and *De Natura Seminis Homani*; and the surgeon Mercuriade (a pseudonym) wrote *De Curatione Vulnerum, De Crisibus, De Febre Pestilenciali* and *De Unguentis*.

Women also joined the university faculties. Costanza Calenda, daughter of a fourteenth-century professor, studied medicine at Salerno and lectured at the University of Naples.[9] Early in the fifteenth century Dorotea Bocchi succeeded her father as professor of medicine and moral philosophy at the University of Bologna. At the age of 25 Maria di Novella became head of mathematics at Bologna.

From the fourteenth to the sixteenth century, human dissections at the Universities of Padua and Bologna resulted in a renaissance in anatomical science and led to improved surgical techniques. Mondino dei Luzzi published his guide to dissection at Bologna in 1316. His student-assistant Alexandra Giliani dissected and prepared the corpses for his demonstrations and lectures. She developed a method for removing blood from arteries and veins and filling the vessels with coloured fluids that solidified, allowing the circulatory system to be studied in detail. Otto Agenius, Mondino's other assistant, was probably Giliani's fiancé. He erected a tablet to her memory in the Church of San Pietro e Marcellino, that reads:

In this urn enclosed, the ashes of the body of Alexandra Giliani, a maiden of Periceto, skillful with the brush in anatomical demonstrations and a disciple, equalled by few, of the most noted physician, Mondinus of Luzzi, await the resurrection. She lived nineteen years; she died consumed by her labours March 26, in the year of grace 1326. Otto Agenius Lustrulanus, by her loss deprived of his better part, his excellent companion deserving of the best, has erected this tablet.[10]

4. Mediaeval Alchemy

A renewed interest in alchemy accompanied the thirteenth-century scientific revival and women retained their fundamental association with this arcane science. But the women alchemists of the Middle Ages were less famous than they were infamous. The theoretical science of the Alexandrian alchemists remained inaccessible, and the majority of these later experimenters were charlatans. Yet even the faking of gold and silver required a knowledge of chemistry. A number of stories attest to the prominence of women chemists in a role they had clung to for nearly 3000 years.

In fourteenth-century Paris the twice-widowed Perrenelle Lethas married Nicholas Flammel, a well-to-do scribe. Together they lived a simple, religious and contented life, until one day there came into Flammel's hands an ancient alchemical manuscript, the Book of Abraham:

> I . . . showed her [Perrenelle] this fair book, whereof at the same instant that she saw it, she became as much enamoured as myself, taking extreme pleasure to behold the fair cover, gravings, images and portraits, whereof, notwithstanding she understood as little as I, yet it was a great comfort to me to talk with her, and to entertain myself, what we should do to have the interpretation of them.

Over the next 21 years the Flammels consulted many people concerning the possible meaning of the book and attempted many experiments themselves – but to no avail. Finally, Flammel travelled to Spain where a Jewish physician named Canche began explaining to him the meaning of the allegorical figures and text. After Canche's death, on the return trip to Paris, the Flammels set to work alone. They laboured for three years. Finally, on Monday, 17 January 1382, they transformed a half-pound of mercury into 'pure silver'. Then, on April 25:

> I made projection of the red stone upon the like quantity of mercury, in the presence likewise of Perrenelle only . . . which I transmuted truely into almost as much pure gold, better assuredly than common gold, more soft and pliable. I may speak it with truth, I have made it three times, with the help of Perrenelle, who understood it as well as I because she helped me with my operations, and without doubt, if she would have enterprised to have done it alone, she had attained the end and perfection thereof.[11]

Before Perrenelle's death in 1397, the Flammels used their treasure for charitable works, endowing hospitals and churches. The Flammels were commonly believed to have discovered the elixir of longevity as well as that of transmutation, for they were reported to be alive in India in the seventeenth century and were spotted at the Paris opera in 1761. Their story did much to improve the reputation of French alchemists.

Whereas the sincerity of the Flammels was widely accepted, the same cannot be said of other women alchemists. For example, there was Barbara, the consort of Emperor Sigismund, owner of the rich gold mines of Hungary:

> It was the gold of these mines that the Empress Barbara, imperious, capricious, dissipated, and thoroughly tired of her husband, sought to get into her possession by a process of extortion from him.

Her plot failed when Sigismund died unexpectedly and his son-in-law seized power, sending Barbara into exile. Unable to live in her accustomed fashion on the allowance granted by her son-in-law, Barbara decided to augment her income by making alchemical gold and silver at her castle at Melnik. Well-versed in the means of deceiving the gold- and silversmiths, as well as in basic chemistry, Barbara was quite successful:

> Especially for making cheap silver, the empress soon found that there was a useful recipe. An ounce and a half of copper was melted in a crucible over a keen fire with an ounce of arsenic and the same quantity of fixed alkali. This produced a brittle metal. But if the mixture was melted four times more, each time adding a new portion of arsenic and alkali, and if the whole was then kept for a time in the fire, there was then produced a malleable white metal.[12]

Soon alchemists were travelling from afar to visit her laboratory. One of these, John von Laaz, who came in 1437, left an account of her questionable procedures:

> As I had heard from various sources that the Consort of His late Majesty King Sigismund was learned in the Natural Sciences, I waited upon her and tried her a little in the Art.
> She knew how to measure her replies with a woman's subtilty.

Before my eyes she took quicksilver, arsenic, and other things which she did not name. Out of these she made a powder, with which copper was dyed white. It stood the test of notching, but not the hammer. With this she has deceived many people.

Similarly I saw her strew heated copper with a powder, which penetrated it. The copper became as refined silver. But when it was melted it was copper once more as before. And she showed me many such deceitful tricks.

Another time she took Iron Saffron and Copper Calx and other Powders, mixed them, and cemented with them equal parts of Gold and Silver. Then the Metal had within and without the appearance of fine Gold. But when it was melted it lost the colour again. Therewith were many merchants duped by her.

As I saw nothing but lying and deception, I reproached her. She was going to have me thrown in prison, but with God's help I managed to get away.[13]

German monks and nuns were also interested in alchemy, despite various edicts prohibiting its practice. The Benedictine Abbey at Lambspringk was home to the 'Lord of Lambspringk', the pseudonym of a nun who wrote an alchemical work in verse with allegorical illustrations.

So it was not only in the alchemical laboratories, the universities and the birthing-rooms that mediaeval women carried on the scientific traditions of the past. It was the convents that linked the women scientists of ancient Greece and Alexandria to the salons of the scientific revolution.

5
'The Sibyl of the Rhine'

> It is hardly too much to say that the Middle Ages studied science
> as though it were theology and Aristotle's *Physics* as though it
> were the Bible.[1]

Hildegard of Bingen (the 'Sibyl of the Rhine') was no exception. Her
science was inseparable from her theology. In fact it was her religious
visions and prophecies that gave her science credibility – making her
the most influential abbess and also one of the most important
scientists of the twelfth century.

The majority of mediaeval scientists, both male and female,
belonged to religious houses. Convents, while varying greatly in the
quality of their educational facilities, provided an attractive alternative to marriage for many women. Although some nuns led
isolated and austere lives devoted to religious duties, many early
mediaeval convents were relatively liberal, affording women a
comfortable life and a variety of opportunities for education and
work. Nuns were frequently physicians and medical instructors, and
most religious houses had infirmaries, featuring clean water and air,
sunshine, wholesome food and sanitary conditions.[2] Many monastic
women did not take permanent vows and were free to come and go as
they pleased.

The majority of these women were from the upper classes or royal
families since convents commonly required a substantial dowry to
'marry Christ'. Abbesses often owned their convents. Sometimes a
wealthy woman would establish a monastic house in order to secure
her property from a husband or other enemy. Such convents thus
served the dual function of boarding school and safe haven for the
daughters of the ruling class. Well-educated abbesses oversaw the

copying and illustrating of manuscripts, although convent libraries were not nearly as complete as those of the much wealthier monasteries.

Especially in Germany, the position of the abbess was often the equivalent of the feudal lord, with political power and jurisdiction over a large domain. Hildegard was to become one of the most scholarly and one of the most powerful of these female ecclesiastics, her influence extending to popes, emperors and kings. She is also the earliest woman scientist whose major works have come down to us intact.[3]

Hildegard was born in 1098 into a family of landed gentry with an estate on the Nahe river. She was a precocious but sickly child, the tenth in the family. At the age of eight she was cloistered in the small Benedictine convent at Disibodenberg where her Aunt Jutta was abbess. In the accompanying ceremony they were given the last rites of the dead, complete with funeral torches:

> On All Saints' Day, 1106 . . . were all three [Jutta, Hildegard and a serving girl] solemnly enclosed at Mount St Disibode, and the entrance to their cells was walled up in the presence of a large crowd. The monk Wibert described this cell as a prison or a mausoleum . . . It . . . was in fact a small convent, which in course of time, as others joined Jutta, was enlarged to accommodate them, and eventually the door was unwalled. (Steele, pp. 18–19)

Jutta was responsible for Hildegard's education which, at a minimum, consisted of Latin, the Scriptures, devotions and music. How much of Hildegard's knowledge was self-taught and how much a result of Jutta's instruction is unknown. Her Latin was interspersed with German and she had a succession of assistants who helped with the language, scripting and illustrating of her manuscripts. Some historians have seized on Hildegard's claim to being a simple, uneducated woman who had read nothing but the Bible as proof that she could not have authored the sophisticated Latin treatises. Hildegard herself maintained that her writings were divinely inspired; that she was merely the vehicle for transmitting God's Word. But she cannot be taken too literally. Just as Maria the alchemist had written under the name of Miriam the Prophetess a thousand years earlier, Hildegard knew that, as a woman, her writings would be taken seriously if they were believed to have come from God. While still a child Hildegard began to have intense religious experiences:

> But from my girlhood, that is to say from my fifteenth year, I felt in myself in a wonderful way the power of the mysteries of secret and wonderful visions. Nevertheless I showed these things to no one except for a few religious people, living in the same way as I was. In the meantime, till God wished His favours to be manifested, I repressed them in quiet silence. (Preface to *Scivias*, Steele, pp. 125-6)

From her childhood Hildegard suffered long bouts of serious illnesses. She came to believe that these illnesses were due to her failure to understand and follow God's wishes and that her recoveries would only occur when she resolved to do His bidding. Her visions, which continued intermittently throughout much of her life, have been attributed by modern scholars to migraine, epilepsy or some similar nervous disorder. Singer has pointed to similarities between her illuminated miniatures – the detailed illustrations accompanying her manuscripts – and the hallucinations experienced by severe migraine sufferers. But there is another explanation:

> From the age of eight, Hildegard was fed on the rich aesthetic fare of Benedictine liturgy, whose ever-present chant provided a 'way in' to deep contemplation and probably to altered states of consciousness.[4]

Whatever their source, the visions served Hildegard well. They became the medium of expression for her scientific ideas as well as her religious views. This was not unusual. Claims of visions were frequent in the twelfth century and remained a common literary device for hundreds of years. The Benedictine *magistra* and physician, Elizabeth of Schönau (1129-65), recorded similar visions, and the two nuns were in frequent communication. That visions were particularly useful to women writers is apparent from the Preface to Hildegard's first book, *Scivias* (*Sci Vias Dei* – 'Know Thou the Ways of God'):

> But I, although I had seen and heard these things, nevertheless because of the doubt and bad opinion and divers remarks of men, refused for a long time the duty of writing, not in obstinacy but in

humility, until I fell on a bed of sickness, cast down by the scourge of GOD, until at length I was compelled to write by many infirmities. (Steele, p. 128)

In 1136 Hildegard succeeded Jutta as abbess. The additional responsibilities, compounded by political difficulties and poor health, interfered with her studies. The rapid growth of the convent and frequent visits by pilgrims further deprived her of the peace and quiet she needed. Conveniently, she had a vision instructing her to leave Disibodenberg and found a new convent on Mount St Rupert near the important mediaeval town of Bingen, at the confluence of the Nahe and the Rhine. Initially there was much opposition to this plan, but she was eventually granted permission to move. The Rupertsberg convent initially had 18 young women in 1150, but it too experienced a period of rapid growth. Disputes raged over the autonomy of the new convent and for several years after the move Hildegard remained gravely ill.

Hildegard began writing *Liber Scivias* in 1141. This included her first complete cosmology and was to become the most influential of her mystical treatises.[5] The Abbot of Disibodenberg took the first two sections of *Scivias* to the Archbishop of Mainz, who in turn transmitted them to Pope Eugenius III and Bernard of Clairvaux at the 1147 Council of Trier. The Pope declared them to be authentic prophecies and officially encouraged Hildegard to continue writing. Bernard, for his part, found her apocalyptic visions useful for arousing enthusiasm for the Second Crusade.

The abbess was a strong and temperamental woman. Although Heinrich, Archbishop of Mainz, had shown her early writings to the Pope and finally granted her permission to transfer to Mount St Rupert, she was not about to let him interfere in her affairs. When he requested that her secretary Richarda be allowed to leave to become abbess of another convent, Hildegard ignored the letter. When he wrote again, she replied that 'the Archbishop, like King Nebuchadnezzar, would be deprived of his office, and would not live much longer.'[6]

Hildegard had reason to feel secure in her political position. With the completion of *Scivias* her fame and prestige were in the ascendant. She undertook an extensive correspondence, acting as consultant and prophet to high church officials and heads of state, her letters usually in the form of prophecies or sermons. She had no qualms about criticising or defying the most illustrious figures of her age; nor was she above flattery when it served her purposes. She warned the Pope of corruption within the Church and her letters reveal her increasing involvement in the political turmoil of the times. She sided with the Roman popes against the Holy Roman Emperor Frederick Barbarossa and the anti-popes, and in her letters praised and encouraged her allies and threatened her adversaries. She accused Frederick of being partially responsible for the schism and diminished authority of the Church, predicting that he would have a long but difficult reign. Frederick found her intimidating: in 1163 he granted the Rupertsberg convent an Imperial Letter of Protection and it was left unmolested when his troops devastated the Rheingau.

From 1155 on Hildegard travelled widely, teaching medicine and theology and spreading religious fervour. She encouraged the persecution of heretical sects, particularly the Cathari with their women priests, who flourished in the Rhineland. Many of her religious pilgrimages were directed against this sect and in 1163 a number of their members were burned at the stake in Cologne.

Between 1150 and 1160 Hildegard worked on her encyclopaedia of natural history (*Liber Simplicis Medicinae* or *Liber Subtilitatum Diversarum Naturarum Creaturarum*). When Schott edited it for publication in Strasbourg in 1533 he renamed it *Physica*. The most scientific of all her works, it proved a popular treatise and was used as a text at the Montpellier medical school. Unlike her mystical writings, *Physica* and her later medical work *Causae et Curae* were divided into books and chapters like other mediaeval treatises on natural science, and were written in a straightforward, didactic style; she did not claim that they were divinely inspired. *Physica* included descriptions of 230 plants and 60 trees, as well as fish, birds, reptiles and mammals, stones and metals. She gave the German term for each entry, along with its medical applications, and developed a German botanical nomenclature that is still in use.[7]

Hildegard began her second book of visions, *Liber Vitae Meritorum*, in 1158. Upon its completion in 1162, she immediately started work on her final visionary cosmology, *Liber Divinorum Operum Simplicis Hominis* (*LDO*) completed in 1170.[8] An expression of her mature cosmology, the visions were illustrated, as in *Scivias*, with detailed explanatory miniatures. *LDO* likewise opened with a Preface explaining that the ideas were not hers but God's. It ended with a vision describing the evils of the age and prophesying the fall of the

Church and the Holy Roman Empire and the coming of the anti-Christ. These prophecies were appropriately ambiguous and firmly based in the political realities of twelfth-century Germany.

Liber Compositae Medicinae or *Causea et Curae* was the last of Hildegard's major works. It consisted of five books of medical theory and remedies, in which she related her mystical concept of the universe – the macrocosm – to specific diseases in the human body – the microcosm. The work was never widely disseminated and only in the last century was an early manuscript copy located in the Royal Library at Copenhagen.

Hildegard also wrote theological treatises, two legendary biographies, poems and hymns, one of the earliest mystery plays (with musical accompaniment) and the earliest surviving mass music composed by a woman.[9] She invented, or at least passed on, a glossary of a coded language with Latin and German equivalents, apparently used for communication by members of the convent in the presence of strangers.

Hildegard died in 1179 at the age of 81. She was investigated for sainthood three times. Although never officially canonised, she was placed in the Roman Martyrology, and the Church permitted her to be honoured as a saint.

Hildegard was responsible for passing on to the twelfth century many of the cosmological ideas of the Judaeo-Christian and Greek traditions. But she was not merely a 'transmitter' – her cosmology was spiced with a great deal of originality.[10] Her visionary works represented an early attempt at expressing a coherent philosophy of the universe using spiritual allegory. Her 'visions' of the physical world were designed to reveal the spiritual world and eternal truths, complicating modern attempts at interpretation, but the miniatures accompanying her manuscripts provide important clues. Hildegard often placed herself in the corner of the illustrations 'recording the vision'.

Hildegard envisioned a spherical earth surrounded by concentric celestial shells that influenced terrestrial events (see Figure 7). This idea, dating back at least to the Pythagoreans, had penetrated Western Europe long before the twelfth century and it is remarkable that Hildegard could present it as a new revelation. But the details of her scheme were unique. In *Scivias*, the earth, made up of the four elements, was surrounded by the spherical atmosphere (*alba pellis* or *aer lucidus*). The four elemental shells of the universe each contained one of the cardinal winds, represented as the breath of a supernatural being, and two accessory winds. The spherical water zone (aer aquosus) was the first of these. The clouds, located in the outer reaches of the aer aquosus, contracted, expanded and blew around, hiding or revealing the heavenly bodies beyond. In the diagram accompanying this vision, Hildegard placed east at the top and north on the left with the east–west axis elongated. Thus the outer zones were egg-shaped. (Most cosmologists conceived of a totally spherical universe, following the design of the ancients.) The oval-shaped purus aether (air) surrounded the aer aquosus and was the widest of all the zones. It held the moon, the inner planets – Venus and Mercury – and the constellations of fixed stars.[11] Next was the dark narrow inner fire (umbrosa pellis or ignis niger), source of hail and lightning. Encompassing it was the lucidus ignis or outer fire, with its eastern (upper) end elongated and pointed. This was home to the sun and the outer planets – Mars, Jupiter and Saturn.

Hildegard envisioned the interior of the earth as made up of two cone-shaped cavities – purgatory and hell. Like her contemporaries, she assumed the underside of the terrestrial globe to be partly under the ocean and partly in the mouth of a monster (the 'Destroyer'). Climate and seasons were reversed in the northern and southern hemispheres. The movement of the celestial spheres and the seasonal changes on earth were facilitated by the winds of each zone. Thus the prevalent winds acted as the motive power, causing the lengthening of days in the spring and their shortening in autumn:

> I looked and behold the east and the south wind with their collaterals, moving the firmament by the power of their breath, caused it to revolve over the earth from east to west; and in the same way the west and north wind and their collaterals, receiving the impulse and projecting their blast, thrust it back again from west to east . . .
> I saw also that as the days began to lengthen, the south wind and his collaterals gradually raised the firmament in the southern zone upwards towards the north, until the days ceased to grow longer. Then, when the days began to shorten, the north wind with his collaterals, shrinking from the brightness of the sun, drove the firmament back gradually southward until by reason of the

lengthening days the south wind began yet again to raise it up.
(Singer, 1928, pp. 209-10)

The four elements of the universe were in harmony until the Fall of
Man. After the Fall, the elements existed in a state of confusion on
the terrestrial globe and there they will remain until the Last
Judgment. This concept reappeared throughout Hildegard's mystical
and naturalistic works. In the celestial spheres, the elements were
still partly in harmony, arranged on the basis of density, with fire
outermost and earth at the centre. Like other mediaeval writers
including Dante, Hildegard realised that there was a serious problem
with this arrangement: obviously the air was directly above the
earth, and water was below the earth and above the air, penetrating
both, rather than in between. In both *Scivias* and *LDO* Hildegard
attempted to rationalise this unlikely arrangement.

By the time she set to work on *LDO*, Hildegard had learned that the
universe was usually represented as concentric spheres. Perhaps
influenced by newly-translated Aristotelian works, she attempted to
bring her visions into line with the accepted scientific theories of the
age, and her egg-shaped universe was abandoned. Recognising that
the water zone must mingle with the earth, she formed the
atmosphere by extending the first water sphere earthwards, with the
cloud zone now in the outer portion of the atmosphere. The second
water sphere was surrounded by the air (*purus aether*) and two outer
circles of fire. She also introduced 'exact measurements' into her
scheme: the superior elements – fire, air and water – were arranged in
three spheres of equal width (see Figure 8).

In the second and third visions of *LDO*, Hildegard attributed to
each of the winds qualities associated with various animals.
Realising that the planets must move independently of their spheres,
she conveniently added a new vision in which a blast, pictured as a
supernatural creature with a human face and located in the outer
fire, moved the planets from west to east in opposition to the
movement of the firmament. From each sphere and astronomical
body and from the winds and clouds, influences, indicated by lines,
extended down to a human figure – the microcosm.

The doctrine of the macrocosm and the microcosm constituted
'the central dogma of mediaeval science'.[12] As a cosmological theory
it lasted well into the Renaissance with such scientists as Paracelsus,
Harvey, Robert Boyle and Leibniz subscribing to it. At the root of the

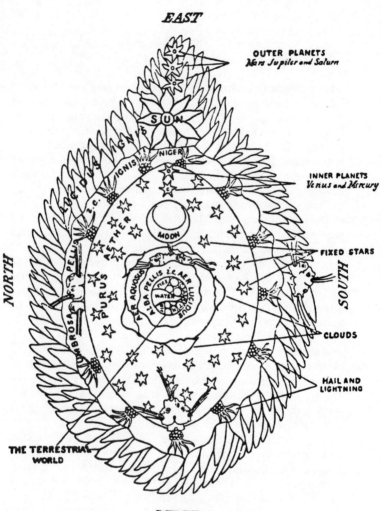

7 Hildegard's first scheme of the universe (simplified by Charles Singer)

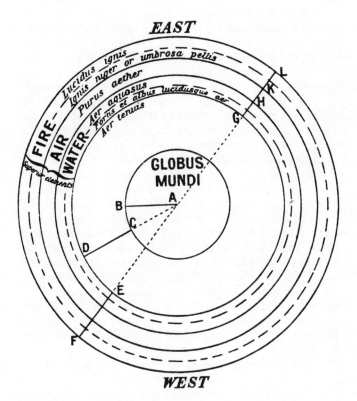

8 *Hildegard's later scheme of the universe (reconstructed by Charles Singer)*

doctrine lay the essential similarity between the structure of the universe and human anatomy and, in Hildegard's view, the qualities of the soul.

As with her vision of the universe as concentric spheres, the macrocosmic–microcosmic theory did not originate with Hildegard's 'divine inspiration', but dated back at least to the Pythagoreans. Nevertheless, Hildegard's work was unique, both in the details of her theory and in her valiant attempts to fit what was known of anatomy and physiology, her concept of the human mind and her theological beliefs into her macrocosmic scheme. The celestial elements influenced the human body by acting, through the medium of the atmosphere, on the blood and humours. Each of the cardinal winds was representative of the elemental zone in which it originated and affected the corresponding humour in the body.

Obviously such doctrines bordered on astrology, as contentious a subject in the twelfth century as it is today. While condemning astrology, Hildegard held that the heavenly bodies could occasionally reveal signs from God. The moon, for example, influenced human nature and human affairs. The blood and brain were augmented when the moon was full and diminished as it waned. As the moon changed, winds stirred the firmament, raising fogs from the sea and other waters. This corresponded to human weeping: as emotion stirred the heart, from joy or sorrow, humours were stirred in the lungs and breast. These humours, rising to the brain, were released through the eyes as tears. The moon had other effects: deformed children were the result of procreating without regard to the phases of the moon.

LDO was devoted almost entirely to the paradigm of the macrocosm–microcosm. Hildegard described the influences of the celestial bodies and the superior elements as revealed by the powers of nature on earth and on humans:

> I saw that the upper fiery firmament [the *lucidus ignis*] was stirred, so that as it were ashes were cast therefrom to earth, and they produced rashes and ulcers in men and animals and fruits ... Then I saw that from the *ignis niger* [inner sphere of fire] certain vapours descended, which withered the verdure and dried up the moisture of the fields. The *purus aether*, however, resisted these ashes and vapours, seeking to hold back these plagues ... And looking again I saw that from the *fortis et albus lucidusque aer* [inner water

sphere] certain other clouds reached earth and infected men and beasts with sore pestilence, so that they were subjected to many ills even to the death, but the *aer aquosus* [outer watery sphere] opposed that influence so that they were not hurt beyond measure ... Again I saw that the moisture in the *aer tenuis* [atmosphere] was as it were boiling above the surface of the earth, awakening the force of the earth and making fruits to grow. (Singer, 1928, pp. 219-20)

In *Causae et Curae* Hildegard discussed the relation of the four humours to health in great detail and more imaginatively: as the humours were disturbed the veins began to boil; a fever might set in, passions such as wrath and petulance aroused, and the mind affected. She defined character types – and in some cases even predicted fates – according to the various combinations of the humours. Describing choleric, sanguine, melancholy and phlegmatic women and men, she forecast their relationships with spouses and the type of children they would conceive. She closed *Causae et Curae* with a description concerning the nature of a person conceived on each day of the lunar month. For example, a woman conceived on the eighteenth day would have health and longevity but with a predisposition toward insanity, and she would be a cunning liar, causing the death of honourable men. Since Hildegard used the day of conception rather than birth, this was not astrology; nor could she be proved wrong.

Some of Hildegard's more interesting biological concepts appeared in *Scivias*.[13] She believed the human body was formed from a seed. Foreshadowing modern hereditary theory, she represented individuals as being unequally endowed with various qualities which, along with physical form, were inherited from the parents. The formless soul came from God, entering the foetus through a long, tube-like structure. *Causae et Curae* included an account of conception and generation, followed by a vivid but matter-of-fact description of male sexual passion, a subject of which Hildegard presumably had scant personal knowledge.

Hildegard's fame as a healer possessed of miraculous powers surpassed even her reputation as a scientific and religious mystic. She was Germany's first important medical writer. Her medicine was a unique combination of Biblical and microcosmic analogies, the Galenic humouralism of popular Benedictine tradition, folk medicine and her own extensive experience. References to specific diseases were vague but, given her own infirmities, it was understandable that she discussed epilepsy, delusions and mental disease in some detail. She emphasised the importance of hygiene and diet, rest and exercise. In Book V of *Causae et Curae* she became the first author to stress the importance of boiling drinking water, especially river and swamp water.

Hildegard subscribed to the common mediaeval belief that each animate and inanimate object was endowed by the Creator with the power to cure or ameliorate a single ailment. Thus *Physica*, the 'Book of Medicinal Simples', functioned as a *Materia Medica*. She prescribed medicine in small doses – simple remedies for the poor and expensive compounds for the wealthy. Although Hildegard inveighed against the diabolical arts and divination, she none the less considered magic to be an integral part of natural substances and phenomena, and so supplied Christian and pagan prescriptions and incantations for counteracting black magic. As with most folk medicine, even some of her more bizarre remedies may have had a physiological basis.

The twelfth century witnessed the beginnings of a scientific renaissance. In Italy and in Spain, wherever the Moslem world touched the European, the influence of Arab science was becoming apparent. The science of the ancient Greeks was being translated from Arabic into Latin, and soon Europe would be rediscovering the knowledge of the ancients, as it had been preserved and improved upon by the Arabs. Hildegard's writings were among the very earliest to exhibit these indirect influences of Arab science on western European thought.

The historian George Sarton called Hildegard the 'most distinguished naturalist' and the most original twelfth-century philosopher in Western Europe.[14] Her writings were renowned in her lifetime and pamphlets and spurious prophecies circulated under her name for many years. Her works were later printed and widely distributed. They continued to affect the direction of scientific thought well into the Renaissance.

Yet Hildegard was not as unique as one might suppose. At the Hohenberg convent on Mount St Odile in Alsace, another twelfth-century abbess was composing an important work of science. Herrad of Landsberg's *Hortus Deliciarum* ('Garden of Delights') was an encyclopaedia of religion, history, astronomy, geography, philosophy, natural history and medical botany. As the technical terms were in both Latin and German, it served as a text for teaching Latin to her nuns. Herrad illustrated the work herself and it was considered of great artistic value. The only manuscript copy was destroyed in the 1870 siege of Strasbourg, but fortunately an early nineteenth-century scholar had copied large sections of it.

As a child, Herrad was sent to study at Hohenberg, succeeding Relind as abbess there in 1167 and assuming responsibility for 47 nuns and 13 novices. The nuns of Hohenberg were Augustinian canonesses, who enjoyed many freedoms. *Hortus Deliciarum* provides a detailed picture of their lives. In 1187 Herrad built a large hospital in the convent grounds where she worked as the chief physician until her death in 1195.

Herrad wrote the greater part of *Hortus Deliciarum* between 1160 and 1170, continuing to make additional entries until 1190. Although based primarily on Biblical sources and her own knowledge and experience, Herrad shared none of Hildegard's reluctance to quote from secular writers and to utilise 'worldly wisdom'.

Although there was no known contact between Herrad and Hildegard, there were resemblances in their work as well as in their lives. Surviving copies of Herrad's illustrations are reminiscent of Hildegard's; Herrad's microcosmic concepts were also similar. She explained more clearly than Hildegard the antipodean inversion of climates, dividing the world into two frigid, two temperate and two tropical zones; and the relationship of the winds to the four elements and their effects on the four humours are also incorporated into Herrad's work.

Hortus Deliciarum included an illustration of the signs of the zodiac and a 'computus' table for determining festival days. Such tables were of the utmost importance in the twelfth century and Herrad's was considered one of the best. She worked out the dates for Easter and the day of the week of Christmas for a cycle of 532 years, from 1175 to 1706.[15]

Herrad and Hildegard were among the last of the scholarly abbesses. Charlemagne's abbey schools had disappeared; in the interests of virtue, many convents were being segregated from the monasteries with which they had previously shared facilities, while the Church hierarchy enacted strict monastic regulations – and occasionally enforced them. Many nuns were cloistered for the first time during the time of Pope Innocent III, and the power and prestige of the abbesses declined. Prioresses in charge of smaller convents were subordinated to male abbots and no new female abbacies were created. By the thirteenth century women were looking to the growing cities, rather than the convents, for educational opportunities.

The late Middle Ages was a time of turmoil and rapid change. Power and influence were shifting from the monasteries and clergy to the towns and the rising middle classes. Once again, learning came to be regarded as a virtue and limited educational opportunities opened up for women outside monasticism. Although misogynist polemics were common, a number of literate upper-class women, such as Christine de Pizan (1364–1430), were writing in defence of women and promoting their education.

With the revival of Greek science, the scholars of the early Renaissance repudiated the achievements of the Middle Ages. Mediaeval women scientists were all but forgotten, but they bequeathed a legacy to the seventeenth and eighteenth centuries. Their heirs were the women of the scientific salons.

6
The Rise of the Scientific Lady

> While learned ladies had always been present among the educated
> nobility, and women had contributed to science and mathematics
> from earliest times, the 'scientific lady' was a product of the
> Scientific Revolution. (Carolyn Merchant, p. 269)

1. Women and the 'Selling' of Science

The Scientific Revolution, beginning with the new astronomy of
Copernicus, changed forever the way educated men and women
viewed their world. Wealthy men of leisure turned to amateur
science, banding together in societies and opening up new vistas for
investigation and discovery: their wives and sisters became 'scientific
ladies'. Although a great many women helped to direct and reflect
scientific thought in the seventeenth and eighteenth centuries, very
few were able to transcend this label. With connotations reminiscent
of the later 'bluestockings', the image of the scientific lady was to
influence the position of women in science for years to come. Long
after men had become professional scientists, women would retain
amateur status in the eyes of society. But if the label was an insult in
the hands of their opponents, it was a source of pride for those
women who attained a level of scientific competency undreamed of
by their mediaeval predecessors. And whilst, with the exception of
religious cosmologists like Hildegard, most women scientists of
the Middle Ages were herbalists or alchemists, midwives or physicians, as the scientific revolution progressed larger numbers of
women took an interest and participated in all areas of scientific
endeavour.

The scientific revolution and the rise of the scientific lady coincided with the beginnings of a controversy over the education of women that was to last for the next 200 years. The centres of science were shifting from Italy – where women scholars had always been respected and honoured – to Northern Europe and England, where women's education had languished. Throughout the Middle Ages the convents had provided women with their only escape from the limitations of married life *and* their only access to an education. With the Protestant Reformation, the convents were dissolved and with them went the educational heritage of women. More often than not, the resources of the convents were turned over to the universities, to the benefit of male scholars. The initial opposition in Northern Europe to the secular education of women, especially in the sciences, was very strong. But learned women also had their supporters, particularly among the Puritans and Quakers. It was the dissenting Protestant sects that were to promote the positive aspects of the scientific lady.

One of the earliest feminists to speak out for women's scientific education was the artist and philosopher, Anna Maria van Schurman of Utrecht (1607–78). A friend of the French philosopher René Descartes, her writings on the education of women were published at Leyden in 1641. Schurman's English disciple was Bathusa Makin. In 1673 Makin drew up a curriculum for women that included scientific study. Following Makin's ideas, Mary Astell (b. 1666) proposed a school along the lines of a mediaeval convent where women could receive an education and live out their lives in peace: 'And I make no question but great Improvements might be made in the Sciences, were not Women Enviously excluded from this their proper Business.'[1] (Although Astell succeeded in raising the money for such a college, the project was blocked by Bishop Burnet as contrary to the spirit of the Reformation.) The utopian authors of the seventeenth century went ever further in their visions of universal education: they would have made scientific studies available to all women, not just those of the upper classes.

Regardless of whether science was deemed suitable for women, in seventeenth-century England and France, for the first time in history, an entire stratum of the female population began to study and speculate about science. The commercialisation of new discoveries and inventions contributed significantly to the rise of the scientific lady. The telescope and microscope became the new 'toys' of the wealthy élite. Society women examined 'wee beasties' with their pocket microscopes and the distant heavens with their telescopes. The manufacturers of optical instruments published scientific books and promoted lecture series aimed at the scientific lady. Efforts to expand the market for their products cut across class lines, reaching rural as well as urban women.

Although reactionaries preached against the proliferation of amateur women scientists, and satirists ridiculed their 'pretensions to learning', it was widely argued that an appreciation of the enormity of the heavens and the abundance of creation would keep women pious and humble: optical instruments would bring women closer to God. As long as scientific ladies confined themselves to the new playthings, avoiding the rigorous study of higher mathematics, physics and medicine (where they would be competing with men), society could accept their new preoccupation with amusement. Indeed, in some aristocratic circles it became socially unacceptable for women to remain ignorant of the latest scientific developments.

In our own age of élitist science, when the most important discoveries are often incomprehensible to the lay person, it is difficult to imagine the tremendous role played by the popularisers of the scientific revolution; but seventeenth-century amateurs hungered for clear explanations of the fascinating new developments. The mechanistic theories of Descartes were popularised by Bernard de Fontenelle. His *Conversations on the Plurality of Worlds* (1686) took the form of a dialogue between a philosopher and the 'Marchioness of G.'. On five consecutive evenings, this beautiful and intelligent 'lady of quality' was escorted through formal gardens while the philosopher instructed her in the intricacies of the Copernican and Cartesian universe. However, the tone throughout was one of condescension: although a woman might not have the mind 'for scientific discovery, she can approach it as many do a romance or novel when they would retain the plot'.[2]

A major attraction of the new astronomy was its emphasis on extra-terrestrial worlds and Fontenelle's book reads almost like a modern work of science fiction. It went through numerous editions and was translated into English in 1688 by Aphra Behn (1640–89). The translation included Behn's commentary on Fontenelle's science. Behn translated Fontenelle because of his tremendous popularity, but her criticisms were so severe that she considered writing her own book on the subject:

I must tell you freely, he hath failed in his Design; for endeavouring to render this part of Natural Philosophy familiar, he hath turn'd it into Ridicule ... And for his Lady *Marquiese*, he makes her say a great many very silly things, tho' sometimes she makes Observations so learned, that the greatest Philosophers in *Europe* could make no better.[3]

The Plurality of Worlds inspired numerous imitations, but by the eighteenth century the scientific popularisers were turning from the Cartesian to the Newtonian universe. Descartes had formulated the first completely mechanistic cosmology – a universe based on matter in motion. The sun and stars of the Cartesian universe were each at the centre of a rotating vortex of matter holding the planets in their orbits. Forty-three years later, in 1687, Isaac Newton's *Principia* substituted mathematical law for Descartes's arbitrary mechanics. Newton's law of universal gravitation explained celestial motion and terrestrial phenomena in a consistent and verifiable mathematical form. The textbooks had to be rewritten.

In Italy Francesco Algarotti's *Il Neutonianismo per le dame* (1737) utilised the now familiar 'philosopher to scientific lady' format for expounding the principles of Newtonian physics and optics. The book was translated into English by Elizabeth Carter (1717–1806) as *Sir Isaac Newton's Philosophy Explain'd For the Use of the Ladies. In Six Dialogues on Light and Colours* (1739). Carter was a member of the Bluestocking Society, a salon of scientists and intellectuals that included Mary Montagu. (The name 'bluestocking' derived from the eccentric dress of botanist Benjamin Stillingfleet, a member of the group; but the term later evolved into a derogatory epithet for educated women.) John Dunton's twice-weekly *Athenian Mercury* (1690–97) was the earliest English periodical to address itself to a female scientific market. The *Mercury* utilised a question-and-answer format in its 'Ladies Day' section, but was so deluged with enquiries that the editors begged their readers to refrain from submitting more.[4] That Dunton and his Athenian Society were made the brunt of several satires in the 1690s was indicative of the journal's popularity.

The Ladies' Diary: or, The Woman's Almanack, Containing many Delightful and Entertaining Particulars, peculiarly adapted for the Use and Diversion of the Fair-Sex appeared annually from 1704 until 1840 when it merged with *The Gentleman's Diary*. In the introduction of the 1718 edition, the editor wrote:

> And, that the rest of the Fair Sex may be encourag'd to attempt
> Mathematics and Philosophical Knowledge, they here see that
> their Sex have as clear Judgements, a sprightly quick Wit, a
> penetrating Genius, and as discerning and sagacious Faculties as
> ours ... and can, carry them thro' the most difficult Problems ...
> This we may glory in as the *Amazons* of our Nation; and Foreigners
> would be amaz'd when I shew them no less than 4 or 5 Hundred
> several Letters from so many several Women, with Solutions
> *Geometrical, Arithemetical, Algebraical, Astronomical* and
> *Philosophical.*[5]

Thus, in addition to the usual almanac-type information, the *Diary*
included articles on astronomy, arithmetic problems and word
puzzles, with prizes awarded for correct solutions. Many women
proposed problems and submitted solutions, although the percentage
of women contributors diminished toward the end of the century.
Women often made their submissions anonymously, by pseudonym
or using only initials. Interestingly, male contributors occasionally
used female pseudonyms.

The scientific entrepreneurs also addressed young women.
Benjamin Martin's *The Young Gentleman and Lady's Philosophy*
and James Ferguson's *An Easy Introduction to Astronomy, for Young
Gentlemen and Ladies* (1768) both featured a pompous young man
who returns from Oxford to initiate his sister into the secrets of
natural philosophy. Martin's text opens with Cleonicus addressing
his sister Euphrosyne:

> Philosophy is the darling Science of every Man of Sense, and is a
> peculiar Grace in the Fair Sex; and depend on it, Sister, it is now
> growing into a Fashion for the Ladies to study Philosophy; and I am
> very glad to see a Sister of mine so well inclined to promote a
> Thing so laudable and honourable to her Sex.

To which Euphrosyne replies:

> I often wish it did not look quite so masculine for a Woman to talk
> of Philosophy in Company ... how happy will be the Age when the
> Ladies may modestly pretend to knowledge, and appear learned
> without Singularity and Affectation![6]

It was no coincidence that Martin and Ferguson were telescope and microscope manufacturers as well as popular lecturers.

Women were also beginning to write and edit their own books and journals. Eliza Haywood's *The Female Spectator* (1744–6) was the first periodical for women published by a woman. It was very popular in North America as well as in England, and the collected issues went through several printings in book-form between 1747 and 1775. Her *Epistles for the Ladies* (1749–50) were almost as popular. Both works emphasised the new revelations of the microscope; but like much of eighteenth-century science digested for ladies, natural history and astronomy were hopelessly intertwined with theology and astrology.

The scientific lady thus found her niche in English society, and as a result, several women scientists rose to prominence. Anne Conway made significant but unrecognised contributions; Lady Mary Montagu's work was praised and appreciated; and Margaret Cavendish brought upon herself both fame and infamy.

2. *'Mad Madge', The Duchess of Newcastle*

Perhaps the best description that can be given of the Duchess of Newcastle is that she was mildly mad and immoderately devoted to Cartesian rationalism. (Gerald Meyer, p. 2)

On 30 May 1667, the newly-formed but already prestigious Royal Society of London opened its doors to a scientific lady. Margaret Cavendish, Duchess of Newcastle, had been invited to visit the Society after considerable debate among its membership (with the dissenters objecting more to her notoriety than to her sex). Arriving fashionably late with a large retinue of attendants, the Duchess looked on as Robert Boyle and Robert Hooke weighed air, dissolved mutton in sulphuric acid and conducted various other experiments for her edification. It was an historic moment for the scientific lady. It was also a personal triumph for the Duchess. She had spent a lifetime trying in vain to win the respect of the male scientific community. Although she achieved a degree of success as a populariser of science, the odds against her were overwhelming. Her sex, her personal eccentricities, and her lack of any formal education assured that her place in the history of science would be that of a singular oddity.

The eighth child of wealthy parents, Margaret Lucas was born into a life of luxury in 1623. At the age of 18, with England embroiled in civil war, she left her sheltered life to become Maid of Honour to Queen Henrietta Maria, wife of Charles I, accompanying her into exile in France after the defeat of the Royalist forces. There she fell in love with and married William Cavendish, a 52-year-old widower.[7] They joined other exiled Royalists in Antwerp where, despite their impoverished state, they rented the mansion of the artist Rubens.

The Cavendishes' informal salon society, 'The Newcastle Circle', included the philosopher Thomas Hobbes and William's brother, Sir Charles. The mechanistic philosophers Descartes and Gassendi numbered among their associates and it was in this group that Margaret Cavendish received her first exposure to science. Eventually, she would help to popularise the mechanistic philosophy of nature that was at the foundation of the scientific revolution.

Late in 1651 Margaret returned to England in a futile attempt to salvage enough of the Newcastle estate to satisfy their legions of foreign creditors. There she first gained a reputation for her extravagant dress and manners as well as for her poetry. Her first anthology, *Poems, and Fancies* (1653), created a sensation in London society – as much for its poor spelling, grammar and rhyming as for the bizarreness of her verse.[8]

Between 1653 and 1671 she wrote 14 'scientific' books, but 'my serious study could not be much, by reason I took great delight in attiring, fine dressing, and fashions, especially such fashions as I did invent myself'.[9] She prided herself on originality rather than scholarship, successfully ignoring the centuries of natural philosophy that had preceded her. She boasted that she would never 'afford boardroom to other people's ideas lest the legitimate offspring of her own brain should be crowded out'.[10] Thus, her scientific theories were unsophisticated and inconsistent at best: at worst they were nonsensical. But she was unrepentant:

> if my *Writing* please the *Readers*, though not the *Learned*, it wil satisfie me; for I had rather be praised in this, by the *most*, although not the *best*. For all I desire, is Fame. . . But I imagine I shall be censurid by my owne *Sex*; and *Men* will cast a *smile* of *scorn* upon my *Book*, because they think thereby, *Women* incroach too much upon their Prerogatives; for they hold *Books* as their *Crowne*, and

the Sword as their Scepter, by which they rule and govern. ('To All Noble and Writing Ladies', sig. A3, 1653)

Margaret had no intention of allowing a lack of knowledge to stand in her way, as she explained in a 1663 preface addressed 'to all Learned Physicians':

> I am to be Pardoned, if I have not the Names and Terms that the Anatomists Have or Use; or if I have Mistaken some Parts in the Body, or Misplaced any; for truly, I never Read of Anatomy, nor never saw any Man Opened, much less Dissected, which for my Better Understanding I would have done; but I found, that neither the Courage of Nature, nor the Modesty of my Sex would Permit me. Wherefore it would be great Chance, even to a Wonder, I would not Err in some; but I have seen the Intrals of Beasts, but never as they are Placed in their Bodies, but as they are cut out to be Drest ... and as for Bones, Nerves, Muscles, Veins, and the like, I know not how they are Placed in the Body. (1663, pp. 249–50)

Undaunted, she proceeded to elaborate her theories on human physiology. Margaret Cavendish presented each of her publications to the universities of Oxford and Cambridge and she resented that her natural philosophy was not taught in academic circles. She ordered a Latin index to accompany the writings she presented to the University of Leyden, hoping thereby to make her work more accessible to European scholars; but her attempts to have her books translated into Latin came to nothing. Her ideas and prose would have baffled the most dedicated translator.

Since the beginning of the century English atomic theory had attempted to explain all natural phenomena on the basis of matter in motion. In the earliest version of Margaret's philosophy, incorporated into *Poems, and Fancies*, atoms all contained the same amount of matter but differed in size and shape, corresponding to the four elements: atoms of earth were square; water atoms round; air particles were long; and fire atoms sharp:

> Small Atomes of themselves a *World* may make,
> As being subtle, and of every shape:
> And as they dance about, fit places finde,

Such *Formes* as best agree, make every kinde.
('A World made by Atomes', 1653, p. 5)

Her theory of disease, based on the old humoural theory, attributed illness to atoms 'fighting' each other, or an overabundance of one atomic shape.

No sooner had Margaret sent her first collection to the printers, than she set to work on a second volume, *Philosophical Fancies* (London, 1653). She was already disavowing her atomic theory, substituting a theory of motion that became the cornerstone of her imaginative natural philosophy. By 1663 she had decided that if atoms were 'Animated Matter', they must have 'Free-will and Liberty'. Thus, like human nations, they would always be at war and could never cooperate to create complex animals, vegetables and minerals: 'And as for Atoms, after I had reasoned with my Self, I conceived that it was not probable, that the Universe and all the Creatures therein could be Created and Disposed by the Dancing and Wandering and Dusty motion of Atoms' (1663, sig. C2^r).

In these early works, including *Nature's Pictures*, Cavendish carried her theories to such extremes that 'she shocked the enemies of atomism, and embarrassed its friends'.[11] Atomists such as Robert Boyle disassociated themselves from such fanciful views. Her writings, and those of Hobbes, with their insistence on the material nature of spirits, also left the atomists open to charges of impiety and atheism. But unlike many seventeenth-century science writers, Margaret seldom mixed theology with her hazy natural philosophy. At the conclusion of *Philosophical and Physical Opinions* she explained that matter and motion expressed God's Divine Plan, but that the Deity would remain incomprehensible and was therefore of no concern to scientists. In the following centuries many natural philosophers would adopt similar arguments to avoid religious controversy.

Margaret was not attacked for her opinions – which were no more absurd than much of what passed for science in the early part of the seventeenth century – rather, she was accused of plagiarism since 'no lady could understand so many hard words'.[12] As a result, she became increasingly defensive and paranoiac. The frontispiece to *Philosophical and Physical Opinions* (1663) pictured her in her study, which was notable for its lack of books. Presumably the empty library supplied proof of her originality.

Although the obscurity of her ideas and her atrocious use of language made it unlikely that anyone would steal her work, she wrote in a concluding epilogue 'to my Just Readers':

I Desire all those, that are Friends to my Book, if not to my Book, for Justice sake, to believe, that whatsoever is New, is my Own, which I hope All is; for I had never any Guide to Direct me, nor Intelligence from any Authors, to Advertise me, but Writ according to my own Natural Cogitations, where, if any do Write after the same Manner, in what Language soever, that they will Remember my Work is the Original of their Discourse; but they that Steal out my Opinions, or Compare them to Old Opinions, that are nothing alike . . . surely they might be Judged to be Fools: But may all such be condemned as False, Malitious, Ridiculous, or Mad. (1663, p. 456)

With the Restoration of the English monarchy and the Cavendishes' return to England, Margaret undertook for the first time a study of the works of other scientists. Not unexpectedly, she found herself in disagreement with almost all of them, including Descartes, Hobbes, Henry More and Francis Mercury van Helmont. Her *Philosophical Letters: or, Modest Reflections upon some Opinions in Natural Philosophy, maintained by several Famous and Learned Authors of this Age, Expressed by way of Letters* (1664) was the result. She sent copies, along with her *Philosophical and Physical Opinions*, by special messenger to the most famous scientists and celebrities of the day, including the Cambridge platonist, Henry More. He mentioned the book in a letter to his friend, the philosopher Anne Conway:

She [the Duchess] is affrayd some man should quitt his breeches and putt on a petticoat to answer her in that disguize, which your Ladiship need not. She expresses this jealousie in her book, but I believe she may be secure from any one giving her the trouble of a reply.[13]

Observations upon Experimental Philosophy, published in 1666 and again in 1668, was a hurried response to Robert Hooke's *Micrographia*. In her 'Preface to the Duke of Newcastle' she wrote: 'I confess, I have but little faith in . . . Telescopical, Microscopical, and the like inspections; and prefer rational and judicious Observations, before deluding-Glasses and Experiments.' In a further preface she added: 'Truly, the Art of Augury was far more beneficial then the lately invented Art of Micrography; for I cannot perceive any great advantage this Art doth bring us.' These new sciences were both unreliable and useless:

> The inspection of a Bee, through a Microscope, will bring him no more Honey; nor the inspection of a grain, more Corn; neither will the inspection of dusty Atoms, and reflections of light, teach Painters how to make and mix Colours ... The truth is, most of these Arts are Fallacies, rather than Discoveries of truth. (1668a, sig. B3)

In fairness to the Duchess, she was not entirely wrong about the new telescopes and microscopes. The lenses were often of very poor quality, distorting images and leading to mistaken interpretations. Nevertheless, her 'science by speculation' could not stand up to Hooke's decisive microscopic discoveries.

Included in the same volume with *Observations* was a semi-scientific utopian romance, *The Blazing World*. This was to prove the most popular of her writings. In this strange tale the Duchess finds herself shipwrecked on an island called 'The Blazing World' where, by marrying the Emperor, she becomes Margaret I: 'I am not Covetous, but as Ambitious as ever any of my sex was, or can be; which makes, that though I cannot be Henry the fifth or Charles the Second, yet I endeavour to be Margaret the First' (1668a, 'To the Reader'). On her imaginary island Margaret learns mathematics, astronomy, biology, alchemy and geology from a bizarre assortment of beast-men, and she founds schools and scientific societies – accomplishments that were unthinkable for a woman in seventeenth-century England.

On occasional visits to London, the Duchess's beauty, wealth and eccentricities – not to mention her intellectual pretensions – made her a popular spectacle: a 'mad, conceited, ridiculous woman', the diarist Pepys called her (XIV, 344). But she fascinated him. He journeyed to Whitehall hoping to catch a glimpse of her entourage: 'There is as much expectation of her coming to Court ... as if she were the Queen of Sheba' (XII, 254).

The wife of John Evelyn described a visit to the Duchess in the same year:

I was surprised to find so much extravagancy and vanity in any person not confined within four walls. Her habit particular, fantastical, not unbecoming a good shape, which she may truly boast of . . . Her mien surpasses the imagination of poets, or the descriptions of a romance heroine's greatness; her gracious bows, seasonable nods, courteous stretching out of her hands, twinkling of her eyes, and various gestures of approbation, show what may be expected from her discourse, which is as airy, empty, whimsical and rambling as her books, aiming at science, difficulties, high notions, terminating commonly in nonsense, oaths, and obscenity.[14]

But the Duchess mellowed with age. *Grounds of Natural Philosophy* (1668) represented the final revision of *Philosophical and Physical Opinions*, and while not abandoning her mechanistic ideas about matter and motion, she now expressed them more briefly and tentatively.

The Duchess acted as her own physician, steadfastly ignoring the counsel of her doctor who diagnosed her chronic illness as a combination of hypochondria and a sedentary lifestyle. With self-inflicted prescriptions, purging and bleeding, her health deteriorated rapidly. She died in 1673 and was buried in Westminster Abbey.

The Duchess of Newcastle's reputation as mad was undeserved; and if her speculations had little impact, she did help to popularise some of the significant new theories of the scientific revolution. Her work spoke out loudly for the education of women – if only to prevent others from repeating her extravagant errors. And her visibility as England's first recognised woman scientist and her outspoken if inconsistent feminism had an impact on the future of women in science.[15] In the next century the fame of Margaret Cavendish was rivalled by only one woman – the feminist, Lady Mary Wortley Montagu.

3. Lady Mary Montagu, Scientist and Feminist

In the eighteenth century smallpox killed approximately 60 million people world-wide. In the British Isles alone, 45,000 people died of the disease annually. Milkmaids had long known that exposure to cowpox provided immunity to smallpox and variolation (a type of immunisation against smallpox) had been practised in China, India and the Middle East for centuries, but it took a brilliant and intrepid

Englishwoman, Lady Mary Wortley Montagu (1689–1762), to introduce the practice to Britain and the rest of Western Europe.

In 1717 Lady Mary travelled to Turkey with her husband, the British Ambassador at Constantinople. There she first witnessed variolation. She described the procedure in a letter to her friend Sarah Chiswell:

> The small-pox, so fatal, and so general amongst us, is here entirely harmless by the invention of *ingrafting*, which is the term they give it. There is a set of old women who make it their business to perform the operation every autumn... People send to one another to know if any of their family has a mind to have the small-pox: they make parties for this purpose, and when they are met (commonly fifteen or sixteen together), the old woman comes with a nut-shell full of the matter of the best sort of small-pox [pus from a victim of a mild attack], and asks what veins you please to have opened. She immediately rips open that you offer to her with a large needle (which gives you no more pain than a common scratch), and puts into the vein as much venom as can lie upon the head of her needle, and after binds up the little wound with a hollow bit of shell... The children or young patients play together all the rest of the day, and are in perfect health to the eighth. Then the fever begins to seize them, and they keep their beds two days, very seldom three ... and in eight days' time they are as well as before their illness... Every year thousands undergo this operation... There is no example of any one that has died in it; and you may believe I am very well satisfied of the safety of the experiment, since I intend to try it on my dear little son ... and I should not fail to write to some of our doctors very particularly about it, if I knew any one of them that I thought had virtue enough to destroy such a considerable branch of their revenue for the good of mankind. (1 April 1717; vol. I, pp. 184–5)

This statement was to prove prophetic. On her return to England, Lady Montagu had her daughter inoculated and she succeeded in interesting Caroline, Princess of Wales, in the procedure. Under Lady Mary's direction experiments were conducted, first on half a dozen condemned prisoners, and then on six orphans. The experiments were successful and the Princess had two of her daughters inoculated. The practice spread rapidly throughout the country despite vehement opposition from both the medical profession and the Church. In a rebuttal to these attacks, Lady Mary published anonymously her 'Plain Account of the Inoculating of the Small-Pox by a Turkey Merchant.' Since variolation did occasionally result in severe disease (fatal in perhaps 2–3 per cent of cases, as compared with 20–30 per cent with naturally contracted smallpox), the popularity of inoculation declined, but not before the practice had spread to continental Europe and North America.

Lady Mary was one of the most fascinating women of the eighteenth century. The great grand-daughter of the diarist Sir John Evelyn, her mother died when Mary was still a young child. Her father, the Duke of Kingston, took scant interest in his family, but Mary set upon a course of self-education, utilising his library. In 1712 she eloped with Edward Wortley Montagu to escape an arranged marriage.

Even as a young woman, Lady Mary was known for her scholarship. At the age of 20 she sent her mentor, the Bishop of Salisbury, her English translation of Epictetus along with a letter:

> My sex is usually forbid studies of this nature, and folly reckoned so much our proper sphere, we are sooner pardoned any excesses of that, than the least pretensions to reading or good sense. We are permitted no books but such as tend to the weakening and effeminating of the mind. . . There is hardly a character in the world more despicable, or more liable to universal ridicule, than that of a learned woman: those words imply . . . a tattling, impertinent, vain, and conceited creature. (Vol. II, p. 5)

Lady Mary became an active and outspoken feminist with 'a tongue like a viper and a pen like a razor'.[16] Her wit and forcefulness (and her stormy relationship with Alexander Pope) soon brought her notoriety. Her volumes of diaries and letters, consciously written for posterity, number among the most important literary documents of eighteenth-century England. In January of 1753 she wrote to her daughter, the Countess of Bute, concerning the proper education of her grand-daughter:

> I believe there are few heads capable of making Sir I. Newton's calculations, but the result of them is not difficult to be understood by a moderate capacity. Do not fear this should make her affect the character of Lady –, or Lady –, or Mrs –: those women

are ridiculous not because they have learning, but because they have it not.

But she concluded the letter with a warning that the child should

> conceal whatever learning she attains, with as much solicitude as she would hide crookedness or lameness; the parade of it can only serve to draw on her the envy, and consequently the most inveterate hatred, of all he and she fools, which will certainly be at least three parts in four of all her acquaintance. (Vol. II, p. 237)

Lady Mary was speaking from experience.

In 1736 Mary Montagu fell desperately in love with the popular science writer Francesco Algarotti. She was 47 and he 24 and her passion was not returned. Nevertheless, three years later she left her husband and followed Algarotti to Italy, but in the meantime Algarotti had moved to Berlin to the court of Frederick the Great. Lady Mary stayed on in Venice, establishing her salon on the Grand Canal. On 10 October 1753 she wrote to her daughter:

> the character of a learned woman is far from being ridiculous in this country, the greatest families being proud of having produced female writers; and a Milanese lady [Maria Agnesi] being now professor of mathematics in the university of Bologna, invited thither by a most obliging letter, wrote by the present Pope... To say truth, there is no part of the world where our sex is treated with so much contempt as in England. (Vol. II, p. 252).

Later in the eighteenth and nineteenth centuries other women scientists would flee the stifling atmosphere of England for the more congenial Italy.

Lady Mary paved the way for public acceptance of scientific inoculation in Europe, and her early work on variolation was a first step toward the formulation of the germ theory of disease. Robert Reid summed up her accomplishments thus:

> she had applied certain scientific principles to her observation. She had, like others before her, thought up a theory to link inoculation of mild smallpox with immunity from smallpox, and had devised experiments, immoral as they undoubtedly were, to

test her theory. Finally she had published her results: broadcast with a fanfare would perhaps be a better description.

Her flair for personal publicity was an important ingredient in her successful impact on eighteenth-century scientific thinking. Without it, without royal patronage and a fashionable following, the discovery might have remained as hidden as it was before Lady Mary appeared on the Turkish scene. In the tradition of the English amateur natural philosopher, the tradition of Bacon and of Boyle, she had made her contribution to science well. (p. 13)

Lady Montagu was one of the last of the great scientific ladies. Women had been educating themselves and making their scientific views heard in the salons of Paris, and a male backlash was inevitable.

4. The Scientific Lady Satirised

It was the salon women of the Age of Enlightenment who encouraged the new philosophies of Descartes, Newton, Leibniz and others, setting the stage for political as well as scientific revolution. But while the works of Descartes were first being followed in the salons of Madame de Sévigné, Madame de Grignan and the Duchesse du Maine, the scientific lady came under attack.

It began with Molière's 1672 satire Les Femmes Savantes (The Learned Ladies). Molière was not attacking the truly intelligent and educated woman, rather he was ridiculing pseudo-intellectual bourgeois society that blindly adopted the rhetoric of science. But misogynists of the day took him at face value, and both French and English playwrights rushed to imitate his successful satire.[16]

Boileau-Despreaux made the eminent salonist Mme de la Sablière, who had undertaken a serious study of maths and astronomy, the butt of his Satire contre les femmes (1694), describing her as spending her nights, astrolabe in hand, observing the planet Jupiter – a nocturnal occupation that he claimed weakened her eye-sight and ruined her complexion.

James Miller's Humours of Oxford, published anonymously in 1726, was one of the bitterest attacks on the scientific lady: 'Lady Science . . . a great Pretender to Learning and Philosophy' spent her days dreaming of life on Jupiter. In a particularly cutting final act, she admitted her folly and vowed to reform:

I will destroy all my *Globes, Quadrants, Spheres, Prisms, Micro-scopes...* I'll Convert my *Air-Pump* into a *Water-Pump,* send all my *Serpent's Teeth, Mummy's-Bones,* and *monstrous Births,* to the *Oxford Museum;* for the Entertainment of other as ridiculous Fools as my self.

The de Goncourt brothers equally left a derogatory account of *les précieuses,* as the French women intellectuals were called by their detractors:

Novels disappeared from the dressing-tables of women; only treatises of physics and chemistry appeared on their *chiffonières...* A woman no longer had herself painted on a cloud of Olympus but in a laboratory... A newspaper arose to fill the need of the times and cater to the tastes of woman. Mingling science and ornamental arts, side by side with Poetry . . . it furnished descriptions of machines, remarks on Astronomy, letters on Physics, excerpts on Chemistry, research in Botany and Physiology, Mathematics, Domestic Economy... and the Proceedings of the Academy... And what prettier picture than all those pretty heads turned towards the doctor enthroned in his curulian chair, at the end of a long table laden with crystallizations, globes, insects and minerals?

 . . . No science repels her; the most virile sciences seem to exercise a temptation and a fascination. The passion of Medicine is almost universal in society; the craze for Surgery is frequent. Many women learn how to wield the lancet, even the scalpel. Others are jealous of the granddaughter of Madame Doublet, the Comtesse de Voisenon. From the physicians received at her grandmother's, she had learned something of the art of healing, and she practiced her cures, at her country seat, among her friends, on anyone she could lay hands on; until at last certain jokers, by inserting a notice in the *Journal des Savants,* made her believe she was elected President of the College of Medicine... For, at this period, Anatomy is among the chief feminine fads. Certain women of fashion even dream of having, in a corner of their gardens, a little boudoir containing those *delights* of Mademoiselle Biheron, the great artist in anatomic subjects, made of wax and of *chiffons,* a glass case filled with corpses! A young miss of eighteen, in fact, the Comtesse de Coigny, was so passionately fond of this horrible study, that she would never travel without taking in the seat of her coach a corpse to dissect, as one takes a book to read. (pp. 279–82)

There is no question that many so-called scientific ladies were in fact intellectual frauds. Observation and experimentation were fashionable and many women pursued the superficialities of scientific discovery, with no real understanding of the underlying physical and mathematical principles. However, countless others took their studies very seriously. And at no other time had so many women been such an integral part of the scientific community.

They obtained their education in the sciences in whatever way they could. In astronomy, chemistry, mathematics and physics, natural history and medicine, women were experimenting, testing, validating and disposing of the new theories of the scientific revolution.

7
From Alchemy and Herbs: Chemists and Physicians of the Scientific Revolution

1. The New Chemists

> [C]hemistry is a science particularly suited to women, suited to their talents and to their situation. (Maria Edgeworth 1795, p. 66)

The seventeenth century witnessed the first major treatise on chemistry written by a woman since Maria the Jewess 1600 years earlier. Marie Meurdrac's *La Chymie charitable et facile en faveur des dames* was published in Paris in 1666 with later editions appearing in 1680 and 1711. Unaware of Maria and the other early alchemists, Meurdrac believed herself to be the first woman to write such a treatise. Her six-part work covered laboratory principles, apparatus and techniques, animals, metals, the properties and preparation of medicinal simples and compound medicines, and cosmetics. The treatise also included tables of weights and of 106 alchemical symbols. She based her work on the alchemical precept that substances were formed of three principles: salt, sulphur and mercury.

In the foreword to her book, Meurdrac described her quandary:

> When I began this little treatise, it was solely for my own satisfaction and for the purpose of retaining the knowledge I have acquired through long work and through various oft-repeated experiments. I cannot conceal that upon seeing it completed better than I had dared to hope, I was tempted to publish it: but if I had reasons for bringing it to light, I also had reasons for keeping it hidden and for avoiding exposing it to general criticism. I remained irresolute in this inner struggle for nearly two years: I

objected to myself that it was not the profession of a lady to teach;
that she should remain silent, listen and learn, without displaying
her own knowledge; that it is above her station to offer a work to
the public and that a reputation gained thereby is not ordinarily to
her advantage since men always scorn and blame the products of a
woman's wit... On the other hand, I flattered myself that I am not
the first lady to have had something published; that minds have no
sex and that if the minds of women were cultivated like those of
men, and if as much time and energy were used to instruct the
minds of the former, they would equal those of the latter.[1]

With the work of Antoine and Marie Lavoisier chemistry joined the
scientific revolution. The Lavoisiers collaborated for many years and
Marie's contributions are impossible to separate from those of her
more famous husband. Together they brought about a fundamental
transition in chemistry, replacing the arcane tenets of alchemy with
systematic scientific principles.

At the age of 14, Marie Anne Pierrette Paulze (1758–1836) had
married the 28-year-old Antoine Lavoisier. It was a marriage of
convenience, contracted by Marie's father to save her from a
proposed match with an elderly and dissipated suitor: it proved to be
one of the most fruitful unions in the history of science.

Antoine Lavoisier, already an established chemist, directed the
interests and education of his remarkably gifted young wife. Marie
began by learning Latin and English in order to translate the
important new chemical treatises from England. Her major translations were to include the works of Joseph Priestly and Henry
Cavendish and Richard Kirwan's crucial papers 'Essay on Phlogiston'
and 'Strength of Acids and the Proportion of Ingredients in Neutral
Salts' (the latter, including her original commentary, appeared in
Annales de chimie in 1792). A talented artist, Marie studied with the
French painter Louis David and illustrated her husband's many publications. She assisted with his experiments, took all the notes, kept
the laboratory records and carried on their scientific correspondence.

Marie turned the Lavoisier home into a popular scientific meeting
place. In 1787 the British agricultural economist, Arthur Young,
visited Paris and left this account:

Madame Lavoisier, a lively, sensible, scientific lady, had prepared a
déjeuné Anglois of tea and coffee, but her conversation on Mr

Kirwan's *Essay on Phlogiston*, which she is translating from the English, and on other subjects, which a woman of understanding that works with her husband in his laboratory knows how to adorn, was the best repast. (p. 78)

In the early eighteenth century, heat and fire remained unexplained phenomena and even the most common gases were unknown to chemists. The phlogiston theory of Stahl and the German iatro-chemists explained the process of burning as the decomposition of compound substances into their simpler components. (Phlogiston was defined as the essential element in all combustible substances.) Heat liberated the phlogiston, leaving behind the calx (a fine powder). Reduction of a metallic calx (nowadays called an oxide) required that the phlogiston be restored. However since phlogiston did not exist, the theory retarded the development of quantitative chemistry for many years. The great English chemists of the eighteenth century – Joseph Black, Cavendish and Priestly – all accepted its existence, although they carried out the experiments that led to its demise in the hands of the Lavoisiers.

It was the fact that combustibles *increased* in weight on burning (taking into account the gaseous products) rather than losing weight as predicted by the phlogiston theory that inspired the Lavoisiers. Shortly after their marriage, they set out to prove or disprove the existence of phlogiston once and for all. In 1774 Priestly visited Paris and told the Lavoisiers of his discovery of 'dephlogisticated air'. It was the component of air that they had been searching for – the gas in the atmosphere that supported combustion. Antoine Lavoisier named it 'oxygen' ('acid-former') because he mistakenly believed that all acids contained this element. In 1783 he announced his revolutionary new theory: combustion and oxidation ('calcination') occurred through the chemical combination of a burnable substance with oxygen, and not through the release of phlogiston. In a dramatic gesture, Marie Lavoisier burned the books of Stahl and the phlogiston theorists.

To inaugurate the new science, Lavoisier and his colleagues revised the chemical nomenclature. In *Traité de chimie* (1789), the first modern chemistry text, Lavoisier redefined the term 'element', listing the 23 known elements as the basis of all chemical reactions. Marie Lavoisier's copperplate illustrations for the *Traité* and her original drawings and watercolours for the series survive as the most famous of her works. Many of her plates depict the apparatus for the section on experimental methods where clarity and accuracy were essential.

The Lavoisiers also established the law of conservation of matter; that is, the weight of the products from a chemical reaction must equal the weight of the reagents. They made important studies of animal metabolism, demonstrating that respiration was analogous to inorganic combustion: physiological processes followed the laws of chemistry! These experiments mark the beginning of the end of the vitalistic theories of Anne Conway and Leibniz (see pp. 4–9).

Despite his politically progressive views, Antoine Lavoisier was an upper-class businessman in a nation where revolution was imminent. He was a member of the *Ferme-Générale*, an association of aristocrats who collected taxes on a profit-sharing basis with the King; as a result, he was among the first victims of the revolutionaries. In 1794 Lavoisier followed Marie's father to the guillotine, while Marie became a fugitive and was briefly imprisoned. The Republic confiscated the Lavoisier estate and Marie was supported by an old family servant until her property was restored in the following year.

In 1805 Marie Lavoisier published *Mémoires de chimie* under her husband's name. Lavoisier had left behind much of the first volume, all of the second and fragments of the fourth of the projected 8-volume work. Marie had begun editing the work in 1796 with the assistance of Lavoisier's collaborator Séguin, but the two quarrelled. She finally completed it alone, adding her own introduction, and distributed it *gratis* to all eminent scientists.

Marie married Count Rumford, an American Tory scientist, in 1805; but she was unwilling to assume the role of subservient wife and they separated four years later. Although she continued as a successful businesswoman and philanthropist, Marie found it increasingly difficult to conduct her scientific work and she died an embittered woman.

Meanwhile, chemistry was becoming increasingly popular among women, and the lecture halls of Paris had to be enlarged to accommodate the crowds. 'I have seen as bright a circle of beauty at the chemical lectures of [Guillaume] Rouelle, as at the court of Versailles,' the English novelist Oliver Goldsmith wrote (p. 300). Several of these women advanced from the lecture halls to the laboratory.

Among them was Claudine Picardet, an important translator of chemical treatises. She was employed in the Dijon laboratory of

Louis Guyton De Morveau, whom she married in 1798 after the death of her first husband. Picardet learned Swedish and German in order to translate Scheele's two-volume *Mémoires de chimie* (1785), which included his own independent discovery of oxygen, and Werner's text on minerals and fossils, *Traité des caractères extérieurs des fossiles* (1790). She also translated some of Kirwan's papers on chemistry and it is probable that she assisted Morveau with the commentary and translation of Bergman's two-volume *Opuscules physiques et chymiques* (1780–85).

Elizabeth Fulhame was an early convert to the Lavoisier theories. Her 1794 publication, 'Essay on Combustion', stimulated interest in the new chemistry. In London she performed experiments for Priestly, and carried out research on the reduction of gold salts by light – experiments which Count Rumford subsequently repeated. In 1810, when her work was reprinted in Philadelphia, Fulhame was made an honorary member of the Philadelphia Chemical Society.

For centuries alchemical principles had been applied to problems in medical science. Soon researchers would be applying the new chemistry instead.

2. Alchemical and Herbal Medicine

In the sixteenth century, as a result of the work of German iatrochemists such as Paracelsus and van Helmont, medical remedies began to include chemical and alchemical components. Women physicians and herbalists added alchemy to their repertoires. Isabella Cortese's *Secreti medicinali artificiosi ed alchemici* includes mineral, medicinal and alchemical recipes, and cosmetics. First printed in Venice in 1561, the year of her death, it was translated into German and reprinted several times over the next 100 years. And Oliva Sabuco des Nantes Barrera (b. 1562) wrote a treatise on human physiological and mental states entitled *A New Philosophy of the Nature of Man, Not Known or Achieved by the Ancient Philosophers, Which Will Improve Human Life and Health*. It was a classical treatise, written in Spanish and Latin and citing Hippocrates, Plato, Pliny and Galen. Barrera believed that the passions (fear, anger, despair, unrequited love, shame, anxiety, compassion, etc.) stimulated the secretions of the brain, affecting health and initiating disease. Dedicated to Philip II of Spain, her work was printed in

Madrid in 1587 and again in 1588. Although all but two copies were destroyed by the Inquisition, it was republished in 1728. [2]

Seventeenth-century English ladies acted as their own physicians, experimenting with chemical and botanical remedies and publishing their collections of medicinal recipes. One of these early books, *A choice Manual of rare and select Secrets in Physick and Chirurgerie, Collected and practised by the Countess of Kent (late dec'd)*, was written by Elizabeth Grey (1581-1651). By 1687 the work had gone through 19 editions. Another book was by Mary Boyle (1626-78) (later Lady Warwick) the sister of the famous chemist Robert Boyle. She utilised his discoveries in her medical practice, and collaborated with her sister Lady Ranelagh on a book of medical recipes, which included an alphabetical list of herbs and their uses, and an index of chemical and astronomical symbols.[3]

One of the most famous herbals of all was written and illustrated by Elizabeth Blackwell (1712-70). Her husband was a physician who abandoned medicine to found a printing business. When this enterprise failed he landed in debtors' prison, but his resourceful wife came to his rescue. Moving close to the Chelsea Botanical Garden she set to work on the 500 drawings and copper engravings for her two-volume herbal. She received assistance with the text from her imprisoned husband and from the garden's curator, Isaac Rand, a Fellow of the Royal Society. The comprehensiveness and accuracy of *A Curious Herbal* (1737-9) made it a particularly useful work and it was so successful financially that the luckless Dr Blackwell soon gained his release. Later he became involved in a conspiracy against the Swedish monarchy for which he lost his head. *A Curious Herbal* was enlarged and reissued by Dr Trew of Nuremberg between 1757 and 1773. Elizabeth went on to study obstetrics with William Smellie, (the leader of the movement that replaced midwives with male physicians) and she became a wealthy and successful general practitioner. The *Blackwellia* genus of plants is named after her.

3. Medicine Becomes a Science

Obstetrics first developed as a science in sixteenth-century France, led by the discoveries of Ambroise Paré and Louyse Bourgeois (1563-1636).

Louyse Bourgeois received a sound education in the wealthy Parisian suburb of Saint-Germain, where she married Martin

Boursier, a student-assistant to Paré, the foremost surgeon of the sixteenth century. Louyse, however, was forced to flee with her mother and three young children when Henri III sacked the suburbs in retaliation for the popular insurrection in May 1588. With Boursier away on active duty, the family was left destitute and Louyse eked out a meagre living selling her embroidery. When peace was restored, the family settled in Paris and Louyse determined to learn midwifery from Paré and her husband. For five years she practised among the poor. When her skills were sufficient she joined the guild and became midwife to the gentry and nobility, attending Queen Marie de Medici through seven deliveries (she was paid 1000 ducats for the birth of a royal son and 600 for a daughter). By 1609 Louyse had attended more than 2000 births.

Bourgeois's major treatise, first published in 1608, was the most comprehensive book on obstetrics since the writings of Trotula. She stressed the importance of anatomical studies for midwives and it was evident that she had participated in post-mortems. The treatise covered female anatomy, diagnoses and stages of pregnancy, abnormalities of labour, the signs of foetal death, abortion and theories of infertility. She gave advice on preventing miscarriage and attributed premature birth and hydrocephalus (fluid on the brain) to poor prenatal nutrition. Bourgeois described 12 positions of the foetus at the onset of labour and directions for turning the child if necessary. She was one of the first to call for induction of labour in the case of severe haemorrhage. She also discussed multiple births, post-natal care and the choice of a wet-nurse. Bourgeois urged obstetricians to avoid patients with smallpox and other contagious diseases, and cautioned against indiscriminate bleeding and strong medicines. Her most important discovery concerned the detachment of the placenta. Bourgeois recognised poor nutrition as a factor in anaemia and she was the first to treat chlorosis (adolescent anaemia) with iron. In keeping with medical tradition, she included an ample number of panaceas and instructions for beautifying the skin.

Bourgeois's common sense made up for her lack of literary skill. It was her determination to treat the cause rather than the symptoms of disease that made her one of the most important writers of the scientific revolution.[4] Other French midwives followed in her footsteps.

Marguerite du Tertre de la Marche (1638-1706), head midwife at the Hôtel Dieu, recorded her experiments on amniotic fluid and blood serum in her 1677 obstetrics text. Her research was soon repeated by other scientists.

Marie Louise Lachapelle and Marie Anne Victorine Boivin were the most important women medical researchers in nineteenth-century France. Marie Louise (1769–1821) came from a long line of midwives. In 1795 when her husband died, she succeeded her mother, Marie-Jonet Dugés (1730–97), as head midwife at the Hôtel Dieu of Paris. This large and very old hospital housed the major school of midwifery in France. Like her mother, Lachapelle wrote several important works. Her three-volume *Practice of Obstetrics* (1821–5) was translated into German and went through many editions. This work contained valuable statistical tables compiled from her 50,000 case-studies.[5]

Marie Anne Victorine Boivin née Gillain (1773–1847) was educated by nuns at a hospital in Etampes. After her husband's death, she became Lachapelle's student, assistant, and eventually her successor. In the course of her work she made original anatomical discoveries, invented a vaginal speculum (an instrument which dilates the vagina, allowing the neck of the womb [cervix] to be examined) and was one of the first to use a stethoscope to listen to the foetal heart. Her *Mémoire de l'art des accouchements* (1812) was in its third edition in 1824 and was translated into several European languages. Boivin translated gynaecological works from English and her thesis on the causes of abortion received a commendation from the Royal Society of Medicine at Bordeaux. Her most important work, on the diseases of the uterus, was used as a textbook for many years. Published in 1833, it included 41 plates and 116 figures which she coloured herself.[5] Boivin was director of several hospitals during her career, and in 1814 she received the Order of Merit from the King of Prussia. The University of Marbourg awarded her an honorary MD degree in 1827. She was also a member of several medical societies.

Germany was known for its well-educated women physicians and midwives, most of whom studied with private tutors. But Justine Dittrichin Siegemundin of Brandenburg (1650–1705) was an exception. After suffering a false pregnancy misdiagnosed by a succession of midwives, Siegemundin began studying anatomy, physiology and medicine on her own, eventually becoming one of the earliest scientific midwives in Germany. After 12 years practising amongst the poor, she became midwife to the Royal Family of Prussia in 1688.

Siegemundin made notes on all her cases, and published her

observations in 1689 at the request of Mary, Queen of England and various German princesses. Although she stressed the importance of allowing labour to follow its natural course, her book was best known for its excellent chapter on internal and external version (turning the foetus in the womb to prevent a breech birth), illustrated with 50 copper-plates detailing foetal positions and methods of turning the foetus. The placenta and various membranes were also illustrated diagrammatically. She concluded her treatise with a chapter on medicines and an index, the latter a rarity in books of the time.[6]

Dorothea Christiane Leporin Erxleben (1715–62) was the most famous German medical woman of the eighteenth century. With her brother, she was taught Latin, basic sciences and medicine by their father, a physician. In 1740 her brother entered the University of Halle, but soon fled the country to avoid conscription. Dorothea petitioned Frederick the Great to allow her brother to return and to permit them both to study at Halle. Her petition was granted in April 1741, but instead of attending the university she married, continuing her medical studies at home. In 1749 Erxleben wrote 'Rational Thoughts on Education of the Fair Sex', which was published anonymously in several journals. It stands as a justification for her study of medicine.

In 1753 three Quedlinburg physicians accused her of the unlawful practice of medicine. So, taking advantage of her special dispensation, she entered the university and obtained her doctorate in 1754, after defending and publishing her thesis based on original research into the curative effects of pleasant-tasting medicine. (At the time it was thought that medicines had to taste terrible in order to be effective.) Erxleben was the first woman to earn a doctorate from a German university although several women had previously received honorary degrees in philosophy.

The anatomist Geneviève Charlotte d'Arconville (1720–1805) wrote prolifically on chemistry, medicine, natural history and philosophy. In 1759 she published her translations of Shaid's *Leçons de chimie* and Alexander Monro's *Osteology*. The latter included beautiful anatomical illustrations prepared under her direction. She also authored a study of putrefaction and 32 substances that caused or hindered the process. The second part of this work included d'Arconville's original researches on the action of strong and weak acids on human and beef bile.[7] In 1766 d'Arconville introduced the use of bichloride of mercury as an antiseptic.

Italian women continued to study medicine, although in fewer numbers than during the Middle Ages; several eighteenth-century women graduated from the universities of Italy. Anna Morandi Manzolini (1716–1774) held the Chair of Anatomy at the University of Bologna and her wax anatomical models filled its museum. Manzolini first studied anatomy to assist her husband in his work. After his death she succeeded him as lecturer of anatomy. In 1760 she was elected professor and *modellatrice*. Manzolini made several original discoveries and was offered the Chair of Anatomy at Milan, but preferred Bologna where she remained until her death.

Marie Dalle Donne (1776–1842) also received a formal medical degree. An intellectual prodigy, she came from a poor family near Bologna and was educated by her uncle, a priest. Later she studied comparative anatomy and experimental physiology with several famous scholars. She passed her public examination for the degree of medicine, becoming a professor of obstetrics and the head of a school of midwifery.

Regina Josepha Henning von Siebold (1771–1849), the wife and student of the court physician at Darmstadt, received an honorary doctorate in obstetrics from the University of Giessen in 1815. Her daughter, Charlotte von Siebold Heidenreich (1788–1859), studied physiology, anatomy and pathology at the University of Göttingen from 1811 to 1812. She received her degree in obstetrics from Giessen in 1817 after successfully defending her thesis on extrauterine pregnancy. She insisted on the traditional public defence of her thesis, setting an important precedent for German universities. Later she became a professor at Giessen.

Aletta Jacobs (1854–1929) was one of the first woman physicians in Holland. She came from a family of doctors and after first becoming an apothecary, entered the medical school at Groningen University in 1871. Jacobs received her degree in 1879 from Amsterdam University. A paediatrician and gynaecologist, she joined the fight for women's rights and, in 1881, undertook the first systematic study of contraception. She was also one of the first professional women to retain her maiden name after marriage. A pacifist as well as a suffragist, she opened the world's first birth control clinic in Amsterdam. (Her vast library on the history of women is located at the University of Kansas.)

By the middle of the nineteenth century, the medical schools of Europe were admitting women. But in Britain, where obstetricians and male midwives had so successfully usurped this traditional female role, the struggle for the medical education of women was reaching its peak.

4. Women Invade the Profession

Midwifery and medicinal botany had remained in the hands of women for most of the eighteenth century, but as the number of university-trained doctors increased, competition for patients became acute and the status of medical women declined, particularly in England. The invention of the forceps by the physicians of the Chamberlen family eventually led to the demise of female midwives who saw forceps as a violent intrusion into the natural process of delivery. The battle-lines were drawn up. The use of the forceps often resulted in the infant being torn apart in the womb, or in the rupture of the womb itself, causing the death of both mother and child. These 'butchers', as male midwives were often called, became the special targets of seventeenth- and eighteenth-century feminists.[8]

In Britain, the fight for the admission of women to professional medical schools – and the acceptance of women doctors by hospitals and medical societies – was fierce, but after the middle of the nineteenth century, women would no longer have to adopt the masquerade of James Miranda Stuart Barry (1795–1865) in order to enter the profession.

In 1812, disguised as a man, Dr Barry graduated from Edinburgh School of Medicine, the future site of a major battle in the fight for medical education of women. She was the protégée and probably the niece of James Barry, a disciple of Mary Wollstonecraft. Apparently aided, both at the university and throughout her career, by certain highly-placed connections, the second James Barry became a successful army surgeon. After being stationed in Africa, the Caribbean, Malta and the Crimea, she was appointed Inspector-General of Canadian Hospitals in 1857.

For thousands of years women had disguised themselves as men to study science and become medical doctors, but never in history was the charade carried on so long and so successfully. Barry's reputation was that of a brilliant and reform-minded, if somewhat effeminate, eccentric. Because of her small stature (she was only 5 feet tall) and high-pitched voice, she received her share of ridicule. She responded angrily and during her career fought several duels and faced court martial proceedings. It was not until Barry's death that the truth came out, and then there was common gossip that she was a male hermaphrodite. Although there was absolutely no evidence for such conjecture, it was assumed that no woman could have achieved her professional success, regardless of the subterfuges employed. The authorities subsequently claimed that she had, in fact, been male – and her records mysteriously disappeared.

At the time of Barry's death, Elizabeth Garrett Anderson (1836–1917) was just beginning her struggle. At the age of 23 she was 'recruited' by Elizabeth Blackwell, the first American woman to receive her MD. In 1860 Garrett became a nurse at the Middlesex Teaching Hospital. She studied with tutors and attended whatever chemistry and anatomy lectures she could. But even this created problems: when Garrett obtained a certificate of honour in each of her class examinations, she was urged to keep her success secret. In June 1861, when a visiting physician asked the class a question that only Elizabeth could answer, the male students petitioned for her dismissal. She was barred from future lectures and subsequently expelled from London Hospital.

The Society of Apothecaries was the only medical examining board whose charter prohibited the exclusion of women. They agreed to admit Garrett to their examinations after she had completed a five-year apprenticeship and lecture course. She received a diploma from the Society in 1865, and her name was added to the Medical Register. Subsequently, the Society revised their charter to ensure that no other woman could follow her example. But Garrett still sought a university degree. Having failed in her attempts to enter Oxford, Cambridge, St Andrews, London and Edinburgh universities, she learned French, and enrolled at the University of Paris which began admitting women to its medical degree course in 1868. She became the first woman to take the medical examinations there, receiving her MD in 1870 after defending a thesis on migraine. The British Medical Register refused to recognise her French degree.

With the support of her father, her new husband James Anderson and Emily Davies, founder of Hitchin College for Women, she now embarked on a successful career as a surgeon and founder of a women's clinic. Later she became president of the new London School of Medicine for Women, and for 19 years was the only woman member of the British Medical Association.

Garrett worked closely – if not congenially – with Sophia Jex-

Blake, (1840–1912) the leader of the 'Battle of Edinburgh'. It is a singular story in the history of women and in the history of medicine. A group of women, led by Jex-Blake, attempted to gain entrance to the Edinburgh Medical School by arranging their own classes and attending lectures and examinations by special dispensation. Unfortunately, the women were too successful in their studies, and so were perceived as a threat by male students and by certain faculty members and physicians, especially obstetricians. The students rioted. The women took their case to the courts, and eventually all the way to Parliament. They lost.

Most of the original group went on to obtain medical degrees at Berne, Switzerland, and in 1878 returned to found their own college, the London School of Medicine for Women. The Irish College of Physicians decided to admit their graduates to the licensing examinations, and finally the Royal Free Hospital began to admit women students for clinical study. In the end they won the war.[9]

8
The New Naturalists

1. Natural History during the Scientific Revolution

Throughout the years of the scientific revolution and the Age of Enlightenment the natural sciences, particularly botany, were looked upon as appropriate subjects for women to study. During the Renaissance artists were encouraged to study nature; at the same time the invention of the printing press revolutionised the production of florals, bestiaries and medicinal herbals. Woodcuts permitted the exact reproduction of illustrations, thereby eliminating the errors of mediaeval copyists, and for the first time since the ancient Greeks, botanical and zoological artists strove for accuracy. Among these new scientific illustrators were many women.

Taxonomy was the biology of the scientific revolution. The opening up of the New World and the Far East provided European scientists with thousands of new species to examine and classify. Establishing botanical gardens, menageries and 'cabinets' of minerals, preserved animal specimens and dried plants were favourite hobbies amongst wealthy collectors. And since the natural sciences were not yet fully recognised by university faculties, these studies remained in the hands of amateurs. Of 48 natural history laboratories in eighteenth-century Paris, seven belonged to women.

In the seventeenth century the newly-invented microscope was turned on insects, revealing for the first time their fascinating anatomy, complex life-cycles and modes of reproduction. Entomology was soon added to the list of subjects seriously studied by women. Most women naturalists stayed at home, classifying the plants and animals of their own locale, or those sent to them from abroad. But some women travelled, enriching their expeditions with botanical and zoological studies.

Maria Sibylle Merian was one of the earliest entomologists. She was also one of the finest botanical artists of the period and a founder of biological classification. She was born in Frankfurt in 1647 of a Dutch mother and a Swiss father, a notable botanical engraver who died when she was still in infancy. Maria's step-father was the Dutch flower painter, Jacob Marrell. Encouraged by her parents, Maria developed her talent for biological illustration. Johann Graff of Nuremberg, who had studied with her step-father, became first her teacher and later her husband.

In 1679 and 1683 Merian published the first two volumes of her work on European insects, illustrated with her own engravings and coloured with the help of her daughter, Dorothea. The insects were depicted in various stages of development, with the plants on which they fed. In 1680 Merian published *Neues Blumen Buch*, a catalogue of her hand-painted engravings of garden flowers, intended as models for embroidery and painting on silk and linen. (She had invented a process for cloth-painting that left the material washable and reversible.)

In 1685, after 17 years of marriage, Merian converted to Labadism, an ascetic Protestant sect that claimed among its adherents Anna Maria van Schurman. Merian left her husband, resumed her maiden name, and took her two daughters to live in the commune of the religion's founder, Jean de Labadie, located at the castle of Bosch in the Dutch province of Friesland. The castle housed an excellent collection of tropical insects from Surinam and, as Merian studied these exotic creatures, she dreamed of travelling to South America herself. In 1698 she set sail with Dorothea.

Mother and daughter spent nearly two years in Surinam, collecting and painting insects and plants, until recurrent yellow fever forced Merian to return home. Back in Amsterdam, they published *Metamorphosis Insectorum Surinamensium* (1705). Merian's elder daughter Johanna later returned to Surinam to supply her mother with drawings and specimens for the second edition of *Metamorphosis*.

Moths and butterflies were Maria Merian's special interest. Despite occasional inaccuracies (such as illustrations of 'composite insects' – the result of tricks by her native guides), her works became fundamental references on entomology. *Metamorphosis* was published simultaneously in Dutch and Latin and was later translated into French. After Merian's death in 1717, Dorothea illustrated and published the third volume of her mother's book on European entomology and published a Latin edition of her earliest work on the life-history of the silkworm.

Entomology was very popular amongst English women in the early eighteenth century. Mary Somerset, the first Duchess of Beaufort, was a famous breeder of insects. She also had one of the world's largest collections of rare and exotic plants.

Anna Blackburne (1726–93) devoted her life to her museum at Orford Hall in Lancashire. She obtained many of her specimens through a barter arrangement with Peter Simon Pallas, a German naturalist employed by the Russian government. She carried on a correspondence with the great Swedish taxonomist Linnaeus, a founder of the modern biological classification system. The North American Blackburnian warbler bears her name, and Linnaeus's student, Fabricius, named a species of beetle after her. Her entomology tutor, Johann Reinhold Forster, called the *Blackburnia* genus of plants after her, based on his *B. pinnata* from 'New Holland'. (The name was later changed to *Zanthoxylum blackburnia*.)

2. Botany, The Female Science

What Miss Edgeworth has said of Chemistry may with equal truth be applied to Botany, and may serve to recommend the study of it, as a branch of general education: – 'It is not a science of parade, it affords occupation and infinite variety, it demands no bodily strength, it can be pursued in retirement; – there is no danger of its inflaming the imagination, because the mind is intent upon realities. The knowledge that is acquired is exact; and the pleasure of the pursuit is a sufficient reward for the labour.' (Jane Marcet, *Conversations on Botany*)

It was the philosopher Jean-Jacques Rousseau – hardly a champion of women's education – who helped to popularise the notion of botany as a suitable science for female study. Addressing his *Essais élémentaires sur la botanique* (1771) to Mme Gautier, he wrote:

I think your idea of amusing the vivacity of your daughter a little, and exercising her attention upon such agreeable and varied objects as plants, is excellent: though I should not have ventured to play the pedant so far as to propose it of myself. Since however it comes from you, I approve it with my heart, and will even assist you in it; convinced that, at all times of life, the study of nature abates the taste for frivolous amusements, prevents the tumult of the passions, and provides the mind with a nourishment which is salutary, by filling it with an object most worthy of its contemplation.[2]

Rousseau's condescending tone was consistent with his belief that scientific study was unsuitable for women:

An inquiry into abstract and speculative truths, into the principles, and axioms of sciences and every thing that render our ideas more general, is not the province of women. Their studies ought to be all practical; it is their business to apply the principles discovered by man, and to make the observations by which our sex is induced to establish those principles... With regard to works of genius, they surpass their comprehension, neither have they sufficient attention and precision to succeed in the mathematics; and as for natural philosophy, it belongs only to that sex which is most active, sees most objects, is possessed of most strength, and exercises it the most, to judge of the relations of sensible beings, and of the laws of nature.[3]

Yet, during the eighteenth century it became a well-established dictum that the study of botany would keep women virtuous and passive. And by the mid-nineteenth century it was even considered 'unmanly' in some circles for men to take an interest in plants.

William Withering's *Botanical Arrangement* was one of the first texts on British plants written in English. He recognised that a sizeable proportion of his readership would be female and felt it necessary to adapt the Linnean classification accordingly:

From an apprehension that botany in an English dress would become a favourite amusement with the ladies, many of whom are very considerable proficients in the study in spite of every difficulty, it was thought proper to drop the sexual distinctions in the titles to the Classes and Orders.[4]

Even such innocent diversions into the gentle science of botany came under attack from some quarters. An extreme reaction was that

of the Reverend Richard Polwhele in his 'poetic' diatribe against the
feminist Mary Wollstonecraft:

> Botany has lately become a fashionable amusement with the
> ladies. But how the study of the sexual system of plants can accord
> with female modesty, I am not able to comprehend. . . I have,
> several times, seen boys and girls botanizing together. (p. 8)

'Botanizing', Polwhele feared, would turn girls into disciples of
Wollstonecraft.

As botany grew in popularity, women published books on the
subject for children as well as for adults. Priscilla Wakefield wrote in
her *Introduction to Botany*:

> Botany is a branch of Natural History that possesses many
> advantages; it contributes to health of body and cheerfulness of
> disposition, by presenting an inducement to take air and exercise;
> it is adapted to the simplest capacity, and the objects of its
> investigation offer themselves without expense or difficulty,
> which renders them attainable to every rank in life; but with all
> these allurements, till of late years, it has been confined to the
> circle of the learned, which may be attributed to those books that
> treated of it, being principally written in Latin; a difficulty that
> deterred many, particularly the female sex, from attempting to
> obtain the knowledge of a science, thus defended, as it were, from
> their approach.[5]

Priscilla Bell Wakefield (1751-1832), a Quaker, specialised in
children's books. She also wrote a number of other works, including
*Domestic Recreation: or Dialogues Illustrative of Natural and
Scientific Subjects* (London, 1805); *Instinct Displayed, or Facts
Exemplifying the Sagacity of Various Species of Animals* (London,
various editions 1811-36); and *An Introduction to the Natural
History and Classification of Insects, in a Series of Letters* (London,
1816). Her *Introduction to Botany*, written in the form of letters from
Felicia to her sister Constance and detailing the Linnean system of
classification, had sold out 11 editions by 1841.

Given the acceptability and popularity of the subject, it is not
surprising that botanical societies were less discriminatory than
other scientific associations. When the Botanical Society of London

was founded in 1836 women made up about 10 per cer.t of the membership. It was the first scientific society that actively encouraged the participation of women; it was an organisation of outsiders to the scientific establishment, subscriptions were relatively low, and the Society took up social problems such as the adulteration of food, diseases of potatoes, and sewage treatment. But in the 20 years of the Society's existence, no woman ever gave a major speech or attained elected office, though they were not forbidden to do so. Most women joined to exchange specimens and a few of them produced exhibits.

Two women members, Margaret Stovin of Chesterfield (1756–1846) and Margaretta Hopper Riley of Nottinghamshire (1804–99), were among the first British botanists to specialise in ferns, a study which became very popular later in the century. Stovin was an established naturalist. Her herbarium filled 20 volumes and she donated many specimens to the Society. But Margaretta Riley was the only woman to contribute scientific papers. Her comprehensive monograph on British ferns was read before the Society in 1840. (The *Annals and Magazine of Natural History* mistakenly attributed the work to her husband. As a result John Riley became a recognised botanist and was elected to several scientific societies.) Margaretta Riley sent at least two other papers on ferns to the Botanical Society and a note to the *Phytologist* in 1841.[6]

Anna Worsley Russell (1807–76) was another Society member who published in scientific journals. In 1835 she contributed a list of flowering plants of the Bristol area to Watson's *New Botanist's Guide*. Two years later she was largely responsible for a plant catalogue of the Newbury area. She published 'Anecdotes of Bats Flying by Day-light' in the *Zoologist* (1843) and also contributed to the *Phytologist* (1849). Although today she is remembered as a botanical artist (over 700 of her drawings of fungi are housed in the British Museum), she was one of the finest field botanists of her day.

Before the age of photography, accurate drawings were essential for distinguishing the newly-classified species and varieties of flowers, trees, shrubs and fruit. The taxonomist and horticulturalist both needed artists and many women naturalists took up botanical illustration.[7] Marianne North (1830–90) was probably the best known, if not the most gifted, of these nineteenth-century artists. Her real contribution though was her introduction of a large number of plant species to Europe. Following her father's death in 1869, with only the vaguest notion of geography she travelled to the United States and Canada to paint 'tropical vegetation'. She continued on to Jamaica, Brazil and the Far East where she collected and painted the largest known pitcher-plants. Sir Joseph Hooker subsequently named these *Nepenthes northiana* after her. Later she journeyed to Chile, Australia and the South Seas. North staged an exhibit of 500 of her paintings at the Kensington Museum, accompanied by a botanical catalogue. Eventually she built a gallery at the Royal Botanical Gardens at Kew to house her collection. North's major interest was in the geographical distribution of plants and among the plant species she discovered were *Northea seychellana, Crinum northianum, Areca northiana* and *Kniphofia northiana*.

North was also interested in zoology and her two-volume autobiography, edited and published in 1892 by her sister Catherine Addington Symonds (a botanical illustrator in her own right), was so successful that a supplementary volume, detailing her first European journeys and her trips to Egypt and Syria, was published in 1893.

By the nineteenth century women were also becoming interested in marine biology. In 1863 Margaret Gatty published *British Seaweeds* which included a special section on suitable attire for women collectors. The genus *Gattya* and a new marine worm, *Gattia spectabilis*, were named after her. A popular magazine noted that conchology (the study of shells) was 'peculiarly suited to ladies; there is no cruelty in the pursuit, the subjects are so brightly clean, so ornamental to a boudoir'.[8]

3. The Women Geologists

The Baroness Martine de Beausoleil was perhaps the first woman geologist. An interest in mineralogy led this French aristocrat to devote 30 years to the study of mathematics, chemistry, mechanics and hydraulics. Her writings, *Véritable Déclaration de la découverte des mines et minières* (Paris, 1632) and *La Restitution de pluton* (Paris, 1640), reported on the mine and ore deposits of France and were designed to demonstrate to the king how he could become the richest ruler in Europe by exploiting the country's mineral resources. Beausoleil discussed general metallurgy, types of mines, smelting, the assaying of ores and scientific methods for locating deposits.[9]

By the early nineteenth century geology was developing into a science, spurred on by the activities of the fossil collectors. Among the earliest English collectors were the Philpot sisters – Mary, Margaret and Elizabeth – of Lyme Regis. By 1831 their 'museum' had become famous and they were supplying material to geologists such as William Buckland, Sir Richard Owen, James Sowerby and Henry de la Beche. Louis Agassiz, the Swiss–American geologist, named a species of fossil fish after Elizabeth.

Mary Anning, a friend of Elizabeth Philpot, supported her family with the proceeds from her fossil finds. She excavated and sold the first complete skeleton of an ichthyosaurus, discovered by her young brother. In 1821 she discovered the first nearly-complete skeleton of a plesiosaurus and sold it to the Duke of Buckingham for £200. The publicity accompanying her success brought fossil-collecting to the attention of the general public.

Marta Graham's 'An Account of some Effects of the Late Earthquakes in Chili' (1823) was the first paper by a woman to be published by the Geological Society of London. In 1862 Miss E. Hodgson of Ulverston published an account of a Diatomaceae-containing deposit she had discovered in an iron mine. By the last two decades of the century women were publishing numerous accounts of their geological and paleontological discoveries.

A number of other English women were active in geology throughout the nineteenth century, though they were not credited for their work. Mary Morland (d. 1857) was already a distinguished naturalist when she married William Buckland, one of the founders of British geology, in 1825. She accompanied Buckland on geological expeditions and identified and reconstructed the fossils they collected. She also edited and illustrated several of his works, including his famous 'Bridgewater Treatise', *Geology and Mineralogy Considered with Reference to Natural Theology* (London, 1858).

Charles Lyell, who documented the antiquity of geological formations, also worked with his wife Mary Elizabeth Horner. An accomplished conchologist, she accompanied Lyell on nearly all his geological expeditions, and the author of Lyell's obituary wrote of her: 'Had she not been part of him she would herself have been better known to fame' (p. 342). The Lyells' circle included a great many women interested in natural history, among them Mary's sister – Lady Frances Bunbury – and Lyell's sisters. Lyell's secretary, Arabella Buckley, was the author of natural science books for young people as well as the editor of the final edition of Mary Somerville's *On the Connexion of the Physical Sciences*.

Charles Lyell's lectures at King's College were so popular among scientifically-minded women that the Bishop of London banned women from the lecture halls. Lyell resigned in protest, transferring his lectures to the Royal Institution. However a similar controversy erupted at the Geological Society over the question of women attending his talks.

4. Women Naturalists Become Biologists

By the eighteenth century, biology – the study of life processes as opposed to the study of nature – was developing into a science in its own right (the term 'biology' did not come into use until the early nineteenth century).

A Swiss entomologist, Maria Aimée Lullin, was one of the earliest women to study insects experimentally. She collaborated with her husband, the blind naturalist François Huber (1750–1831), at their home near Paris. Maria carried out their investigations and made all the observations for their classic work on bees published under her husband's name. Their discoveries included the functions of the bee's antennae, the expulsion of drones from the hive, and the fertilisation of the queen in flight.

Eleanor Ormerod (1828–1901) was perhaps the first woman to attain the status of professional entomologist. She was educated by her mother, a botanical artist. Three of her brothers became naturalists. Eleanor often worked in collaboration with her sister, Georgiana, a fellow of the Entomological Society of London. She first began studying entomology in 1852 with insects collected by workers on her father's estate. Soon she had become a self-taught expert on insect infestations of vegetables, crops, forests and domestic animals. She also studied snails, slugs, worms, spiders and fungi, and the biological balances of nature.

Ormerod never married. She was wealthy enough to subsidise the publication and distribution of her work, which included original drawings and diagrams. Her first paper was published in the *Journal of the Linnaean Society* in 1873, and four years later she issued a pamphlet on harmful insects. Soon she was receiving reports and papers from entomologists throughout the world. Her scientific correspondence grew to some 1500 letters a year. In 1881 she published *Manual of Injurious Insects, with Methods of Prevention and Remedy* (a second enlarged edition appeared in 1890). In 1884 she published her 'Guide to Methods of Insect Life'; in 1898, the *Handbook of Insects Injurious to Orchard and Bush Fruits, with Means of Prevention and Remedy*; and in 1900, an 80-page pamphlet, 'Flies Injurious to Stock'. Ormerod also published a number of smaller leaflets that she distributed free. Her most ambitious undertaking was her Annual Report on economic entomology, published between the years 1877 and 1900.

Many of Ormerod's writings were based on original observations and her own anatomical discoveries. She appeared as an expert court witness on infested food shipments and the like, carrying out work usually performed by salaried government entomologists.[10]

Ormerod's recommended methods for pest control included chemicals, mineral oil, kerosene, soap and water, and manual methods such as pruning and burning. She introduced and lobbied extensively for 'paris-green', a controversial, arsenic-based pesticide.

Ormerod was awarded numerous honorary memberships and fellowships including a Doctor of Law degree from the University of Edinburgh in 1900, the first woman to be so honoured. From 1882 to 1892 she was Consulting Entomologist to the Royal Agricultural Society. A political conservative, Ormerod objected vehemently when feminist Lydia Becker (see p. 181) held her up as an example of what women could accomplish with their own resources. In 1889 she was recommended for a newly-created lectureship in agricultural entomology at Edinburgh University but, as she wrote at the time, 'Lady Professors are not admitted in Scotland' (p. 200). It is hardly surprising that the election committee had a difficult time filling the post – when Eleanor Ormerod began her research, economic entomology was an unknown field. She was one of the prime movers in its transformation into an important speciality within the fields of biology and agricultural science. Yet, as a woman, she was never able to attain professional status. The same was true of the women who collaborated with two of the most famous biologists of the era, Lazzaro Spallanzani and Louis Pasteur.

Spallanzani first became interested in science through the influence of his cousin, Professor Laura Bassi, (see p. 136) with whom he studied mathematics at the University of Bologna. It was through her intervention that his parents agreed to let him abandon his law studies for science. Spallanzani's interests were shared by his sister Marianna, a naturalist, and Eleonora of Naples (b. 1768), the Marchioness of Fonseca, who assisted him with his fundamental experiments that helped to overthrow the doctrine of spontaneous generation.

Marie Laurent worked with Pasteur after their marriage in 1849. Over the years she became increasingly involved in his research, working in the laboratory, and writing papers. She assisted her husband during the long search for a rabies vaccine and when Pasteur became paralysed in 1868, it was Marie who supervised their experiments.

When Charles Darwin's theory of evolution by natural selection was published in 1859 the scientific world was shaken as never before. A philosopher, physicist, anthropologist and archaeologist, Clemence Augustine Royer (1830–1902) translated Darwin's *Origin of Species* into French in 1862. Her preface to the work landed her firmly in the company of other scientific 'heretics'. In 1870 she published an expanded discussion of the theory of evolution, *Origine de l'homme et de sociétés*.

These women were pioneers. By the twentieth century all the biological sciences would be considered appropriate fields for women.

Margaret Dutchess of Newcastle.

Margaret Cavendish, Marchioness of Newcastle in her
library: the absence of books is conspicuous. A poem beneath
the engraving reads: 'Her Library on which She look's / It is
her Head her Thoughts her Books. / Scorninge dead Ashes
without fire / For her owne Flames doe her Inspire.
Frontispiece to *Philosophical and Physical Opinions.*

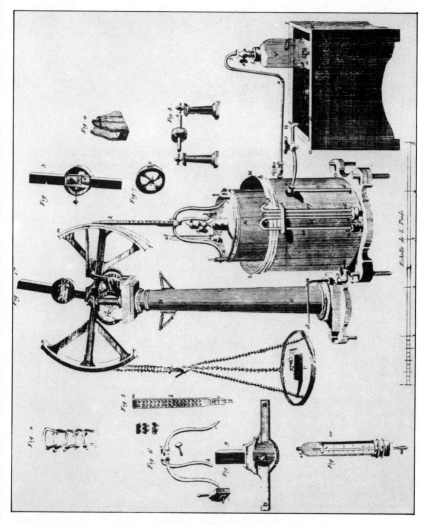

Marie Lavoiser's copperplate illustration of the 'gazometer', an instrument that provided a 'uniform and continued stream of oxygen gas'. Plate VIII from the second volume of *Traité élémentaire de chimie* (1789).

Anna Morandi Manzolini (1716–74) Professor of
Anatomy at the University of Bologna.

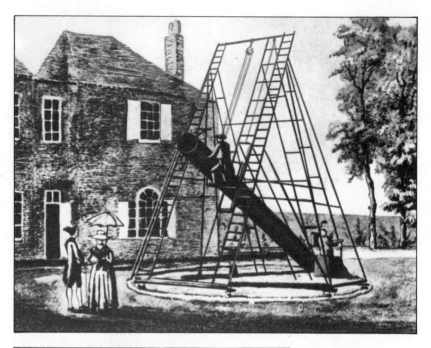

Caroline Herschel
geb d 16ten März 1750
+ d 9ten Januar 1848

Caroline Herschel in her old age.

(left) The Herschels' house at Datchet with the 20-foot telescope.

(bottom left) Herschel's 40-foot telescope.

Emilie du Châtelet.

Ada Lovelace, aged 19.

Sóphia Kovalévsky in the 1870's.

Mary Somerville.

9
The Women Astronomers

1. The Copernican Revolution

Women astronomers played a significant role in the day-to-day work of the scientific revolution. They came from star-gazing families and their contributions to astronomy were in the realm of the mundane – the tedium of observation and calculation. What is notable about the female astronomers of the seventeenth and eighteenth centuries is that there were so many of them.

A century before Newton, Copernicus had revolutionised astronomy by placing the sun at the centre of the universe, with the earth orbiting around it and spinning daily on its axis. The self-taught astronomer and alchemist Sofie Brahe (c. 1556–1643) worked with her more famous brother Tycho at his observatory at Uraniborg. There they made the crucial new observations that enabled Johannes Kepler to determine the elliptical orbits of the planets. Meanwhile Galileo was taking up the battle for the new cosmology. A number of 'forgotten' women astronomers set to work filling in the details, initiating a tradition that would culminate early in the twentieth century with the famous women astronomers of the Harvard College Observatory.[1]

Maria Cunitz was the first woman to attempt to correct Kepler's *Rudolphine Tables* of planetary motion, a problem of major concern to seventeenth-century science. Born in Silesia in 1610, the eldest daughter of a physician, Maria developed an early interest in astronomy. At the age of 20 she married Elias von Löwen, a physician and amateur astronomer, and with his encouragement, set about making new reductions of old observations in order to simplify the *Rudolphine Tables*. But Cunitz was at a disadvantage: without financial resources or observational instruments, she was limited to manual calculations, and although she managed to correct many errors in the original sources, her tables were simpler than Kepler's primarily because she neglected small terms in the formulae. And so she introduced a number of new errors.

Cunitz's *Urania Propitia* was compiled during her life as a refugee from the Thirty Years' War (1618–48). Written in both German and Latin, it was finally published at Frankfurt in 1650. (In a gratifying role-reversal, the preface acknowledged her husband for his able assistance.) Maria Cunitz died in 1664 while again fleeing from the ravages of war.

Another Polish women, Elisabeth Korpmann, was by then making the new, more accurate observations needed to improve upon Cunitz's work. At the age of sixteen she married Hevelius, a wealthy Danzig engraver and amateur astronomer. Hevelius was engaged in compiling a new star catalogue and revising Kepler's tables, for which purpose he had constructed an observatory on the roof of their house. But Hevelius was a hard taskmaster: his first three assistants died shortly after undertaking the observations and the string of household servants he subsequently enlisted proved equally unsatisfactory. Finally, in desperation, he opened the observatory to his wife. Elisabeth was the most accurate and diligent of astronomical observers. She worked at her husband's side for ten years, until 1679, when a great fire swept through Danzig. The observatory, all their data and most of the printed copies of Hevelius's *Machinae Celestae* were destroyed. Hevelius died a broken man, but Elisabeth carried on their work, publishing *Firmamentum Sobieskanum* and *Prodromus Astronomicae*. The latter, a catalogue of the positions of 1888 stars, was not only the largest star catalogue ever compiled, but the last compiled without a telescope. An engraving in *Machinae Celestae* pictures Elisabeth and her husband observing with a large brass sextant (see Figure 9).

As telescopic observations increased, illustrations became an important adjunct to astronomical treatises. Maria Clara Eimmart (1676–1707) was one of the earliest of these astronomical artists. The daughter of a successful painter, engraver and amateur astronomer, she used telescopic observations to illustrate her father's *Micrographia Stellarum Phases Lunae Ultra 300*. Their Nuremberg workshop and observatory were home to a number of dedicated astronomers, including Maria's husband, Johann Heinrich Müller, who later became an astronomy professor at Altorf. Maria used her engraving skills to depict comets, sunspots, eclipses and the mountains of the moon – the observations that overthrew once and for all the 'perfect and immutable heavens' of Aristotle.

Maria Müller died too young to achieve the renown of her contemporary, Maria Winckelmann Kirch. Born near Leipzig in 1670, Maria Margarethe Winckelmann received her early training from Christoph Arnold, the so-called 'astronomical peasant'. In 1692 Maria married Gottfried Kirch, an astronomer who had studied with Hevelius in Danzig. Settling in Berlin, Kirch directed his wife's studies as he had those of his three sisters. Even after his appointment as Royal Astronomer in 1700, these women continued to support themselves by producing calendars, almanacs and other books of observations and computations.

Maria Kirch discovered the comet of 1702, although it was not named after her and she did not receive recognition. Her observations on the aurora borealis (1707) and her writings on the conjunction of the sun with Saturn and Venus (1709) and on the approaching conjunction of Jupiter and Saturn in 1712 (including the obligatory astrological predictions) became her more lasting contributions to astronomy.

Following her husband's death in 1710, Maria Kirch trained her 16-year-old son Christfried as her assistant. In 1712 Maria, her eldest daughter Christine (c. 1696–1782) and Christfried went to work in the well-equipped observatory of their patron the Baron von Krosigk. There they continued to calculate calendars and almanacs until the Baron's death in 1714. Two years later, when Christfried was elected director of the Berlin Observatory, his mother and sister became *his* assistants. But the role-reversal did not decrease Maria's status: her friend Leibniz presented her at the Prussian Court and soon after she received an invitation from Peter the Great, Tsar of Russia. However Maria Kirch chose to remain with her son, continuing to calculate the calendars for Breslau, Nuremberg, Dresden and Hungary. Her daughters calculated the almanacs and ephemerides (tables of the positions and motions of the heavenly bodies) of the Berlin Academy of Sciences long after their mother's death in 1720.

The Swedish astronomer Andreas Celsius met the Kirch women while studying with Christfried in Berlin, and in Paris he encountered another devoted astronomer, the sister of Joseph Delisle. Then, on arriving in Bologna to study with the director of the observatory, he

9 Elisabeth Hevelius and her husband Johannes observing with a large
brass sextant; from an engraving in *Machinae Celestae*.

found that his new teacher also had two sisters, Teresa and Maddalena Manfredi, both well-educated and collaborating with their brother on the preparation of the solar, lunar and planetary ephemerides of Bologna. Agnes Manfredi, a third sister, may also have assisted with the calculations. Celsius later wrote to Kirch:

> I begin to believe that it is the destiny of all the astronomers whom I have had the honour of becoming acquainted with during my journey to have learned sisters. I have also a sister, although not a very learned one. To preserve the harmony, we must make an astronomer of her.[2]

The fate of this neglected sister has gone unrecorded.

Meanwhile in Paris in the 1680s, Jeanne Dumée set out to prove that women are not incapable of study, 'if they wish to make the effort, because between the brain of a woman and that of a man there is no difference'.[3] At the age of 17, having sent her husband off to war, Dumée was free to devote herself to astronomy. Her treatise, *Entretiens sur l'opinion de Copernic touchant la mobilité de la terre*, demonstrated how the observations of Venus and the satellites of Jupiter proved the motion of the earth and the validity of the Copernican and Galilean theories. Her unpublished manuscript survives in the National Library in Paris.

Soon French women were moving toward the frontiers of astronomy, led by Nicole-Reine Étable de la Brière Lepaute (1723–88), the wife of the royal clockmaker. Her first important investigation involved the oscillations of pendulums of varying lengths. An account of this work appeared in her husband's *Traité d'horlogerie* (1755). Working with him, she gained a reputation as one of the best 'astronomical computers' of the day.

In 1757 astronomers were expecting the return of Halley's comet (it had previously appeared in 1531, 1607 and 1682) and Jérôme Lalande, director of the Paris Observatory, therefore approached the mathematician Alexis Clairaut for help in predicting the comet's return by solving its orbit. Clairaut, who had previously collaborated with Emilie du Châtelet (see pp. 140–1), requested the assistance of Mme Lepaute.

The problem was immense. Indeed, in our age of electronic computers it seems incredible that such a project could have been completed by brainwork alone:

During six months we calculated from morning to night, sometimes even at meals. . . The assistance rendered by Mme Lepaute was such that, without her I should never have been able to undertake the enormous labour, in which it was necessary to calculate the distance of each of the two planets Jupiter and Saturn from the comet, separately for each successive degree for 150 years.[4]

Finally, on 14 November 1758, they reported the dates for the return of the comet to the Academy of Sciences. It was the first time that scientists had predicted a perturbed comet's return to perihelion (the point of its orbit closest to the sun). And they were just in time. Halley's comet was first sighted on 25 December and it reached perihelion on 13 March – within the dates set by the team of astronomers. It was another triumph for Newtonian science. In his *Comets*, Clairaut gave Lepaute full credit for her work, but he later retracted it. Today, Clairaut alone is usually credited with the prediction.

Meanwhile Lepaute turned her attention to the coming eclipses of 1762 and 1764, calculating and publishing a chart of the path of the 1764 eclipse for every quarter-hour for all of Europe. She also published a separate chart for Paris, showing the different phases of the eclipse. Her calculations required that she prepare a table of parallactic angles (the angle of displacement of an object caused by a change in the observer's position), her extended version of which was published by the French government.

Mme Lepaute also published a number of astronomical memoirs including one based on all the observations made of the 1761 transit of Venus. From 1759 to 1774 she and Lalande were in charge of the *Connaissance des Temps*, the Academy of Sciences' annual publication for astronomers and navigators. In 1774 she took over the *Epheméris*, publishing the seventh volume covering the decade to 1784, and the eighth volume (1783) covering the period up to 1792. For this last volume she alone made all the computations for the positions of the sun, moon and planets. A crater on the moon is named in Lepaute's honour.

Mme Lepaute was not Lalande's only female collaborator. His friend Louise Elisabeth Félicité Pourra de la Madeleine du Piéry (b. 1746) computed most of the eclipses used by Lalande for his study of lunar motion. She also computed a variety of astronomical tables, and it was to Mme du Piéry that Lalande dedicated his *L'Astronomie des dames* (1786).

Lalande also published an appreciation of the work of his niece by marriage, Marie-Jeanne Amélie Harlay Lefrançais de Lalande (1768–1832), who lectured on astronomy in Paris, and worked independently as well as in collaboration with her husband:

> My niece aids her husband in his observations and draws conclusions from them by calculation. She has reduced the observations of ten thousand stars, and prepared a work of three hundred pages of horary tables – an immense work for her age and sex. They are incorporated in my *Abrégé de Navigation*.
>
> She is one of the rare women who have written scientific books. She has published tables for finding the time at sea by the altitude of the sun and stars. These tables were printed in 1791 by the order of the National Assembly... In 1799 she published a catalogue of ten thousand stars, reduced and calculated.[5]

Mme Lalande named her daughter after the great German–English astronomer Caroline Herschel (see below). Caroline Lalande was born on 20 January 1790, the day Herschel's comet was first seen in Paris.

2. Caroline Herschel and her Comet Sweepers

> I did nothing for my brother but what a well-trained puppy-dog would have done: that is to say, I did what he commanded me. I was a mere tool which *he* had the trouble of sharpening. (Caroline Herschel, 1876, p. 142)

Thus wrote Caroline Herschel of the work that was to make her the most famous and admired woman astronomer in history. Never has a woman scientist so underestimated her own abilities and denied her own accomplishments; caught, as she was, in the contradiction between her achievements and the prevailing social attitudes that defined woman's role in science as that of uncredited assistant. Yet Caroline's excessive self-deprecation is understandable, for the limitations of her background and education made her scientific successes unprecedented.

Fortunately, Caroline Lucretia Herschel left a detailed account of

her life. Unlike some of her contemporaries, her personal communi-
cations were never intended for publication. Quite the opposite, for
Caroline Herschel was the most private of women. She destroyed
much of her diaries and correspondence, and certainly would have
destroyed them all if she had thought that they would ever be made
public.

Nothing in Caroline's early life hinted at what she would later
achieve. Born into a large family of Hanover musicians in 1750, a
traditional upbringing contributed to her low self-esteem. Caroline's
father, who was interested in astronomy, thought she should receive
some education: her mother disagreed, believing that Caroline's duty
was to become a good housekeeper and take care of her brothers.
Although she never overcame her distaste for housekeeping, in
caring for her brothers Caroline far exceeded her mother's expecta-
tions, becoming 'almost pathological in her selflessness'.[6] But,
without formal education, her future looked bleak:

> and for a Governess I was not qualified for want of knowledge in
> languages. And I never forgot the caution my dear Father gave me;
> against all thoughts of marrying, saying as I was neither hansom
> nor rich, it was not likely that anyone would make me an offer.[7]

It was her brothers William and Alexander, both musicians in
England, who came to her rescue. So, in 1772, at the age of 22,
Caroline set out for England to train as a singer.

Caroline did indeed become a successful soprano, but William's
interest was turning from music to astronomy, and since Caroline
refused to perform except under his direction, she was now forced to
give up her new-found career and with it, all hope of earning her own
living and thus becoming financially independent of her brother.
Instead she began her training as an assistant astronomer.

With the completion of William's early telescopes and his
discovery of the planet Uranus in 1781, he gave up music altogether,
and was appointed King's Astronomer, but with an annual salary of
only £200 to cover all household and professional expenses. From
that time on Caroline never stopped worrying about money.

Caroline's interest in, and love for, science developed slowly.
William gave her lessons in mathematics and astronomy, which she
carefully copied down in her commonplace book. Early in 1787
William wrote to Lalande (see pp. 123–5), sending his sister's

compliments to Mme du Piéry, and adding: 'Caroline would think herself happy indeed if she were able to calculate fluxions, as she heard that her *happy rival* could do; but that following such a glorious example, she would not cease to beg her brother to teach her that sublime science.'[8] But for the most part Caroline taught herself science and mathematics piecemeal.

It was an exhausting life – observing at the telescopes all night and spending the days making laborious calculations and reductions, writing up the night's observations and writing papers. Much has been made of how, in those early years from 1775 to 1783, Caroline hand-fed William and read to him from novels while he polished the mirrors for his telescopes. But Caroline did much more than that. She shared in every success and failure, from the construction of the first 7-foot telescope to that of the ponderous 40-foot one, for which she made the first pasteboard model.

William Herschel's experiments with new and larger telescopes enabled him to study the distant stars, whereas other astronomers were forced to confine their observations to the moon, planets and comets. Together, the Herschels founded sidereal astronomy – the study of stars – advancing astronomy from the science of the solar system to the science of stellar systems. Between 1783 and 1802 the Herschels discovered 2500 new nebulae and star clusters, visible evidence of distant galaxies, with their 20-foot reflecting telescope.

The years 1784 to 1787 were given over to the construction of an even greater telescope with a focal length of 40 feet. The mirrors were 4 feet in diameter, and each one weighed a ton. During the casting of the great mirrors, Caroline's job was to pound bushels of horse manure in a mortar and pass it through a fine sieve to make the material for the mould. At one point she supervised two crews of 12 men each, working day and night grinding and polishing the giant mirrors. The great telescope was a disappointment scientifically, but it earned prestige and renown for both William Herschel and his patron, King George III, and was referred to in the popular press as one of the 'Wonders of the World'.[9] In her Diary of 1786, Fanny Burney spoke of walking upright *through* the telescope itself. It was rarely used, but on those occasions when it was, Caroline sat in a little hut at its base receiving William's reports through a speaking tube.

In 1782, as soon as they had moved their astronomical instruments from Bath to Datchet, William gave Caroline a small refracting telescope adapted to sweeping the sky for comets. The 'comet sweeper' was to occupy her during William's frequent absences from home, and proved to be the beginning of her career as an independent observer. Her earliest discoveries included three new nebulae, listed in William's *Catalogue of One Thousand New Nebulae* with a note crediting Caroline.

In the summer of 1783 William built her a new Newtonian sweeper, with a focal length of 27 inches. Caroline was occupied that summer with assisting her brother and measuring double stars and determining their positions. By the end of the year, she had discovered several star clusters and 14 new nebulae, including the companion to the Andromeda nebula, but no comets.

With their final move to Slough, Caroline was given what amounted to her own small observatory. On 1 August, 1786, she became the first woman to be recognised for discovering a comet. The entry in her journal reads:

> *August* 1. – I have counted one hundred nebulae to-day, and this evening I saw an object which I believe will prove to-morrow night to be a comet.
>
> *2nd.* – To-day I calculated 150 nebulae. I fear it will not be clear to-night. It has been raining throughout the whole day, but seems now to clear up a little.
>
> 1 o'clock. – The object of last night *is a comet.* (p. 64)

Caroline sent an account of her discovery to Dr Charles Blagden, Secretary of the Royal Society:

> In consequence of the friendship which I know to exist between you and my brother, I venture to trouble you, in his absence, with the following imperfect account of a comet: –
>
> The employment of writing down the observations when my brother uses the twenty-foot reflector does not often allow me time to look at the heavens, but as he is now on a visit to Germany, I have taken the opportunity to sweep in the neighbourhood of the sun in search of comets; and last night, the 1st of August, about 10 o'clock, I found an object very much resembling in colour and brightness the 27 nebula of the *Connoissance des Temps*, with the difference, however, of being round. I suspected it to be a comet; but a haziness coming on, it was not possible to satisfy

myself as to its motion till this evening. I made several drawings of the stars in the field of view with it, and have enclosed a copy of them, with my observations annexed, that you may compare them together. . . .

You will do me the favour of communicating these observations to my brother's astronomical friends. (1787, pp. 1–2)

The same day she wrote a similar letter to her friend Alexander Aubert. Both letters contained precise descriptions of the comet's position.

Her letter to Blagden was read to the Royal Society on 9 November and published in the *Philosophical Transactions* of 1787, along with her illustrations of the comet's position and remarks on the new comet by William. Fanny Burney was present on the occasion when William, summoned by the King, pointed out Caroline's comet to the Royal Family. Fanny wrote in her Diary: 'The comet was very small, and had nothing grand or striking in its appearance; but it is the first lady's comet, and I was very desirous to see it' (p. 18). Comets were to remain Caroline Herschel's field of expertise – William himself never discovered one.[10]

In 1787, the King granted William additional funds for the completion and maintenance of the 40-foot telescope and also settled an annual salary of 50 pounds on Caroline. It was the first time that a woman had been appointed assistant to the court astronomer: this was 'the first money I ever in all my lifetime thought myself to be at liberty to spend to my own liking' (pp. 75–6).

As a result of her brother's marriage to Mary Pitt, the 10-year period from 1788 to 1798 was a most unhappy time for Caroline, who still thought of herself primarily as housekeeper to William. The marriage contract called for Caroline to live in separate lodgings, and reluctantly she moved, first into the Cottage Observatory at Slough, and then to private lodgings, finally settling at Upton House, her sister-in-law's former home. After the marriage Caroline was in charge of the observatory and instruments only during the summer when William and his family were on holiday. Yet these years were Caroline's most productive. Freed from domestic responsibilities, she devoted herself completely to astronomy. She made many observations and drawings of the satellites of Saturn and 'Georgium sidus' (William's name for Uranus) and kept up an extensive scientific correspondence. She also became something of a local celebrity and for the first time was able to cultivate her own friendships. Mme Beckedorff (a fellow pupil at the Hanoverian dressmaking school of her youth), now at Queen Charlotte's court, became Caroline's one close friend. The royal princesses were well-educated and interested in astronomy, and sought out the company of the famous woman scientist; Caroline became particularly friendly with Princess Sophia Matilda.

Late in 1790 William completed a new telescope for Caroline, a larger Newtonian 'comet sweeper' with a focal length of 5 feet. Before the end of 1797, Caroline had announced the discovery of seven more comets and was known throughout Europe as a distinguished astronomer. Accounts of each discovery were sent to the Royal Society, and were subsequently published in the Society's *Philosophical Transactions*. Whereas her first account was hesitant and apologetic, her later publications were appropriately professional.

The Herschels continued their observations of the planets, double stars and various other phenomena. With Caroline's assistance, William discovered 1000 double stars. They were able to demonstrate that many of these stars were binary systems connected by mutual attraction – the first evidence of the force of gravity operating outside the solar system. Years later, at the age of 81, Caroline wrote to her nephew that their 'observations on double stars were from first to last the most interesting subject; he [William] never lost sight of it in his papers on the construction of the heavens, &c' (p. 247).

In 1787 Caroline undertook an immense project for her brother: the *Catalogue of 860 Stars Observed by Flamsteed, but not included in the British Catalogue* and *A General Index of Reference to every Observation of every Star in the above-mentioned British Catalogue*, published by the Royal Society in 1798.

In 1808 Dietrich Herschel arrived at Slough 'ruined in health, spirit and fortune' and expecting Caroline to care for him. This she did for the next four years while never neglecting her scientific work: 'the time I bestowed on Dietrich was taken entirely from my sleep or from what is generally allowed for meals. . .' (p. 116). Caroline was finally beginning to resent her role as her brothers' keeper, especially when it conflicted with her astronomy.

William Herschel died in August of 1822, following a long illness. Immediately after the funeral Caroline left England, her home for the past fifty years. Feeling herself to be 'a person that has nothing more to do in this world' (p. 134), she returned to Hanover to a home that no longer existed. There Caroline Herschel was to live on for another quarter of a century.

At the age of 75 she completed her immense work of the positions of some 2500 nebulae – *A Catalogue of the Nebulae which have been observed by William Herschel in a Series of Sweeps*. It was for this work that Caroline received the Gold Medal of the Royal Astronomical Society in 1828. The unanimous resolution read:

> That a Gold Medal of this Society be given to Miss CAROLINE HERSCHEL, for her recent reduction, to January 1800, of the Nebulae discovered by her illustrious brother, which may be considered as the completion of a series of exertions probably unparalleled either in magnitude or importance, in the annals of astronomical labour.[11]

Initially Caroline was thrilled when John Herschel, president of the Society, accepted the medal on her behalf. However the correspondence between them that followed reinforced her reluctance to claim credit for her work. It is not clear whether John was concerned about his aunt's private and modest nature or whether he truly felt she did not deserve the recognition. In any case, he wrote to her on 28 May, 1828: 'Pray let me be well understood on one point. It was none of my doings. I resisted strenuously... The Society have done *well*. I think they might have done *better*, but my voice was neither asked nor listened to' (p. 227). He added that the question of awarding her a medal had also been discussed at the Royal Society.

Whatever John Herschel may have intended by his letter, Caroline replied on 21 August:

> What you tell me ... concerning the medal, has completely put me out of humour with the same; for to say the truth, I felt from the first more shocked than gratified by that singular distinction, for I know too well how dangerous it is for women to draw too much notice on themselves. And the little pleasure I felt at the receipt of the few lines by your hands, was entirely owing to the belief that what was done was both with your approbation and according to your recommendation. Throughout my long-spent life I have not been used or had any desire of having public honours bestowed on me; and now I have but one wish, that I may take *your* good opinion with me into my grave ... Whoever says *too much of me*

says too little of your father! and only can cause me uneasiness. (pp. 231-2)

Although more honours followed, Caroline was never again able to accept them graciously as her long-overdue reward. In February of 1835 at their annual meeting, the Royal Astronomical Society voted unanimously to bestow honorary membership on the two leading women scientists of the early nineteenth century – Caroline Herschel and Mary Somerville. In recommending the honours the Report of the Council concluded:

> that while the tests of astronomical merit should in no case be applied to the works of a woman less severely than to those of a man, the sex of the former should no longer be an obstacle to her receiving any acknowledgement which might be held due to the latter.[12]

Election to the Royal Irish Academy followed in 1838, and in 1846, on the occasion of her 96th birthday, she received the Gold Medal for Science from the King of Prussia. But after a lifetime of hard work without adequate recognition or compensation, this showering of awards angered her: 'the premium of the King of Denmark's medal, for the discovery of telescopic comets, provokes me beyond all endurance, for it is of no use to me. One of my eyes is nearly dark' (p. 254).

In Hanover Caroline Herschel was recognised as one of the most learned women of the age. Despite failing eyesight, she continued to read all the latest scientific papers when she could get them, and eagerly anticipated visits from scientists with whom she could discuss the newest developments in astronomy. Her activities and continuing interest in astronomy belie the contentions of historians who claim that she had no real interest in science. She was, in fact, a talented and devoted astronomer who was confined by society's prejudice against women, and her own lack of self-confidence, to the role of assistant.

Caroline Herschel died on 9 January 1848, at the age of 97. Her niece Anna Knipping wrote to John Herschel on 13 January:

> I felt almost a sense of joyful relief at the death of my aunt, in the thought that now the unquiet heart was at rest. All that she had of

love to give was concentrated on her beloved brother. At his death she felt herself alone. For after those long years of separation she could not but find us all strange to her, and no one could ever replace his loss. . . Time did indeed lessen and soften the overpowering weight of her grief, and then she would regret that she had ever left England, and condemned herself to live in a country where nobody cared for astronomy. I shared her regret, but I knew too well that even in England she must have found the same blank. She looked upon progress in science as so much detraction from her brother's fame, and even your investigations would have become a source of estrangement had she been with you.[13]

Caroline Herschel occupies a unique place in the history of women in science. Her personality, her relationship with her brother William, and her attitudes toward science in general – and toward her own scientific achievements in particular – present a tangle of contradictions. Yet without any systematic education or training she became a great astronomer, and helped to open up astronomy to other women of the nineteenth century.

Contemporaries of Caroline Herschel included Wilhelmine Bottcher Witte, born in Hanover in 1777, and her daughter Minna who worked with her husband, the astronomer Maedler. Using a fine telescope, Wilhelmine made a model of the moon with details drawn from her own observations. At the request of Alexander von Humboldt, ever the champion of women scientists, she made a duplicate for Friedrich Wilhelm III. Frau Rumker worked with her husband, the director of the Hamburg Observatory, computing the orbits of comets. On 11 October 1847 she became the first in Germany to sight the famous comet of the American astronomer Maria Mitchell.

Following the work of the Herschels, Mme Yvon-Villarceau computed the orbits of various binary stars after first verifying the mathematical formulae used in such computations.

On 1 April 1854 Caterina Scarpellini also discovered a comet. As a child she had been encouraged to study astronomy by her uncle, Feliciano Scarpellini, the founder of the Capitoline Observatory. In 1866 she observed the Leonides shower (a group of meteors which appear to come from the constellation Leo) and compiled the first Italian meteor catalogue; she also organised the Meteorologico

Ozonometric station in Rome and edited its monthly bulletin. Scarpellini authored several studies on the possible influence of the moon on earthquakes and was an honorary member of several European learned societies. In 1872 she was awarded a gold medal by the Italian government in recognition of her statistical work.

10
The Philosophers of the Scientific Revolution

> It was a brilliant age because the women in it were brilliant, combining brains with beauty beyond any precedent. (Will and Ariel Durant, p. 302)

In sixteenth-century France Catherine de Parthenay, the Princess de Rohan, spent many years studying mathematics and astronomy with François Viète. His work on mathematical analysis, *In Artem Analyticam Isagoge*, was dedicated to her:

> It is to you especially, august daughter of Melusine, that I am indebted for my proficiency in mathematics, to attain which I was encouraged by your love for this science, as well as your great knowledge of it, and by your mastery of all other sciences.[1]

Following the Princess de Rohan, the women philosophers of the scientific revolution were first and foremost mathematicians.

1. The Women Philosophers of Italy

Seventeenth- and eighteenth-century Italy witnessed a resurgence of women scientists including Elena Cornaro Piscopia (1646–84), who received her doctorate of philosophy from the University of Padua, where she became a mathematics lecturer in 1678; Diamente Medaglia, who wrote a dissertation on the importance of mathematical study for women; Cristina Roccati who taught physics at the Scientific Institute of Rovigo for 27 years; Maria Angela Ardinghelli of Naples, a student of mathematics and physics and the Italian translator of Stephen Hale's work on biophysics, *Vegetable Staticks* (1727); and Laura Bassi.

Laura Maria Catarina Bassi (1711–78) was a child prodigy. She was educated in mathematics, philosophy, anatomy, natural history and languages by Dr Gaetano Tacconi, a professor at the college of medicine. At the age of 21, she engaged in a public debate with five philosophers. Bassi went on to receive her doctorate in philosophy from the University of Bologna in 1733 and the Senate granted her a pension to continue her studies. She eventually became a professor, publishing many papers on Cartesian and Newtonian physics. Two of her Latin dissertations on mechanics and hydraulics were published in the *Commentaries of the Bologna Institute* and many of her physics lectures are extant in manuscript form. By the end of her life she was famous throughout Europe as one of the most able of eighteenth-century women scientists.

But it was Maria Gaetana Agnesi (1718–99) who was to become the most celebrated Italian woman of the scientific revolution. Her father was mathematics professor at the University of Bologna. He recognised Maria, the eldest of his 21 children, as a prodigy, and anxious to capitalise on her talents, he engaged as her tutor Don Ramiro Rampinelli, Professor of Mathematics at the University of Pavia. Soon local and visiting intellectuals were attending the Agnesi salon to hear Maria expound on mathematical and philosophical subjects. De Bosses, a French traveller, described one such *conversazione*:

Count *Belloni* . . . made a fine harangue to the lady in *Latin*, with the formality of a college-declamation. She answered with great readiness and ability in the same language; and they then entered into a disputation, still in the same language, on the origins of fountains and on the causes of the ebbing and flowing which is observed in some of them, like the tides of the sea. She spoke like an angel on this subject; and I never heard it treated in a manner that gave me more satisfaction. Count *Belloni* then desired me to enter with her on the discussion of any other subject I should choose to pitch upon, provided that it related to Mathematicks or Natural Philosophy . . . and we afterwards disputed on the propagation of light and prismatick colours. *Loppin* then discoursed with her on *transparent bodies*, and on *curvilinear figures* in

Geometry, of which last subject I did not understand a word . . .
After she had replied to *Loppin*, the conversation became general,
every one speaking to her in the language of his own country, and
she answering him in the same language: for her knowledge of
languages is prodigious. She then told me that she was sorry that
the conversation at this visit had taken that formal turn of an
Academic Disputation, declaring that she very much disliked
speaking on such subjects in numerous companies.[2]

Maria's father finally discontinued these spectacles when, with the
death of his wife, responsibility for the enormous household fell on
his eldest daughter.

Despite her extraordinary talents, Maria's one ambition was to
enter a convent; but since her father refused his permission, she
devoted the next 20 years to the education of her younger brothers
and to her own mathematics. At the age of 17 Maria wrote a
privately-circulated commentary on the Marquis de L'Hôpital's
analysis of conic sections.[3] In 1738 she published her collection of
190 essays on philosophy, logic, mechanics, elasticity, celestial
mechanics and Newton's theory of universal gravitation. Included in
Propositiones Philosophicae was a plea for the education of women.

Agnesi completed her most important mathematical work while
still in her twenties. Written in Italian as a text for her younger
brothers, *Analytical Institutions* was a clear and concise synthesis of
the new mathematics. The first volume dealt with the analysis of
finite quantities (algebra and geometry); the second covered the
differential and integral calculus (analysis of variable quantities and
their rates of change) recently invented independently by Leibniz
and Newton. Agnesi included many examples and problems, original
methods and generalisations. It was the first systematic work of its
kind and was widely translated.[4] Fifty years later it was still the most
complete mathematical text in existence.

Maria Agnesi was elected to the Bologna Academy of Science in
1748, the year *Analytical Institutions* was published in Milan.
Although the French Academy of Sciences denied her admission, the
committee secretary wrote her a commendation:

Permit me, Mademoiselle, to unite my personal homage to the
plaudits of the entire Academy. . . I do not know of any work of this
kind which is clearer, more methodic or more comprehensive than

your Analytical Institutions. There is none in any language which can guide more surely, lead more quickly, and conduct further those who wish to advance in the mathematical sciences. I admire particularly the art with which you bring under uniform methods the divers conclusions scattered among the works of geometers and reached by methods entirely different.[5]

Analytical Institutions was dedicated to 'her Sacred Imperial Majesty, Maria Teresa of Austria, Empress of Germany, Queen of Hungary, Bohemia, &c. &c.':

none has encouraged me so much as the consideration of your sex, to which Your Majesty is so great an ornament, and which, by good fortune, happens to be mine also. It is this consideration chiefly that has supported me in all my labours, and made me insensible to the dangers that attended so hardy an enterprise. For, if at any time there can be an excuse for the rashness of a Woman, who ventures to aspire to the sublimities of a science, which knows no bounds, not even those of infinity itself, it certainly should be at this glorious period, in which a Woman reigns, and reigns with universal applause and admiration. Indeed, I am fully convinced, that in this age, an age which, from your reign, will be distinguished to latest posterity, every Woman ought to exert herself, and endeavour to promote the glory of her sex... Hence it was, that the Sciences so early took possession of your mind, and that you became well acquainted with the whole circle of them. (pp. xvii–xviii)

In 1748 Maria Agnesi took over her father's lectures at the university, and two years later the Pope appointed her to her father's Chair of Mathematics and Natural Philosophy. However, she became disillusioned with her mathematical studies while still quite young, devoting the last 40 years of her life to charitable works and establishing a small hospital in her home. In 1762, when asked to review an exciting new paper by the French mathematician Lagrange, she replied that 'such matters no longer occupy my mind'.[6]

Although Maria Agnesi received more recognition than most of her contemporaries, her historical reputation was distorted by a curious incident. Her section on analytical geometry in *Analytical Institutions* included a discussion of the versed sine curve. As a result of an inaccurate English translation, the curve became known as the 'Witch of Agnesi' – and as such was Maria Agnesi immortalised in the annals of mathematics.

2. The Marquise du Châtelet

> She was a great man whose only fault was in being a woman. A woman who translated and explained Newton . . . in one word, a very great man.[7]

So wrote Voltaire of his friend, collaborator and lover, Gabrielle-Emilie Le Tonnelier de Breteuil, the Marquise du Châtelet-Lomont (1706–49). Whereas Maria Agnesi was one of the earliest expounders of the calculus of Newton and Leibniz, her contemporary, the French scientist Emilie du Châtelet, was among the first to popularise both the physics of Newton and the vitalistic natural philosophy of Leibniz. Although Newton's law of universal gravitation was much more appealing than the Cartesian theory of vortices, Newtonian science had not received general acceptance in continental Europe. It was the Marquise du Châtelet, more than any one else, who brought about the transition in France from the outmoded Cartesian science to the Newtonian cosmic order. In doing so, she made a major contribution to the furtherance of the scientific revolution.

Emilie de Breteuil was born into an aristocratic society that expected its women to be clever and witty as well as beautiful. Yet French society had never before witnessed in a woman the precocious combination of intelligence and scholarly determination that characterised the flamboyant marquise. She was to move far beyond the accepted realm of the educated woman of the Enlightenment. No doubt some people came to perceive Emilie du Châtelet as challenging the foundations of a patriarchal society based on the premise of male superiority. As a result, both her contemporaries and later historians, while not ignoring her, dismissed her scientific work and chose to focus instead on her relationship with the great poet, historian and philosopher Voltaire, her affairs with other men, her eccentricities, and her physical attributes. Her writings were overshadowed by the volume and variety of Voltaire's work, while her personality, and her open relationship with the most notorious satirist of the age, made her many enemies.[8] With few exceptions, her influence on Voltaire's intellectual development and her own impressive scientific accomplishments have been ignored.

As a child, Emilie showed no promise of ever possessing the one attribute that truly mattered for women of her position – beauty. Her father, the Baron de Breteuil, Chief of Protocol at the Court of Louis XIV, wrote of her:

> My youngest is an odd creature destined to become the homeliest of women. Were it not for the low opinion I hold of several bishops, I would prepare her for a religious life and let her hide in a convent. She stands as tall as a girl twice her years, she has prodigious strength, like that of a wood-cutter, and is clumsy beyond belief. Her feet are huge, but one forgets them the moment one notices her enormous hands.[9]

At five feet nine inches she towered over most eighteenth-century men. Convinced that she would never find a husband, her parents determined to make her spinsterhood more tolerable by providing her with the best education available. However by the age of 16, when she was introduced to the court at Versailles, Emilie had matured into an attractive, intelligent and sharp-tongued woman. Determined to control her own life, she began to search for a husband – someone older, wealthy and preferably away as much as possible: in the Marquis Florent-Claude du Châtelet-Lomont she found her ideal match. The marquis owned a number of large estates, had a passion for war, and the couple had nothing in common. They were married in 1725.

With her two children being raised by nurses and governesses, and her husband off with his troops, Emilie could enjoy life at one of the most decadent courts of all time – but after nights of dancing, flirting and gambling, she always returned home to her studies. One of her lovers, the statesman, scholar and godson of Louis XIV, the Duc de Richelieu, encouraged Emilie to begin advanced studies in physics and mathematics. Her social position enabled her to obtain as tutors some of the greatest eighteenth-century scientists. She studied algebra and Newtonian physics with the flamboyant mathematician and explorer Pierre Louis de Maupertuis and with his protégé, Alexis-Claude Clairaut.[10] Maupertuis was to provide both Emilie and Voltaire with their most valuable instruction. Clairaut's lessons for the marquise were collected and printed as his *Eléments de géometrie*.

The 1730s marked the beginnings of the Parisian café society, but courtesans were the only women allowed in these establishments. Emilie, masquerading as a man, would join her friends Maupertuis and Moreau at the café where scientists gathered to discuss philosophy. No one was fooled by her disguise, but in this way the marquise was able to penetrate the 'old-boy' scientific network to a greater extent than many of her twentieth-century counterparts.

Although Emilie had studied Descartes, she was drawn to the newer philosophies of Newton and Leibniz. At that time, Maupertuis and Clairaut were probably the only Newtonians in the French Academy, but they were soon to find allies in Emilie and Voltaire. Voltaire's *Letters on the English* (1734) included discussions of both the natural philosophy of Sir Isaac Newton and Lady Montagu's recent introduction of inoculation against smallpox (see pp. 88–92) and from then on, his vehement attacks on the Church and state, the monarchy and the aristocracy were conducted in the name of Newtonian science.

Emilie first met Voltaire in 1733. Soon after, hounded by the secret police, he was once again forced into exile. This time he had the perfect retreat. The new lovers settled at Cirey: a run-down thirteenth century estate owned by Emilie's husband and located in the independent Duchy of Lorraine. They had the large house completely remodelled – bringing in thousands of volumes for their library and transforming the great hall into a laboratory complete with air pumps, furnaces, a telescope, microscopes and a variety of other scientific apparatus. Here the marquise performed her experiments on Newtonian optics. All this was accomplished with the blessing of Emilie's husband who was delighted at having his property restored and maintained at Voltaire's expense – provided that Voltaire built him a game reserve!

Cirey proved the ideal home for scholars. Although they had frequent visitors (who were usually treated to a production of Voltaire's latest play – with Emilie invariably in the leading role), Emilie and Voltaire spent most of their time shut away in their separate apartments, working and studying. Soon Cirey had become the French centre of Newtonian science, with Maupertuis, Algarotti, Samuel Koenig, Clairaut and the Bernoullis in attendance, and close connections established with Frederick the Great of Prussia and the scientific academies of Berlin, Scandinavia and Russia.

Emilie was never taken seriously as a scientist within her own aristocratic social circle, but among other scientists and mathematicians she was well known and respected. Equally, her intellectual influence on Voltaire should not be underestimated. It was she who turned Voltaire from poetry and playwriting to physics and metaphysics – the story goes that she hid Voltaire's half-finished manuscript of *Siècle de Louis XIV*, directing him to study science instead – and throughout their life together, Emilie remained the better mathematician.

In the 1730s when the spectre of Newtonian science overthrowing the Cartesian system was raising a storm of controversy in the French Academy of Sciences, Mme du Châtelet was amongst those dedicated to the ultimate triumph of the Newtonian system. Late in 1735 Francesco Algarotti arrived at Cirey where, in consultation with the marquise, he completed his *Il Neutonianismo per le dame*. He proved an inspiration to the couple and they immediately began work on their own popular account of Newton's theories for the French audience. When word of their collaboration leaked out in 1736, the newspapers of Paris had a field-day ridiculing the idea that Voltaire would collaborate with anyone on anything, much less with a woman on such a difficult undertaking as the philosophy of Newton. *Eléments de la philosophie de Newton* was officially attributed to Voltaire, but he stated repeatedly that Mme du Châtelet had been his guide to Newton and that it was she who had explained the more complex aspects of the cosmology. In the dedication of the first edition in 1738, Voltaire implied that the contribution of 'Lady Newton' was the greater of the two.[11]

The chapters on optics were largely Emilie's work. A few of her papers are included in the Voltaire collection in the Leningrad public library. Among them is a 35-page manuscript dealing exclusively with the formation of colours. This is the fourth chapter of Châtelet's lost 'Essai sur l'optique', probably written in 1736; although a popularisation of Newton's *Optics*, it is more advanced than her treatment of the subject in *Eléments*.[12] Emilie probably had less of a hand in the remainder of *Eléments* which deals with Newtonian attraction. Her 'Lettre sur les éléments de la philosophie de Newton', a review and defence of the theory of attraction as presented in *Eléments*, appeared in the September 1738 issue of the *Journal des sçavans*. The article ended with a call for a comprehensive physics text in French – a subtle promotion for her own *Institutions de physique*, the first draft of which she had already completed.[13]

In 1737 the Academy of Sciences announced a competition for the best essay on the nature of fire. In the preceding 100 years astronomy, optics and mechanics had advanced as sciences, but chemistry was still in its infancy. The nature of fire was a controversial question in eighteenth-century science, centring on whether heat was a material substance or a form of energy. Shortly after the announcement, Voltaire determined to enter the competition, and together with Emilie began experimenting. Newton had believed that heat was energy resulting from the motion of molecular particles, but had been unable to produce a convincing thesis to support his theory. Most scientists clung to the idea that heat was a material substance possessing weight: thus an object should get heavier when heated. This hypothesis was disproved in Châtelet and Voltaire's experiments with various masses of hot and cold iron. (Subsequently scientists adopted the theory that heat was a weightless fluid.)

A month before the closing date for the competition the marquise decided to enter independently. Working at night and in secret, she completed her 'Dissertation sur la nature et la propagation du feu' just before the deadline. Having performed the same experiments, there were similarities between the lovers' essays, but their conclusions were different – and both were notably original. Châtelet, contradicting Voltaire, argued that light and heat were the same substance: luminous when the particles moved in a straight line, generating heat when they moved irregularly. She also asserted that different colours of light emitted different amounts of heat.[14]

Both Emilie and Voltaire were convinced that the other would win the competition, and they were bitterly disappointed when the prize was divided between Leonhard Euler and two others. But through Voltaire's influence, and because of the couple's notoriety, the Academy agreed that it would be good publicity to publish both of their essays along with those of the three winners.

Emilie du Châtelet's next work, *Institutions de physique*, was published anonymously in November of 1740, and from the first it was a controversial work.[15] She needed an up-to-date introductory physics text for her son's instruction. *Eléments* had too narrow a focus for this purpose and the classic French text by Rohault was over 80 years old, pre-dating both Newton and Leibniz. Emilie's friend and neighbour, Mme de Champbonin, urged her to undertake such a work in secret.

Institutions remained faithful to Newtonian physics, but Newton's purely scientific, materialistic philosophy did not completely satisfy the marquise. She believed that scientific theory demanded a foundation in metaphysics and this she found in Leibniz. Early in 1738 she came to accept the *forces vives* - the vital monads of Conway and Leibniz - and she determined to rewrite the early chapters of *Institutions* to reflect her new bias. She never doubted that Leibnizian metaphysics was reconcilable with Newtonian physics, as long as the implications of the Newtonian system were limited to empirical physical phenomena. *Institutions* went beyond the philosophies of Newton and Leibniz. Châtelet included historical background and the most recent developments in physics. In this way she managed to summarise almost all of seventeenth-century science and philosophy. But she was courting disaster.

The original manuscript of *Institutions* had already been approved and the printing begun when Châtelet asked Maupertuis to come to Cirey to assist with the revisions. He arrived in March of 1739, accompanied by Koenig and Johann Bernoulli. Koenig stayed on as mathematical tutor to Châtelet and Voltaire, travelling with them to Brussels in May. Official praise and approval for the completed draft of *Institutions* had greatly increased the marquise's self-esteem and she confided to Koenig her authorship of the manuscript, enlisting his help with the revision of the early chapters on Leibnizian metaphysics.

Back in Paris in September, Koenig revealed her secret and - incredibly - claimed that he had dictated the work to her. It was a particularly blatant example of the appropriation of women's scientific work by men. Châtelet hurriedly completed the early chapters and appealed to Maupertuis and the Academy for support against Koenig's accusations. But it was not until after her death that she was completely vindicated.

The publication of *Institutions* triggered new conflicts. In February 1741 Jean Jacques Mairan, a Cartesian and the perpetual secretary of the French Academy, published a strong reply to Châtelet's explanation of the *forces vives,* further accusing her of plagiarising Koenig. The marquise responded with a direct attack in an essay published in Brussels in the same year. The Academy of Sciences, so recently converted from Descartes to Newton, and always anxious for controversy, embarked on a Newton–Leibniz debate and narrow-minded disciples of Newton saw Châtelet as a traitor to the cause.

Despite Koenig's claims, no one could seriously deny that

Institutions was Châtelet's own work. (It could not be attributed to Voltaire – he was publicly disavowing Leibniz.) This was serious science and it greatly enhanced the marquise's reputation. It also silenced her many critics among the aristocracy who for years had refused to recognise her as anything but Voltaire's mistress. Now younger scientists were arriving at Cirey to study with her. The ardent pupil had become teacher, and Emilie du Châtelet was never again to be taken lightly by the intelligentsia of Europe.

Châtelet's two-volume translation of Newton's *Principia* was the culmination of her life's work. It included her commentaries, the first part of which was purely mathematical and the second, a 6-chapter revision of, and vast improvement over, the *Eléments*. Her work remains the only French translation of Newton. With its publication, Newtonian scientific method became an integral part of the French Enlightenment for the first time.

It is uncertain exactly when Mme du Châtelet began work on the *Principia*, but by 1745 she was devoting most of her time to it. The following year Clairaut began collaborating with her and by the spring of 1747 the translation was completed, the commentaries outlined, and printing begun. It was not published until 1759, ten years after her death.

In 1748 at Lunéville, the court of the exiled Polish King Stanislaus, Emilie met the Marquis de Saint-Lambert, an army officer ten years her junior. They fell in love and embarked on a stormy affair. Emilie du Châtelet's letters to her new lover were among the most passionate of the century, surpassing even Voltaire's erotic correspondence with his latest lover, his niece, Louise Denis. Then, at the age of 42, the marquise found herself pregnant. Since the child could claim no father, Voltaire suggested that they classify it among her 'miscellaneous works'.[16]

Emilie did not expect to survive childbirth and she was determined to finish her work on Newton before her confinement. In February 1749, Châtelet and Voltaire moved to Paris so she could work with Clairaut. On 18 May and again two days later, she wrote to Saint-Lambert:

> Do not reproach me for my Newton; I am sufficiently punished for it. Never have I made a greater sacrifice to reason than in remaining here to finish it. . . . . . . I get up at nine, sometimes at eight; I work till three; then I take my coffee; I resume work at four;

PRINCIPES
MATHÉMATIQUES

DE LA

PHILOSOPHIE NATURELLE,

Par feue Madame la Marquise DU CHASTELLET.

TOME PREMIER.

A PARIS,

DESAINT & SAILLANT, rue S. Jean de Beauvais.
Chez { ET
LAMBERT, rue & à côté de la Comédie Françoise,
au Parnasse.

PRÉFACE HISTORIQUE.	HISTORICAL PREFACE
CETTE traduction que les plus savans Hommes de France devoient faire, & que les autres doivent étudier, une femme l'a entreprise & achevée à l'étonnement & à la gloire de son pays. Gabrielle-Emilie de Breteuil, Marquise du Châtelet, est l'Auteur de cette Traduction, devenue nécessaire à tous	This translation which the most learned Men of France should have done, and which others should study, a woman has undertaken and achieved to the astonishment and to the glory of her country. Gabrielle-Emilie de Breteuil, Marquise du Châtelet, is the author . . .

10 *Title page to Emilie du Châtelet's translation of Newton's* Principia,
followed by Voltaire's Preface to her work.

at ten I stop to eat a morsel alone; I talk till midnight with M. de Voltaire, who comes to supper with me, and at midnight I go to work again, and keep on till five in the morning.... I must do this ... or lose the fruit of my labours if I should die in child-bed.... I finish it from reason and honour; but I love only you.[17]

Emilie du Châtelet's daughter was born at Lunéville on 4 September. (Voltaire put out the story that she gave birth while working at her desk, placing the newborn on a volume of geometry while she summoned a maid.) A few days later Emilie died of puerperal fever.

Emilie du Châtelet made major contributions to the development of French scientific thought. More than any other individual, she was responsible for the introduction and diffusion of the Newtonian and Leibnizian philosophies in France, although it is Voltaire who usually receives the credit. She once wrote to Frederick of Prussia:

Judge me for my own merits, or lack of them, but do not look upon me as a mere appendage to this great general or that renowned scholar, this star that shines at the court of France or that famed author. I am in my own right a whole person, responsible to myself alone for all that I am, all that I say, all that I do. It may be that there are metaphysicians and philosophers whose learning is greater than mine, although I have not met them. Yet, they are but frail humans, too, and have their faults; so, when I add the sum total of my graces, I confess that I am inferior to no one.[18]

Emilie du Châtelet could have been speaking for 2000 years of women scientists.

11
The Nineteenth-Century Mathematicians

All abstract knowledge, all knowledge which is dry, it is cautioned, must be abandoned to the laborious and solid mind of man. 'For this reason,' it is further reasoned, 'women will never learn geometry.' (Immanuel Kant, quoted in Griffin, p. 14)

1. The Mathematical Contributions of Sophie Germain

During the Napoleonic era Paris was the European centre of science and mathematics was enjoying a golden age. When the physicist Ernest Chladni visited Paris and demonstrated the reproducible patterns produced by sprinkling sand on a plate and striking the edge with a violin bow, he created a sensation. Interest in the resonant vibration of elastic bodies dated back to the Pythagoreans, but there was no mathematical theory to explain the phenomenon. Napoleon urged the First Class of the Institut de France (the mathematics and ⌐hysical sciences section of the reconstituted French Academy) to establish a *prix extraordinaire* – a 1 kilogram gold medal worth 3000 francs – for an analysis of the modes of vibration of these elastic plates.

Pierre Laplace organised the competition in 1809, hoping that it would establish the reputation of his own protégé, Siméon Denis Poisson. But Poisson in fact did not enter the competition – at least not officially. Instead, at a public session of the Institute on 8 January 1816, the prize was awarded to Sophie Germain. Yet despite this accomplishment, Germain's story is that of a woman who was prevented from achieving her full potential by an all-male scientific establishment.

Marie-Sophie Germain was born into a bourgeois Parisian family in 1776. As a child she sought refuge from the revolutionary turmoil of the streets in her father's library. There, at the age of 13, she discovered mathematics. Despite her family's attempts to discourage such interests, she spent the years of the Reign of Terror (1793–4) teaching herself differential calculus.

When the École Polytéchnique opened in 1795, Sophie obtained the lecture notes from Fourcroy's chemistry course and Lagrange's course on analysis. At the end of the term, Sophie submitted a paper to Joseph Lagrange, under the name of the student LeBlanc. Lagrange was impressed by the work and, on learning the true identity of its author, went to congratulate her in person. It was the start of one of the strangest careers in the history of science. News of this young female mathematician spread through Paris and Sophie received numerous offers of assistance from mathematicians, but none of these potential tutors was prepared to offer her a complete and serious mathematical curriculum.

Inspired by Karl Gauss's 1801 dissertation on number theory, Sophie began to study this branch of higher arithmetic on her own. In 1804 she wrote to Gauss, once again using the name LeBlanc. Gauss sent her an encouraging reply and she forwarded other samples of her work. But Gauss was so absorbed in his own monumental research, that he only responded when her work related to his own theorems. He never commented on her original mathematics: 'Only on one occasion did Gauss respond promptly and with real enthusiasm – upon discovering that Monsieur LeBlanc was, in reality, a woman.'[1] In 1806 Napoleon's armies were fighting the Prussians, and Sophie became concerned for the safety of her mentor. She asked the commander of the French artillery, an old family friend, to ensure Gauss's safety. The mathematician was confused by this attention, for the only woman he knew in Paris was Madame Lalande. Sophie now felt obliged to tell him the truth, to which Gauss replied:

The taste for the abstract sciences in general and, above all, for the mysteries of numbers, is very rare: this is not surprising, since the charms of this sublime science in all their beauty reveal themselves only to those who have the courage to fathom them. But when a woman, because of her sex, our customs and prejudices, encounters infinitely more obstacles than men in familiarizing herself with their knotty problems, yet overcomes these fetters and penetrates that which is most hidden, she doubtless has the most noble courage, extraordinary talent, and superior genius.[2]

Sophie continued to write to Gauss for many years, but he stopped answering her letters in 1808. However, his letters to other correspondents indicate that he continued to admire her work, and that she sometimes stimulated his mathematical thinking.[3]

Sophie Germain worked outside the scientific community: much more so than most other women scientists who had fathers, brothers and husbands to open doors that would otherwise be closed to them. For Sophie:

> Every conversation was a formal social event requiring letters of invitation, planning for transportation, requests for permission. Sophie Germain could not stop to chat with friends at meetings of the Institute nor get into serious conversation over cigars and brandy after dinner.[4]

Her isolation did not pose a particular problem in her work on number theory since Paris mathematicians had little interest in so abstract a subject. When she moved into the new field of mathematical physics with its numerous applications though, she was at a major disadvantage – she lacked the methodology for approaching a problem such as the Chladni plates (see Figs. 11-12), and Lagrange tried to discourage her. But, excited by one of Chladni's demonstrations, she began studying Euler, laboriously translating his mathematical physics from the Latin in which she had no formal training. Her one advantage proved to be her lack of preconceived notions and her ignorance of contemporary thinking on the subject.

Originally, Germain had not intended entering the competition for the *prix extraordinaire*. Her anonymous entry was completed in the first eight months of 1811 and submitted on 21 September. It was the only entry. Of the judges – Legendre, Laplace and Lagrange – only Legendre was aware of her authorship, and he not only kept her informed of the committee's progress, he also let her add a supplement to her submission which he distributed to the other judges. This was clearly unethical, although it was probably not unusual. (Here the evidence exists in Germain's correspondence with Legendre, whereas within the male scientific community such information would have been exchanged on a informal daily basis.)

In December, the committee informed Germain that the principal equation in her entry was wrong, and the competition date was extended until October 1813. But when Lagrange used Sophie's equation to derive the correct one, her self-confidence increased. For the next year and a half she worked alone, convinced that her approach to the problem was right. She began questioning the abilities and impartiality of the judges. In October 1813 she wrote to an unknown correspondent (possibly Legendre):

> I enjoin your probation of memoir No. 1 carrying this epigram:
>> But by far the greatest obstacle to the progress of science and to the undertaking of new tasks and provinces therein is found in this: that men despair and think things impossible.
>
> If I had found the occasion, I would have consulted you before adopting this quotation, since it has an air of pretentiousness, which hardly suits me, having so many reasons to mistrust my own skills and, indeed, not seeing any strong objections to my theory other than the improbability of having it meet with justice. I fear, however, the influence of opinion that M. Lagrange expressed. Without doubt, the problem has been abandoned only because this grand geometer judged it difficult. Possibly this same prejudgment will mean a condemnation of my work without a reflective examination.[5]

Once again Germain's was the only entry, and this time Poisson joined Laplace and Legendre in evaluating her work. Legendre wrote to Sophie on 4 December 1813 in reply to her request to add another supplement:

> Mademoiselle,
> I do not understand the analysis you send me at all; there is certainly an error in the writing or the reasoning, and I am led to believe that you do not have a very clear idea of the operations on double integrals in the calculus of variations. Your explanation of the four points does not satisfy me any more... There is a great lack of clarity in all of this.
> I will not try to point out to you all the difficulties in a matter that I have not especially studied and that does not attract me; therefore it is useless to offer to meet with you and discuss them. Besides, the thing is over with; there is nothing further to change in the memoir, and with all my good will I can do nothing. . .

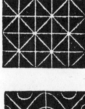

CHLADNI'S MUSICAL SAND-FIGURES,

11 *From Mary Somerville's* Of the Connexion of the Physical Sciences

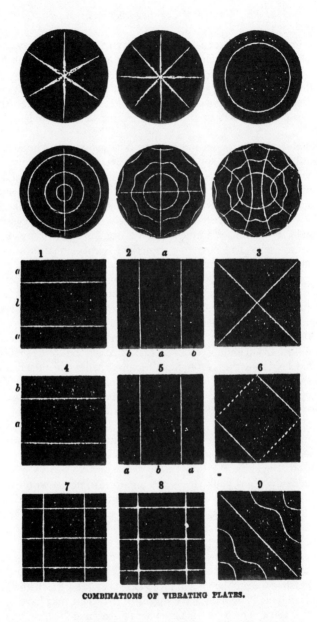

COMBINATIONS OF VIBRATING PLATES.

12 From Mary Somerville's Of the Connexion of the Physical Sciences

In any case, there is the possibility of having your research published, reestablishing the correct analysis or downplaying it, and your work will bring you honor. This was perhaps the proper thing to have done in the first place. But I promise you always the deepest secrecy, and, if you have not committed some other indiscretion, it will be as though the thing were null and void.[6]

Sophie Germain's second memoir was awarded an honorable mention – and the competition was extended again. Poisson's appointment to the Physics Section of the First Class had disqualified him from entering the competition. Nevertheless, at a session of the First Class in August 1814, he began reading a memoir on the theory of elastic surfaces. Legendre immediately objected, a discussion ensued, a committee formed, and Poisson finished his reading. Poisson's work had obviously benefited from Germain's second memoir. His derivation of the central equation – the one that Lagrange had derived from Germain's first memoir – was no better than hers; but it was Sophie's second memoir that had shown how useful this equation could be. Once again a woman's work had been appropriated without acknowledgement.

Although the competition was still open, Poisson now proceeded to publish his memoir in a journal that he edited, expecting that the prize would be withdrawn – after all, Laplace had established it with Poisson in mind, and Poisson had now produced an analysis that was acceptable to most of his colleagues! Germain's initial response to Poisson's memoir was to stop working on the problem:

She found herself somewhat in the position of a mystery writer who has been working in almost total isolation on an intricate and fascinating plot that will make her name known as author. Suddenly a new book appears by an already famous writer with virtually the same plot, but far more brilliantly motivated and cogently argued. The novice author may suspect plagiarism, but is quite helpless. She has no choice but to give up the project.[7]

To make matters worse, Poisson would be among the judges and Germain, unimpressed by his solution, was not about to abandon her approach to the problem. Then she changed her mind; the historians, Bucciarelli and Dworsky, have suggested that there may have been an oral agreement between Legendre, Poisson and Laplace; that if

Legendre would drop his complaint against Poisson, the competition could continue and the prize be awarded to Sophie Germain – presuming that her third entry was at all worthy.

Germain's third memoir was half the length of her second and substantially different: this time, she attempted to derive one of Poisson's equations using her own methods. Since Poisson's work was wrong, so was hers. Sophie's one consolation was that, in the end, her approach proved to be more correct than Poisson's.

The committee of the First Class used Germain's experimental attempts, rather than her mathematics, as the pretext for finally awarding her the prize. At the formal presentation a large crowd assembled to see the famous female mathematician, but they were disappointed. Sophie Germain chose not to participate.

Despite its many defects, Germain had to publish her work on elasticity to prevent Poisson from receiving all the credit. She had her *Recherches sur la théorie des surfaces élastiques* published privately in 1821 and she continued to study elasticity. In 1824 she submitted another manuscript to the Academy for approval. Laplace, Poisson and the Baron de Prony were chosen to report on whether the Academy should publish her memoir; but no report was ever made. *Mémoire sur l'emploi de l'épaisseur dans la théorie des surfaces élastiques* remained in Prony's estate until 1879.[8]

In 1826 Germain wrote yet another memoir: *Remarques sur la nature, les bornes et l'étendue de la question des surfaces élastiques* (Paris: Huzurd-Courcier). This time, at the urging of Augustin Cauchy (who wanted to spare the Academy the embarrassment of reporting on it), she published it herself before sending it to the Academy. Lacking both formal training in mathematics and access to the most recent publications and the latest thinking in her chosen field, Sophie was writing memoirs that were clearly inadequate and could not be approved by the Academy. At the same time the members felt that, out of respect for her sex, they could not reject her work outright as they would that of a professional colleague. It was an impossible situation. Originally, Germain had been the only one working on elasticity and her knowledge of mathematics was the limiting factor. Now there was widespread interest: an interest that had been stimulated by Germain's results. But the work was all being done within a community that excluded her so completely that she did not even realise what was happening. It was her sex, not her mathematical ability, that was the determining factor.

Ironically, although it was the *prix extraordinaire* that guaranteed Sophie Germain a place in the history of science, her real contributions to mathematics lay elsewhere. She returned to her work on number theory, to a problem that has fascinated mathematicians for centuries: a proof of Fermat's last theorem. (For any integer $n > 2$, it is impossible to find any positive whole numbers, x, y and z, such that $x^n + y^n = z^n$.) As naive as ever, Sophie originally attempted to find a general proof of the theorem. Legendre persuaded her to try for a limited but valuable contribution to the problem. Sophie Germain's theorem demonstrated that for all prime numbers $n < 100$, there are no solutions to the equation, for the case in which none of the three numbers x, y and z is divisible by n. Her theorem has since been generalised and improved, but not replaced. Other mathematicians using her methods extended her result to integers higher than 100. Her work appeared as a footnote in Legendre's 'Recherches sur quelques objets d'analyse indéterminée et particulièrement sur le théorème de Fermat'.

With the revolution of July 1830, Sophie Germain retreated to her study as she had done at age 13. There she wrote two final memoirs, one on surface curvature and one on number theory, summing up work she had completed years earlier. They were published in *Crelle's Journal* after her death in 1831.[9]

Sophie Germain's friendship with Joseph Fourier eventually enabled her to participate in the scientific community in a limited way. In 1822 Fourier was elected Permanent Secretary of the Academy of Sciences, in part due to Sophie's influence on a few of the Academy's members. One of Fourier's first official acts admitted Sophie to all public sessions of the four Academies comprising the Institute. (It was not that women were excluded, merely that the few available tickets usually went to wives of members.)

After she developed breast cancer, Sophie gave up mathematics to devote herself to more general cultural and philosophical questions. An unfinished essay, 'Considérations sur l'état des sciences et lettres', deals with the relationship between scientific and artistic endeavours, the history of intellectual development and the nature of society. Her ideas were similar to the philosophy of positivism later developed by Auguste Comte. Sophie's nephew published the essay two years after her death.[10]

Sophie Germain was a competent natural scientist as well as a brilliant, if untrained, mathematician. But she was viewed by her contemporaries as a phenomenon, not as a serious student in need of teaching and guidance. It was an obstacle faced by other women mathematicians of the nineteenth century.

2. Ada Lovelace and the Beginnings of Computer Science

Mathematics may have been thriving in Paris but in England it had reached an all-time low. Only Charles Babbage and Augusta Ada Lovelace were making important advances, and they were so far ahead of their time that the significance of their work would not be appreciated for another century.

Ada Byron Lovelace (1815–52) spent her life in the shadow of a domineering mother, whose marriage to the poet Lord Byron lasted only a few months. Their legal separation, however, was a bitter, prolonged and very public battle. Lady Byron had studied algebra, geometry and astronomy with the Cambridge don, William Frend, and Byron once referred to his wife as the 'Princess of Parallelograms'.[11] She had her daughter carefully tutored. It was to Frend that Ada went with some of her first scientific questions.

Although Ada was an insular and unhealthy child who suffered from migraines, temporary paralysis (her mother's home remedies included frequent leeching and blood-letting) by the age of 14 she was competent in mathematics, astronomy, Latin and music. At 17, she was aspiring to be a greater mathematician than Mary Somerville, who wrote in her autobiography:

> All the time we lived at Chelsea we had constant intercourse with Lady Noel Byron and Ada, who lived at Esher, and when I came abroad I kept up a correspondence with both as long as they lived. Ada was much attached to me, and often came to stay with me. It was by my advice that she studied mathematics. She always wrote to me for an explanation when she met with any difficulty. Among my papers I lately found many of her notes, asking mathematical questions. (p. 154)

It was about this time that Ada first made the acquaintance of Charles Babbage, who would eventually be recognised as the inventor of the forerunner to the modern computer. In 1834 Ada Byron attended a series of lectures on Babbage's difference engine (see below) at the Mechanics' Institute. She also went to the horse races for the first time. These two events were to be determining factors in her future.

Ada was an extremely ambitious woman who, above all else, longed to become a famous scientist. In this she had the support and encouragement of both her mother and her husband, William King (the Earl of Lovelace). But she was first frustrated and then tormented by her inability to find a suitable mathematics tutor, without whom even the most brilliant student could not hope to become successful. She longed to study with Charles Babbage but he was occupied with raising money to design and build his calculating engines, and with the business of founding scientific societies. Undaunted, Ada began studying finite differences (the mathematical basis of Babbage's difference engine) but, like Sophie Germain, her work lacked guidance and a definite goal, and she came near to abandoning mathematics to pursue her musical interests.

Then, in 1842, an Italian engineer, L.F. Menabrea, published a theoretical and practical description of Babbage's latest concept – the analytical engine. Charles Babbage wrote in his autobiography:

Some time after the appearance of his memoir on the subject in the 'Bibliothèque Universelle de Genève', the late Countess of Lovelace informed me that she had translated the memoir of Menabrea. I asked why she had not herself written an original paper on a subject with which she was so intimately acquainted? To this Lady Lovelace replied that the thought had not occurred to her. I then suggested that she should add some notes to Menabrea's memoir; an idea which was immediately adopted.

We discussed together the various illustrations that might be introduced: I suggested several, but the selection was entirely her own. So also was the algebraic working out of the different problems, except, indeed, that relating to the numbers of Bernoulli, which I had offered to do to save Lady Lovelace the trouble. This she sent back to me for an amendment, having detected a grave mistake which I had made in the process.

The notes of the Countess of Lovelace extend to about three times the length of the original memoir. Their author has entered fully into almost all the very difficult and abstract questions connected with the subject.

These two memoirs taken together furnish, to those who are capable of understanding the reasoning, a complete demonstration

– That the whole of the developments and operations of analysis are now capable of being executed by machinery. (p. 68).

In the first of her seven notes Ada distinguished between the difference engine and the analytical engine. The difference engine was a mechanical device for computing and printing tables of mathematical functions by addition, using the method of finite differences. (Babbage was to spend several decades, and some £17,000 of public funds as well as much of his personal fortune in unsuccessful attempts to get the machine built.) His analytical engine was a completely different and much more sophisticated concept. It could add, subtract, multiply and divide directly, and the plans called for programming it with punched cards. (Today it would be considered a fully-automated, general-purpose, digital computer.) Babbage never got it past the planning stage.

Ada Lovelace's original contributions concerned the programming of the analytical engine and she devised several programmes for performing advanced mathematical calculations. She also made some remarkable predictions concerning both the applications of the analytical engine (including the composing of music) and some of the problems which might arise in dealing with such a machine:

It is desirable to guard against the possibility of exaggerated ideas that might arise as to the powers of the Analytical Engine. . .

The Analytical Engine has no pretensions whatever to *originate* anything. It can do whatever we *know how to order it* to perform. It can *follow* analysis; but it has no power of *anticipating* any analytical relations or truths. Its province is to assist us in making *available* what we are already acquainted with. This it is calculated to effect primarily and chiefly of course, through its executive faculties; but it is likely to exert an *indirect* and reciprocal influence on science itself in another manner. For, in so distributing and combining the truths and the formulae of analysis, that they may become most easily and rapidly amenable to the mechanical combinations of the engine, the relations and the nature of many subjects in that science are necessarily thrown into new lights, and more profoundly investigated. (p. 284)

Ada's translation and notes were published in *Taylor's Scientific Memoirs* in 1843 – although Babbage thought her notes should have appeared as a separate paper. The notes comprise her most important mathematical work. They were signed with her initials since, although she wanted credit for her work, it was considered undignified for women of the aristocracy to publish under their own names.

Most women scientists were modest and humble, and not since the seventeenth-century exuberance of the Duchess of Newcastle had England seen the likes of the Countess of Lovelace. While working on her notes, she wrote to Babbage:

> I hope another year will *really* make me something of an *Analyst*. The more I study the more irresistible do I feel my genius for it to be. I do *not* believe that my father was (or ever could have been) such a poet as I shall be an *Analyst* & Metaphysician, for with me the two go together indissolubly.[12]

And again in July 1843:

> I cannot refrain from expressing my amazement at my own child. The *pithy & vigorous* nature of the style seem to me to be most striking; and there is at times a *half-satirical & humorous dryness* which would I expect make me a most formidable *reviewer*.
>
> I am quite thunderstruck at the *power* of the writing. It is especially unlike a *woman's* style surely; but neither can I compare it with any man's exactly.[13]

Soon after, Ada became engrossed in cybernetics, the mathematics of brain function as she called it. She was working within the framework of the mediaeval macrocosm–microcosm paradigm yet, like the Duchess of Newcastle, she saw herself as original:

> I have my hopes, & very distinct ones too, of one day getting *cerebral* phenomena such that I can put them into mathematical equations; in short a law or laws for the mutual action of the molecules of the *brain*; (equivalent to the law of *gravitation* for the planetary and *sidereal* world).
>
> I am proceeding in a track quite peculiar & my own, I believe. There are many and great difficulties but at present I see no reason to think them insurmountable. . . The grand difficulty is in the *practical experiments*. In order to get the exact effects I require I

must be a most skilful practical manipulator in experimental tests; & that, on materials difficult to deal with; viz. the brain, blood, & nerves of animals.

In time I will do all I dare say . . . I hope to bequeath to future generations a *Calculus of the Nervous System*.[14]

Ada's plans were both naive and ambitious. Her husband had himself elected to the Royal Society so that she could have access to scientific books and papers which he painstakingly copied for her. Although she tried to obtain permission to use the Society's library in her husband's name early in the morning (since, as she wrote, the secretary was a discreet man and 'would not talk about the thing & make it notorious'), the Royal Society was not about to make an exception to their rule barring women. But Ada's central interest was still the work of Babbage, and she hoped to continue their collaboration with the goal of developing the analytical engine into a practical machine. But the collaboration would be on her own terms:

My channels for developping [sic] & training my scientific & literary powers are various, & some of them very attractive. But I wish my old friend to have the *refusal*.

Firstly: I want to know whether if I continue to work *on & about* your own Great Subject, you will undertake to abide wholly by the judgment of myself (or of any persons whom you may *now* please to name as referees, whenever we differ) on all *practical* matters *relating to whatever can involve relations with any fellow-creature or fellow-creatures*.

Secondly: can you undertake to give your mind *wholly & undividedly*, as a primary object that no engagement is to interfere with, to the consideration of all those matters in which I shall at times require your intellectual *assistance & supervision*; & can you promise not to *slur & hurry* things over; or to mislay & allow confusion & mistakes to enter into documents &c?

Thirdly: If I am able to lay before you in the course of a year or two, explicit & honorable propositions for *executing your engine* . . . would there be any chance of your allowing myself & such parties to conduct the business for you; your own *undivided* energies being devoted to the execution of the work . . .?[15]

The real problem was that the design of the analytical engine was far too advanced for the precision engineering of the time. But Ada had come up with a new scheme for raising the money with which they believed they could complete the project.

Ada apparently convinced Babbage and her husband to join in her supposedly infallible system for winning at the horse races. The Earl of Lovelace backed out early on, cutting his losses and assuming that Ada would do the same. For his part, Babbage seems to have acted as intermediary between Ada and the bookies. The results were disastrous, and Ada found herself being blackmailed. It took the Earl of Lovelace, Lady Byron and Mary Somerville's son, the barrister Woronzow Greig, years to untangle the mess Ada had made of her finances and her reputation. She destroyed most of her letters from 1844 on and Babbage likewise burned anything that might have further damaged her already tarnished reputation.

Ada had other difficulties too. When she fell ill in 1843 her mother had her treated with blood-letting, laudanum (tincture of opium), a new experimental drug called morphine and alcohol (as a stimulant). As a result, she became drug-dependent and by the end of the year she was vacillating between despondancy and ecstasy. When her health finally improved, she turned to experimenting with chemistry and electricity, writing to Sophia De Morgan (the wife of the mathematician Augustus De Morgan) that '*Many causes* have contributed to produce the past derangements; & I shall in future avoid them. *One* ingredient, (but only one among many) has been *too much Mathematics*.'[16] Professor De Morgan wrote to Lady Byron in 1844 in support of this view:

> The power of thinking on these matters [mathematics] which Lady L. had always shown from the beginning of my correspondence with her, has been something so utterly out of the common way ... but this power must be duly considered by her friends, with reference to the question whether they should urge or check her obvious determination to try not only to reach, but to go beyond, the present bounds of knowledge ... the very great tension of mind which they [mathematical studies] require is beyond the strength of a woman's physical power of application ...

For this reason De Morgan never told Ada his opinion of her mathematical abilities:

The tract about Babbage's machine is a pretty thing enough, but I could I think produce a series of abstracts, out of Lady Lovelace's first queries upon new subjects, which would make a mathematician see that it was no criterion of what might be expected from her.[17]

But there was little time left to worry about the physical effects of too much mathematics. Ada had overcome her addiction to laudanum, but she continued to incur huge gambling debts, and was finally forced to confess to her husband that she had twice pawned his family jewels. She was also terminally ill with cancer. She died in 1852 aged 36.

3. The Mathematical Mind: The Story of Sóphia Kovalévsky

It was not a nihilistic, scarcely a political, movement. It was an eager striving after knowledge and mental development; and it had spread so far and wide that at this moment hundreds of young girls belonging to the best families abandoned their homes and betook themselves to foreign universities in order to study science. (Anna Carlotta Leffler, p. 159)

Thus Sóphia Vasilevna Kovalévsky rebelled against her family and left home to find a new life. It would be a life made exciting by the political milieu of the times; a life made tragic by her own psychological and emotional needs; and a life made brilliant by her mathematical and literary genius. It is one of the most fascinating stories in the history of science. Yet the story of her life should not overshadow the fact that Sóphia Kovalévsky was first and foremost a great mathematician.

Sóphia (usually known as Sonya) was born in 1850. Her maternal grandfather was an eminent German mathematician and astronomer, and her mother was well-educated. Sonya's early interest in mathematics was awakened in a curious way – lacking sufficient wallpaper for all the rooms of their spacious country home in Byelorussia, one of the children's rooms was covered with sheets from Ostrogradsky's lithographed lectures on differential and integral calculus, and Sonya spent hours trying to decipher the formulae and text. Many years later, when she took her first calculus lesson with Alexander Nikolaevitch Strannoliubsky, she was already familiar with the notation and formulae of advanced mathematics. Her early education was in the hands of tutor Joseph Ignatevich Malevich, who believed she had a future as a writer. Her uncle, Peter, however, enjoyed talking to her about mathematics.

In 1864 Sonya began studying the *Elements of Physics* written by their neighbour, Professor Nicholas Tyrtov. In the process she taught herself trigonometry, working out the concept of 'sine' in the same way it had originally been invented. Tyrtov was greatly impressed and urged her father, General Krukovsky, to have Sonya tutored in higher mathematics. The General was himself interested in mathematics and he encouraged her studies – up to a point. Sonya bought a microscope and began studying biology as well.

During the 1860s the young people of the Russian aristocracy were rebelling against all forms of authority. Many became nihilists. They were enthusiastic about education, the advancement of women, the emancipation of the serfs and science. It was the son of the local priest who introduced first her sister Aniuta, and then Sonya herself, to radical politics.

In 1868 the family moved to the capital, St Petersburg, to further Sonya and her brother's education. Here she was taught analytical geometry and calculus by Strannoliubsky, who encouraged her involvement with the cause of women's education. Years later Sonya and Strannoliubsky worked together on a committee to raise money for women's colleges. Within a short time Sonya was ready for university.

In 1861 the University of St Petersburg had opened its lecture halls to women but shortly afterwards the government closed the schools because of the students' political agitation. When they reopened, the privilege of women's education had been withdrawn. Many aristocratic Russian women determined to study abroad, but an unmarried woman could not obtain a passport without her parents' permission. To overcome this, it became common in radical student circles for women to enter into marriages of convenience in order to travel to foreign universities where their 'husbands' would leave them to study in peace. The young couples considered this a higher form of marriage than a mere 'love-match'.

Sonya's sister Aniuta had no preparation for a university education, yet she longed to escape abroad. Sonya was considered too young to marry. But if either Aniuta or her friend Anna Mikhailovna Evreinova (Zhanna) could arrange such a marriage, the other – and presumably Sonya as well – would be allowed to accompany her. Maria Alexandrovna Bokova had entered into such a marriage in order to study medicine in Zurich, and was now practising as a surgeon in Russia. Maria had helped other women with such marriage arrangements. But she refused to propose to the physiology professor Ivan Sechenov on their behalf. Sonya and Aniuta were unaware that Maria herself had fallen in love with him, and was now living with him and her husband in a discreet *ménage à trois*. Instead, Maria approached Sechenov's friend, Vladimir Onufrievich Kovalévsky.

Kovalévsky was supposedly studying law, but he spent his time translating and publishing the works of Charles Darwin, Thomas Huxley, Louis Agassiz, and other natural philosophers. Vladimir agreed to wed either Aniuta or Zhanna, but upon meeting the beautiful and intelligent Sonya, he changed his mind and insisted on marrying her. This was a problem, for Sonya was very young and Aniuta, six years older, was expected to marry first. Their father asked for a long engagement but capitulated when Sonya pretended to elope with Vladimir.

Sonya and Vladimir continued their studies in St Petersburg while trying to arrange a similar match for Aniuta. Sonya had determined to devote herself to the study of mathematics when, in April 1869, the Kovalévskys left for Vienna. But the city was too expensive for their modest allowance and Sonya found the mathematics inferior. They moved on, spending the summer in England. Here they became acquainted with Charles Darwin, Thomas Huxley and the novelist George Eliot. It was in Eliot's home that Sonya found herself heatedly debating the question of women's intelligence with a male guest. The man was Herbert Spencer. Eliot and Sonya became close friends and years later Sonya wrote her 'Recollections of George Eliot', published in Russia in 1886 and subsequently translated into a number of languages.

In the autumn, the Kovalévskys moved to Heidelberg where Vladimir studied palaeontology and Sonya eventually succeeded in obtaining permission to attend mathematics and physics lectures under a special dispensation. They were joined by Zhanna's cousin, Julia Vsevolodovna Lermontova. Thanks to Sonya's success at Heidelberg, Julia had a much easier time obtaining permission to attend chemistry courses. But R.W. Bunsen (who introduced spectral analysis, discovered caesium and invented the gas burner that bears his name) was an inveterate misogynist who had maintained for years that no female would ever enter his laboratory. Sonya went to see him and he eventually agreed to accept both women as students. (Bunsen was later to warn Karl Weierstrass that Sóphia Kovalévsky was a dangerous woman who had tricked him with her charms!)

Julia left the following account of their life in Heidelberg:

> I remembered those first happy months in Heidelberg; those enthusiastic discussions on every kind of topic, and her poetical relationship to her young husband, who in those days adored her with quite an ideal love... Her youth was really filled with noble feelings and aspirations, and she had at her side a man, with his feelings completely under control, who loved her tenderly. This was the only time I have known Sónya to be really happy... From the first Sónya attracted the attention of her teachers by her extraordinary talent for mathematics... Her behavior enchanted the German professors, who always admire bashfulness in a woman, especially in one so charming and young, and, withal, one who was studying so abstract a science as mathematics.[18]

But Zhanna's father was still refusing to allow her to study in Germany with her friends. Finally, in desperation, she fled across the border by a smuggler's route, and arrived in Heidelberg in November 1869. Aniuta was now back from Paris, the Kovalévsky apartment was severely overcrowded, and Vladimir, made to feel unwelcome by the disapproving newcomers, moved out. He subsequently left Heidelberg, completing his doctorate at Jena with a treatise that established him as one of the founders of the science of evolutionary palaeontology.

After three terms at Heidelberg Sonya decided to go on to Berlin to study with Weierstrass, the 'father of mathematical analysis'. It was a decision that would determine the future course of her life. Although she had no hope of being allowed to attend lectures there, as she had at Heidelberg, she appealed to Weierstrass personally. She brought excellent recommendations from her Heidelberg professors but Weierstrass had no interest in a woman student, and assigned her difficult problems just to be rid of her. But so impressed was he by her solutions that he accepted her as a private pupil, tutoring her without charge for the next four years. In Berlin Sonya again lived with Julia who had arranged to study chemistry privately.

For a time Sonya's studies were interrupted by her concern for her sister's safety. Aniuta had returned to France, where she had become an outspoken feminist and a leader of the Paris Commune. One spring night in 1871, Sóphia and Vladimir succeeded in passing through the German lines and rowed across the Seine into Paris, where fighting had just broken out between the Republicans and the Communards. Unable to convince Aniuta to leave Paris, they returned to Germany a month later. Eventually, after the fall of the Commune, the sisters were forced to appeal to their father for help in securing Aniuta's escape.

It was at this point that Sonya's parents discovered that not only was their older daughter living with a man to whom she wasn't married, but their younger daughter was married to a man with whom she had never lived. Soon the entire family was pressing Sonya to consummate her marriage. But Sonya was now single-mindedly devoted to mathematics.

Weierstrass proved to be the intellectual challenge she needed. And she, in turn, challenged him. Their relationship moved beyond that of teacher and pupil. They became colleagues and the closest of friends. It took Weierstrass a long time to obtain permission for Sonya to use the university library. Next he began lobbying his former student, Lazarus Fuchs, to grant her a doctorate *in absentia* from the University of Göttingen. Weierstrass was worried that if Sonya were required to take an oral examination, she would not try for her degree out of shyness and insecurity about her spoken German. So he stressed her mathematical achievements and heritage, her struggle to obtain an education and her femininity. Finally he cited Karl Gauss's arguments for granting Sophie Germain an honorary degree from Göttingen.

The university agreed to accept as her dissertation *The Theory of Partial Differential Equations* (1875), which included the famous Cauchy-Kovalévsky theorem on the existence and uniqueness of solutions to such equations. (Neither she nor Weierstrass were aware of Cauchy's earlier work and Kovalévsky's was much more general than that of Cauchy). In addition she submitted two other works – one on the rings of Saturn and one on elliptic functions – that equally qualified as doctoral theses. Following Laplace, Sóphia assumed that the rings of Saturn were liquid, and she showed that their stable form would be oval in shape. Many years later the rings were revealed to be made up of solid particles, but her mathematical approach to the problem was of lasting value. Her paper 'On the

Reduction of a Certain Class of Abelian Integrals of the 3rd Rank to Elliptic Integrals' was published in *Acta Mathematica* in 1884. After solving a problem to her satisfaction Sonya often lost interest, sometimes not bothering to publish at all.

Sóphia Kovalévsky was granted her degree *in absentia* and *summa cum laude* in 1874. But Julia Lermontova was made to take both oral and written examinations in addition to presenting her thesis *On the Knowledge of Methylen Compounds*. It was a terrible ordeal for a woman who had never in her life taken an exam and Weierstrass later learned that several of the examiners had come planning to fail her. Nevertheless Julia was awarded her chemistry degree *magna cum laude* from the University of Göttingen and went to work in a private organic chemistry laboratory in Moscow. Kovalévsky and Lermontova were the first; but within a few years, Göttingen would be known throughout the world as a haven for women scientists and mathematicians.

Sóphia now had her degree, but nowhere in Europe was there a position for a female doctor of mathematics. The Kovalévskys returned to Russia where the only job available to her was teaching arithmetic to elementary schoolgirls. (Sonya commented: 'I was, unfortunately, weak in the multiplication table.'[19]) She applied for the master's examination that would allow her to teach in a Russian university. The Minister of Education refused her.

She appeared to abandon her interest in further studies, in spite of Weierstrass's attempts to persuade her to continue. For about two years she refused to reply to his letters. It was not until 1885 that she revised and published her 'Supplementary Remarks and Observations on Laplace's Research on the Form of Saturn's Ring in *Astronomische Nachrichten*. Weierstrass's student, Gösta Mittag-Leffler, on a visit to St Petersburg reported back that Sonya had abandoned mathematics, and was now a theatre reviewer and science reporter for a newspaper. It was about this time that Sonya and Vladimir consummated their marriage.

In 1878, while awaiting the birth of her daughter Sóphia (Fufu), Sonya returned to mathematics. In January of 1880 (probably at the instigation of Weierstrass) she was invited to speak on Abelian integrals to a convention of Russian naturalists and physicians. Mittag-Leffler travelled to St Petersburg to hear her.

By this time the Kovalévskys were deeply in debt. Their property speculations and publishing ventures had failed miserably, and early in 1880 they were forced to move into Julia's small Moscow apartment. At Sóphia's suggestion the three scientists set about trying to perfect an electric light bulb, unaware of Thomas Edison's recent success. (Sóphia noted in her diary that in 1880 70 patents were awarded to women around the world.[20]) She studied geology and natural history, hoping to encourage Vladimir in his work, and helped him translate Brehm's *Birds*. It was useless. Leaving her child with Julia, Sóphia left for Berlin in the autumn of 1880. Once there, Weierstrass suggested she should work on the refraction of light in crystalline media. Although she returned to Moscow in January, relations with Vladimir were severely strained, and she left for Paris at the end of the month, taking her daughter with her.

The previous year, Mittag-Leffler had tried to get Sonya a position at the University of Helsingfors, but the faculty refused to accept a Russian woman. Now as professor of mathematics at Stockholm, Mittag-Leffler was anxious to secure for that university its first great woman mathematician. Sonya was flattered but hesitant:

> I have never looked for any other appointment than this, and I will even admit that I should feel less bashful and shy if I were only allowed the possibility of applying my knowledge in the higher branches of education. I may in this way open the universities to women, which has hitherto only been possible by special favour – a favour which can be denied at any moment, as has recently happened in the German universities. Without being rich, I have still the means of living independently. The question of salary is, therefore, of no importance to me in coming to a decision. What I wish, above all, is to serve the cause in which I take so great an interest; and, at the same time, to be able to live for my work, surrounded by those who are occupied with the same questions – a piece of good fortune I have never enjoyed in Russia, but only in Berlin.[21]

Sonya felt she should finish her papers first: 'On the Propagation of Light in Crystalline Media' was published in *Acta Mathematica* in 1883; and a second paper followed in 1884. However Kovalévsky and Weierstrass were both embarrassed to learn that the work contained a serious error, copied from an earlier mathematician, in which a multi-valued function was treated as if it had a single value.

Early in 1882 Sóphia went to live in Paris where she was elected to the Mathematical Society. She sent her daughter back to Russia and there, on 15 April 1883, Vladimir Kovalévsky committed suicide. In August 1883 Sonya left for Odessa, to address the Congress of Russian Naturalists and Physicians on her work with crystals, and in 1884 she moved to the University of Stockholm.

It was a new and progressive university. But Sonya's reception was mixed. One newspaper welcomed her as 'a princess of science' to which she responded: 'a princess! If only they would assign me a salary.'[22] Her most outspoken Swedish adversary was the playwright, August Strindberg: 'A female professor of mathematics is a pernicious and unpleasant phenomenon – even, one might say, a monstrosity; and her invitation to a country where there are so many male mathematicians far superior in learning to her can be explained only by the gallantry of the Swedes toward the female sex.'[23]

Sóphia replied: 'I think he is right, only I wish he would prove clearly that there were plenty of mathematicians in Sweden better than I am, and that it was only *galanterie* that made them select me!'[24] Despite vehement opposition she was awarded a five-year salaried professorship at the end of her first year.

Initially Sóphia found life in Stockholm challenging: lecturing three times a week on the newest and most advanced topics in analysis, tutoring a large number of students and carrying out the most important research of her career. She wrote a short treatise that Weierstrass published in *Borchardt's Journal* and began a collaboration with Mittag-Leffler on a large mathematical work. That summer she returned to Berlin expecting that now, as a university professor, she would finally be allowed to attend lectures. But once again Weierstrass's petition on her behalf was turned down.

Sóphia became an editor of *Acta Mathematica*, an international journal founded by Mittag-Leffler in 1882, in which she published her translations of two papers by the great Russian mathematician P.L. Chebyshev. In 1885 she became professor of mechanics as well as mathematics at the University of Stockholm.

But by 1886 Sonya had grown bored with life in Stockholm:

[she] could not work, but she maintained with more and more eagerness that work – especially scientific work – was no good; it could neither afford pleasure nor cause humanity to progress. It was folly to waste one's youth on work, and especially was it

unfortunate for a woman to be scientifically gifted, for she was thus drawn into a sphere which could never afford her happiness.[25]

She desperately missed the intellectual stimulation of Paris and St Petersburg, and without brilliant mathematical colleagues to inspire her, she turned instead to literature.

Mittag-Leffler's sister and Sóphia's close friend, Anna Charlotte Leffler-Edgren, was a well-known novelist and feminist. In 1887 the women began writing a play. Leffler wrote: 'I do not think two women-friends have ever enjoyed each other's society so much as we do – and we shall be the first example in literature of two women-collaborators' (p. 242). *The Struggle for Happiness*, actually two plays, was printed under the pseudonym Korvin-Leffler.

Sóphia Kovalévsky referred to her literary work as her 'child' – the word Ada Lovelace had used for her mathematics. In French, Swedish and Russian, Sóphia wrote short stories, magazine articles, a collection of verses, and a reminiscence of the Polish uprising; and she began collaborating with Leffler on a play based on an unfinished manuscript by Aniuta. Her reputation as a writer was firmly established with the Russian publication of her autobiography, *Recollections of Childhood* (1890). It was widely translated and was popular in Sweden as a novel, *From Russian Life: The Raevsky Sisters* (1889). From her unrevised manuscripts, Sóphia's friends edited *Vera Barantzova* after her death. First published in Sweden in 1892, the novel told the story of a young revolutionary martyr; as *A Nihilist Girl*, it was published in Russia in 1906 and translated into six other languages. Fragments of other novels were found among Sóphia's papers after her death.

In the summer of 1886, Sóphia learned that the *Prix Bordin*, the highest award of the French Academy of Sciences, would be offered for the best paper on the rotation of a rigid body about a fixed point. It was the fourth time this had been made the subject of a competition, Euler, Lagrange and Poisson having all failed to solve the problem. Sóphia had worked in this area before and, returning to Stockholm with her 8-year-old daughter, she began lecturing on the rigid body question.

Sóphia Kovalévsky worked very hard to win the *Prix Bordin*. Yet she came close to not completing her entry, when she fell in love with Maksim Maksimovich Kovalévsky (distantly related to her husband's family) an eminent Russian sociologist and historian.

Finally, she succeeded in solving the problem, but there was no time to revise the manuscript. She wrote to her friend, the mathematician Charles Hermite, asking if she could submit her draft and substitute the final version later. This was arranged and her anonymity preserved.

In December of 1888 at a solemn session of the French Academy, Sóphia Kovalévksy was awarded the *Prix Bordin*. It was, as her friend Anna Leffler wrote, 'the greatest scientific honour which any woman has ever gained; one of the greatest honours, indeed, to which any one can aspire' (p. 266). It was announced that the winning entry, chosen from 15 anonymous submissions, was so elegant that an additional 2,000 francs had been added to the prize. Sóphia broadened and refined her work in 1889 and the Swedish Academy of Science awarded her a prize of 1,500 kroner. Her solution was so general that no new case of rotatory motion about a fixed point has been researched since.

In 1889 Mittag-Leffler secured for her a professorship for life in Stockholm. She tried, however, for a position in Paris, and when that failed, she again lobbied for a post in Russia. Her colleague Chebyshev succeeded in having her named the first woman corresponding member of the Imperial Academy of Science, an action which required a charter amendment. It was a small consolation. Returning to St Petersburg that summer to find a publisher for her *Recollections*, she tried to arrange full membership in the Academy. This would have guaranteed her a salary and required only two months' residency each year. But she could not even gain admittance to the Academy meetings.

She was briefly reconciled with Maksim but while climbing near Nice with him, she suffered a heart attack. She returned to Stockholm in February 1891, having made her decision. She would relinquish her professorship to marry Maksim and devote herself to mathematical research. Within a few days she was dead. Her last mathematical paper was a note on potential theory in *Acta Mathematica* (1891).

Life had not been easy for this great woman mathematician. In her character and her literary work she was very much a woman of the nineteenth century. But her mathematical brilliance required a more liberal age. Her basic shyness, romantic nature and emotional dependence were in constant conflict with her professional ambitions. Anna Leffler wrote of her:

Sonya perhaps exaggerated her fear out of coquetry. She possessed to a high degree that feminine grace so highly appreciated by men. She loved to be protected.

To a quite masculine energy and genius, and, in some ways, an inflexible character, she united a very feminine helplessness. She never learned her way about Stockholm... She could look neither after her money matters, her house, nor her child... But she never failed to find some devoted friend who made her interest his own, and on whom she could throw all the burden of her affairs... It was such a delight to her to be thus assisted and cared for in trifles that, as I said before, she rather liked to exaggerate her fears and helplessness. Notwithstanding all this, there was never a woman who, in the deepest sense of the word, could be more independent of others than she... Mittag-Leffler often told her that her love of and desire for sympathy was a feminine weakness. Men of great genius had never been dependent in this way on others. But she asserted the contrary, enumerating a number of instances in which men had found their best inspiration in their love for a woman. (pp. 222–23, 230)

12
The Popularisation and Professionalisation of Science

Instead of being ashamed that so little has been hitherto done by female abilities, in science and in useful literature, I am surprised that so much has been effected. Till of late, women were kept in Turkish ignorance; every means of acquiring knowledge was discountenanced by fashion, and impracticable even to those who despised fashion. Our books of science were full of unintelligible jargon, and mystery veiled pompous ignorance from public contempt; but now, writers must offer their discoveries to the public in distinct terms, which everybody may understand; technical language will no longer supply the place of knowledge, and the art of teaching has been carried to great perfection by the demand for learning: all this is in favour of women. Many things, which were thought to be above their comprehension, or unsuited to their sex, have now been found to be perfectly within the compass of their abilities, and peculiarly suited to their situation. Botany has become *fashionable*; in time it may become useful, if it be not so already. Science has *'been enlisted under the banners of imagination'*, by the irresistible charms of genius; by the same power her votaries will be led *from the looser analogies which dress out the imagery of poetry, to the stricter ones which form the ratiocination of philosophy*. (Maria Edgeworth, 1795, pp. 64–6)

Although primarily a novelist, Maria Edgeworth (1767–1849), like so many other educated women of her day, maintained a lifelong interest in science. A true woman of the Enlightenment, her circle included many famous scientists: Erasmus Darwin, Sir Humphry

Davy, William Wollaston, Joseph Priestly, Sir John Herschel and his wife, and Charles Babbage, as well as many of the women central to science – Marie Lavoisier, Jane Marcet and Mary Somerville. The latter two were numbered among her closest friends. *Letters for Literary Ladies*, Edgeworth's first publication under her own name, was a plea for the education of women.

The nineteenth century witnessed the beginnings of a pseudo-science that attempted to 'prove' the intellectual inferiority of women; in particular, that women were intellectually and morally unfit for scientific work. For every Maria Edgeworth, there were 100 men fighting to keep education out of the hands of women. But it was too late. Throughout Europe women and men were demanding equality in education.

In Naples in 1876, Angiulli published a plea for a lay system of female education identical to that for males:

> But let us consider, point by point, how the need to teach girls some science arises from the duties they will have to fulfil as wives, mothers, and educators.
>
> Women must know something of the fundamental laws which explain the cosmic system of our planet and the simpler facts of meteorology and physics. Without such information, one does not, nowadays, possess human dignity. It is only thanks to such study that women can cease peopling the heavenly spaces with imaginary entities and acquire that freedom of mind which is the first step toward educating ourselves and others. They will [then] be able to stop believing and making their children believe – thereby stunting the development of their intellects – that rain is sent to us by Jesus, that thunder is the sign of divine anger and menace, and that successful crops and a good or bad harvest are to be attributed rather to the will of Providence than to the merits of work and the course of natural events.[1]

Science became increasingly popular during the nineteenth century. The spread of elementary education, for girls as well as boys, made new developments more accessible to the general public. Rapid technological advance, spurred on by the industrial revolution, brought home the importance of scientific knowledge. Books, magazines and the new regional scientific societies catered to this widespread interest in scientific research.

1. Jane Marcet's 'Conversations'

> It may be due to the author of the admirable 'Conversations on Chemistry,' to mention, that the title of the present volume was chosen, because it was the only one that seemed to be adapted to the nature of the subject, which had not been appropriated by preceding writers.

Thus wrote Jane Marcet in the preface to her *Conversations on Botany* (pp. iv–v). It was a spoof, for Marcet herself was the author of *Conversations on Chemistry* as well as other popular science books, but many of her readers would have missed the point, since her books were usually published anonymously, under one of several pseudonyms, or were wrongly attributed.

Jane Haldimand (1769–1858) was born in London of Swiss parents. In 1799 she married Alexander Marcet, a Swiss physician who later became an experimental chemist. The Marcets were at the centre of London literary and scientific circles, and with her husband's encouragement Jane attended Sir Humphry Davy's lectures at the Royal Institution. Soon she was Davy's student.

Elementary science texts were practically unknown when Jane Marcet published *Conversations on Chemistry, intended more especially for the Female Sex* in 1805. The two-volume work appeared anonymously:

> IN venturing to offer to the public, and more particularly to the female sex, an Introduction to Chemistry, the author, herself a woman, conceives that some explanation may be required; and she feels it the more necessary to apologize for the present undertaking, as her knowledge of the subject is but recent, and as she can have no real claims to the title of chemist. (p. v)

Despite this, most readers assumed the author was a man, and her true identity was not made public until the 13th edition was published in 1837.

Using the classic formula – a dialogue between the teacher, Mrs Bryan, and her students Emily and Caroline – Marcet described the important new discoveries in chemistry. Mrs B. and Emily were as serious as could be but Caroline had no interest in chemical theory. She loved spectacular experiments, especially explosions. It was the character of Caroline that allowed Marcet to enliven her text with detailed descriptions of experimental methods. She had studied painting with Sir Joshua Reynolds and Thomas Lawrence and illustrated the apparatus and experiments using her own woodcuts and drawings.

The science of chemistry was advancing at a phenomenal pace during the early nineteenth century, and *Conversations on Chemistry* went through 16 English editions, each carefully updated by the author. There were two French translations and at least 15 American editions. (The book was usually referred to as 'Mrs. Bryan's Conversations' in the United States where it had sold some 160,000 copies before 1853.) However, American editors took many liberties with the text, occasionally plagiarising it outright. An indignant supporter of Marcet wrote: 'We are informed by one of the American editors of this work that his reason for not placing the name of Jane Marcet on the title-page, was because scientific men believed it fictitious!'[2]

References to 'Mrs Bryan' (the name of the teacher in the text) added to the confusion. *Conversations on Chemistry* was often attributed to Margaret Bryan, a London schoolteacher who had published the lectures, experiments and problems she used in her female seminary, in the form of two relatively sophisticated textbooks, *A Compendious System of Astronomy* (1797) and *Lectures on Natural Philosophy* (1806). (Many of the subscribers for these books were women.) Marcet's books were also attributed to her husband, who handled much of her correspondence, or to her editor.

The great chemist Michael Faraday, as a young apprentice to a bookbinder, was first introduced to chemistry while binding Marcet's *Conversations*. They later became good friends, and Marcet always included his new work, as well as Davy's, in each edition. However Marcet was criticised for her ready acceptance of Davy's more questionable results, and it was probably at his suggestion that she chose to ignore John Dalton's theory of the atom, atomic weights and symbols. (Dalton showed that elements combine into compounds in simple numerical ratios and postulated that atoms of the same element were all identical, while those of different elements differed in size and weight [1808]; it was many years before the significance of his work was widely appreciated by chemists.)

Conversations on Botany, written for young people and published anonymously in 1817 and 1820, was commonly attributed to Elizabeth and Sarah Mary Fitton. This volume of conversations between 'Mother' and 'Edward' included 20 coloured plates and utilised the Linnaean system of classification (see p. 110 above). Marcet's *Conversations on Vegetable Physiology* (1829) was inspired by her close association with the naturalist August de Candolle. *Conversations on Natural Philosophy*, her first book, was eventually published in 1819 to serve as an introduction to *Conversations on Chemistry*. Like her other books, it was plagiarised in the United States, with only the American editor's name appearing on the cover and title-page.

But there was another current in the structure of nineteenth-century science: one that conflicted with its increasing popularity.

2. The Universities and the Scientific Societies

As science became increasingly complex, specialised and profes-sionalised, so it became an established subject in the universities. The great École Polytechnique in Paris was founded in 1794, but women were not admitted until 1972. Likewise (except in a few special cases), women were barred from the most important nine-teenth-century centres of science – the universities of Germany.

In Britain women fared somewhat better. Although Arthur Cayley had failed in his attempts to open mathematics at Cambridge University to women early in the nineteenth century, by the middle of the century women could study mathematics at their own colleges: Queen's College opened in 1848 with 200 students – among them Sophia Jex-Blake (see pp. 106–7) who would go on to lead the fight for women's medical education. Although women were still not admitted to the universities of Oxford, Cambridge or London, nevertheless they were applying in large numbers – and were dutifully given entrance examinations. In 1863 the Cambridge papers of 83 girls were assessed for grading by a committee of the National Association for the Promotion of Social Science. Their excellent results in science and mathematics were discussed at a meeting of the Association, and an expert assured the gathering that encouraging girls to use their brains would not cause them to go insane. To prove the point, girls at a village school were taught botany by a university professor, and were later reported to be 'unusually intelligent, orderly and neat in their appearance and in special request as nursery maids.'[3]

It would be many years before universities admitted women on an equal basis with men, but the struggle for acceptance was also being waged in the Societies and Academies. The Italian scientific societies had been the earliest in Europe and had welcomed women members, but most of these organisations were closed by the Inquisition, and the most influential European scientific societies were founded in the mid-seventeenth century, as tribunals to approve or criticise new research, to encourage the investigation of pressing social problems and issues, and to disseminate knowledge of new discoveries through their journals. By the eighteenth century these societies had begun to control the direction of scientific research.

Women were instrumental in the establishment of some scientific societies. Sophia Charlotte, Queen of Prussia, helped found the Berlin Academy in 1700; Richelieu, founder of the French Academy, was inspired by the academy-like salon of Madame de Rambouillet; and the St Petersburg Academy of Sciences operated under the patronage of Empresses Catherine I, Anna and Catherine the Great. Princess Catherine Dashov (1748–1810) reorganised and revitalised the Academy when she became its director in 1783; she was an enthusiastic naturalist and her friend Benjamin Franklin arranged for her unanimous election as the first woman member of the American Philosophical Society in 1789. Yet even in the late nineteenth century the St Petersburg Academy still prohibited female members.

In Britain, the Royal Society remained an association of men, but the Royal Institution, founded in 1799 by Count Rumford to promote scientific research, depended on the subscriptions of its members of both sexes. Fashionable London ladies flocked to Albemarle Street to attend lectures at the Institution.

The popularity of nineteenth-century science and its increasing importance in industrial regions resulted in a number of new scientific associations that were less steeped in male tradition. From its founding in 1831, the British Association for the Advancement of Science struggled with the 'woman question'. President-elect of the BAAS, the Reverend William Buckland, wrote to Roderick Murchison on 27 March 1832:

Everybody whom I spoke to on the subject agreed that if the Meeting is to be of scientific utility, ladies ought not to attend the reading of the papers – especially in a place like Oxford – as it would overturn the thing into a sort of Albemarle dilettanti meeting instead of a serious philosophical union of working men. I did not see Mrs Somerville, *but her husband decidedly informed me that such is her opinion of this matter*, and further I fear that she will not come at all.[4]

(Mary Somerville – the most respected of all nineteenth-century women scientists – was not one to attend a function where she was not welcome!)

The officers of the BAAS consequently decided that women could attend the social functions but not the meetings of the Association. But Charles Babbage objected – albeit because of the women's 'enchanting smiles' and because more members would attend if they could bring their wives and daughters along to be entertained.[5] He prevailed, and women were invited to the general meeting and occasional evening lectures as 'Members' Philosophical Associates'.

But the women were not satisfied. In 1833 they packed the galleries and platform seats at BAAS meetings and by 1834 were outnumbering the men. To overcome this, strict rules were established for the issuing of ladies' tickets. Nevertheless, at the 1835 meeting in Dublin women disregarded the rule barring them from sectional meetings, and in 1837, fearing that women would again gate-crash the sections, they were officially invited to the geology and natural history divisions where they were confined to special galleries. (However, Caroline Fox (1819–71) managed to attend the section on physical sciences without incident.)

In 1838 1,100 women and 1,300 men attended the BAAS meeting at Newcastle upon Tyne, and for the first time women were admitted to the majority of sections. (They were, however, excluded from the natural history section 'on account of the nature of some of the papers belonging to the Zoology division'.[6] The ban was ignored.) Finally, in 1839, women were admitted to all sections (though confined to separate galleries or railed-off areas). Thus, by the simple tactic of invasion, women gained admittance to the meetings of the British Association.

From the outset, some BAAS members had recognised that women were crucial to both the success and the style of the Association – and soon they were vital to its finances as well; although Humphrey Lloyd wrote to Edward Sabine, 'The only thing that seems to me doubtful is the propriety of the *Association itself meddling with the ladies*, or taking their money. Is it not rather *American*?'[7] For the most part, the women who participated in the BAAS did so out of a sincere interest in science, but were not taken seriously by most of the men. Nevertheless women scientists benefited from the Association. Although the first woman member, Miss Bowlby of Cheltenham, was not admitted until 1853, from 1840 onwards women were active participants.

Paulina Jermyn (1816–66), a naturalist and geologist, met her future husband, the geologist Walter Calverley Trevelyan, at the 1833 meeting in Cambridge, and was active in the affairs of the Association. She was treated as a colleague by its leading scientists. During the 1840s, Mrs Davies Gilbert read papers to the statistics section on the need for agricultural education in industrial schools, and exhibited specimens of her intensively cultivated wheat. The first work on pure science delivered to the Association by a woman may have been Miss R. Zorubin's 1858 paper, 'On Heat and on the Indestructibility of Elementary Bodies'. Lydia E. Becker (b. 1827), author of *Botany for Beginners* (1864), contributed a number of papers over the years, including one in 1868 to the section of economic science and statistics, arguing that there were no intellectual differences between the sexes. The following year she led a group lobbying for the election of women to the Association committees and offices. (They were told there was no rule to prevent such election, but in 1876 the Council ruled against them on the grounds that there had never been any women officers.)

Such controversies were common in natural history clubs and societies throughout the nineteenth century. From their founding the London Botanical Society, the Zoological Society of London (1827) and the Royal Entomological Society (1833) admitted women on the same terms as men. However, the Linnaean Society of London, the Royal Microscopical Society, the Geological Society and the prestigious Royal Society did not admit women until the twentieth century.

3. Mary Somerville: 'The Queen of Nineteenth-Century Science'

We have spent two days pleasantly here with Dr Wollaston, Dr and Mrs Somerville . . . besides our own dear friend, Mrs Marcet. Mrs Somerville is the lady who, La Place says, is the only woman in England who understands his works. She draws beautifully; and while her head is among the stars, her feet are firm upon the earth. (Maria Edgeworth 17 January 1822, (1895) p. 398)

When she died in 1872, Mary Somerville was hailed by *The London Post* as 'The Queen of Nineteenth-Century Science'.[8] John Stuart Mill wrote that she 'alone perhaps of women, knows as much of mathematics as is now needful for making any considerable mathematical discovery' (p. 286); and Margaret Fuller asked: 'Since Somerville has achieved so much, will any young girl be prevented from seeking a knowledge of the physical sciences, if she wishes it?' (p. 94).

During her lifetime Mary Somerville was a heroine in scientific and feminist circles. Yet unlike so many other women scientists she never deviated – at least in public – from the preoccupations and conduct considered socially acceptable for women and perhaps this in part was the key to her success. Her contemporaries all emphasised Somerville's femininity – in a letter informing her that the Royal Society had voted unanimously to place her bust in its Great Hall, J.G. Children wrote that the Society's members would

> honour Science, their country and themselves, in paying this proud tribute to the powers of the female mind – and at the same time establish an imperishable record of the perfect compatibility of the most exemplary discharge of the softer duties of domestic life, with the deepest researches in Mathematical Philosophy.[9]

Children did not bother to add that, as a woman, Mary Somerville could not set foot in the Great Hall of the Royal Society. In *Nature*, a reviewer of her *Personal Recollections* wrote:

> No one ... could possibly have afforded a stronger refutation of the axiom, almost universally upheld half a century ago, that scientific acquirements of a high order are wholly incompatible with the proper exercise of the natural and ascribed functions of a woman's destiny. (p. 417)

Mary Somerville was, in fact, something of a paradox. She was an outspoken feminist (hers was the first signature on John Stuart Mill's petition for women's suffrage) yet she saw herself as a woman who had been granted rare opportunities and believed that women scientists lacked originality and creative genius.

Born Mary Fairfax in Scotland in 1780, she received only the most rudimentary formal education – one year at a Miss Primrose's boarding school, where

I was enclosed in stiff stays with a steel busk in front, while, above my frock, bands drew my shoulders back till the shoulder-blades met. Then a steel rod, with a semi-circle which went under the chin, was clasped to the steel busk in my stays . . . (p. 22)

Back home again, she amused herself by studying birds and teaching herself Latin 'for the sake of having something to do' (p. 36). It was hardly a childhood calculated to produce one of the finest scientists of the nineteenth century. But her uncle Dr Somerville (later her father-in-law) inspired her with stories of the great women scholars of the ancient world.

Mary studied the mathematical puzzles included in women's journals but she had never heard of algebra and had no idea what the 'x's and 'y's meant. From her younger brother's tutor she obtained copies of Euclid's *Elements* and Bonnycastle's *Algebra*. Her father objected: 'we shall have Mary in a strait jacket one of these days. There was X., who went raving mad about the longitude!' (p. 54). But when her parents removed the candles to prevent her from reading at night, Mary memorised the books and worked out the problems in her head.

In 1804 she married Samuel Greig, a captain in the Russian navy, who 'had a very low opinion of the capacity of my sex, and had neither knowledge of nor interest in science of any kind' (p. 75). Three years later she was left a widow with two young sons. Now free to pursue her own interests, she won a silver medal for her solution to a problem on Diophantine equations (see p. 44) in William Wallace's *Mathematical Repository*. Wallace, who was later to become professor of mathematics at Edinburgh University, and her friends at the *Edinburgh Review* encouraged her to continue her studies. Soon she was reading Newton's *Principia*.

She married again – this time her cousin William Somerville, a physician who shared her interest in natural history. Mary could not have found a more supportive husband. As a Fellow of the Royal Society, he could use its library to her advantage and introduce her to distinguished scientists and years later, when she was the leading science writer of the day, her husband edited and recopied her manuscripts, compiled her bibliographies, and handled her corres-pondence with scientists and publishers. Meanwhile they studied geology together and collected a cabinet of minerals, and by the age of 33, Mary was progressing from Greek and botany to meteorology, astronomy, higher mathematics and physics.

In 1816 the Somervilles moved from Edinburgh to London, where they found themselves at the centre of an exciting and progressive circle of amateur and professional scientists. Mary's close friend, William Wollaston, added to her mineral collection and presented her with the prism he had used to discover the solar spectrum; within hours of his discovery, Thomas Young was explaining to her his method for dating Egyptian papyruses astronomically; Sir James South taught Mary how to observe binary systems; Sir Edward Parry brought her seeds and minerals from the Arctic, where he named an island after her; and Lady Bunbury taught her the classification of seashells. She admired Charles Babbage's calculating engines, and became mentor to the young Ada Lovelace (see pp. 157–63). The Somervilles were also frequent visitors to the Herschels' observatory at Slough. In Paris and Switzerland they met the greatest scientists of the day. Mary's friends sent her books and papers, performed experiments for her, invited her to their meetings and lectures, and answered all her questions. She was in a perfect position for writing about science.

Mary Somerville's first paper, 'On the Magnetizing Power of the More Refrangible Solar Rays', was communicated to the Royal Society by her husband. With apparatus consisting only of a non-magnetic steel sewing-needle, paper and a prism, she concluded that magnetism was induced by the blue-green-violet end of the solar spectrum.[10] (Her results and conclusions were at first widely accepted, and stimulated further investigation of the question, but were later disproved.)

Somerville published two other research papers: 'Experiments on the Transmission of Chemical Rays of the Solar Spectrum across Different Media' appeared in the French Academy of Sciences' *Comptes Rendus* in 1836, and 'On the Action of the Rays of the Spectrum on Vegetable Juices', extracted from a letter to Sir John Herschel, was published by the Royal Society in 1845.

Mary was, however, aware of the limitations of her experimental work. In a draft of her autobiography she wrote:

> In the climax of my great success the approbation of some of the first scientific men of the age and of the public in general I was highly gratified, but much less elated than might have been expected, for although I had recorded in a clear point of view some of the most refined and difficult analytical processes and

astronomical discoveries, I was conscious that I had never made a discovery myself, that I had no originality. I have perseverance and intelligence but no genius, that spark from heaven is not granted to the sex, we are of the earth, earthy, whether higher powers may be allotted to us in another existence God knows, original genius in science at least is hopeless in this.[11]

Such thoughts reflected contemporary attitudes to scientific women, who were permitted to study botany or describe the discoveries of male scientists, but not to conduct original investigation or experimentation; these were considered either inappropriate or beyond their capabilities.

On 27 March 1827 Lord Henry Brougham, the High Chancellor, wrote to Dr Somerville asking if Mary would undertake the translation of Laplace's *Mécanique Céleste* for his Society for Diffusing Useful Knowledge. Mary was hesitant. By interpreting the observed motion of comets, planets and satellites using Newton's theory of gravitation, Laplace had shown that the solar system was a stable and perfectly self-regulating mechanism. It was a long and extremely complex work. In an 1808 review John Playfair commented that there were scarcely a dozen mathematicians in Britain capable of even reading it.[12] It was said that in 1817 when the Somervilles dined with Laplace in Paris, he remarked to Mary, unaware of the identity of her first husband: 'I write books that no one can read. Only two women have ever read the *Mécanique Céleste*; both are Scotch women: Mrs Greig and yourself.'[13]

Mary finally agreed to the project, with the provision that her manuscript be burned if it were found unacceptable. She worked on her book in secret for the next four years, all the while carrying on a busy social life and supervising the education of her young daughters. As she wrote in her autobiography: 'A man can always command his time under the plea of business, a woman is not allowed any such excuse'. (pp. 163–4)

Mary Somerville's *Mechanism of the Heavens* was much more than a translation of Laplace. Her lengthy 'Preliminary Dissertation' included the basic mathematics necessary for understanding Laplace's ideas, as well as a history of the subject and an explanation of Laplace's work with her own drawings, diagrams, mathematical derivations and proofs. (The 'Dissertation' was later reprinted and sold separately.)

But Brougham had decided that *Mechanism of the Heavens* was too long and sophisticated for his Library of Useful Knowledge, so Dr Somerville now sent the manuscript to the publisher John Murray, with a favourable assessment by Sir John Herschel. Murray did not expect it to sell but agreed to print 750 copies. It not only received enthusiastic reviews, it was a financial success:[14] *Mechanism of the Heavens* was to remain a standard text in higher mathematics and astronomy for the rest of the century.

Mary's second book, *On the Connexion of the Physical Sciences*, emphasised the increasing interdependence of the various branches of science. Although she devoted over a third of the book to her favourite subject – physical astronomy – she also covered mechanics, magnetism, electricity, heat and sound. Her discussion of optics strongly supported Thomas Young's wave theory of light and she argued cogently for the adoption of the French metric system. Her meteorology and climatology were also advanced for the day. She included diagrams of Chladni's experiments with vibrating plates – the phenomenon that had occupied Sophie Germain for so many years (see pp. 150–5 and Figs. 11-12). Many scientists – and Michael Faraday in particular – contributed their knowledge and advice to each revised edition.

Physical Sciences was a descriptive work. It utilised examples and analogies, included a glossary, and confined mathematical formulae to the notes. In her 1834 dedication to Queen Adelaide, consort of William IV, Somerville wrote that she had tried 'to make the laws by which the material world is governed more familiar to my country-women'. But she never sacrificed accuracy for readability.

The book was even more successful than *Mechanism*. It went through 10 editions in the next 40 years and was translated into French, German and Italian (and was pirated in the United States). With each edition, outdated material was eliminated and new discoveries included, resulting in a fourfold increase in length over the years. In particular the development of electricity and magnetism into crucial nineteenth-century sciences can be traced through the successive editions of *Physical Sciences*. *The Athenaeum* called the book 'delightful' and 'with the exception of Sir John Herschel's treatises, the most valuable and the most pleasing work of science that has been published within the century' (p. 202). It was in his review of *Physical Sciences* that William Whewell coined the word 'scientist' (as opposed to 'philosopher') to 'designate the students of the knowledge of the material world collectively' (p. 59).

Physical Sciences proved an important book for other scientists as well as for the general public. In the sixth and seventh editions (1842 and 1846) Somerville wrote:

> Those [tables of motion] of Uranus, however, are already defective, probably because the discovery of that planet in 1781 is too recent to admit of much precision in the determination of its motion, or that possibly it may be subject to disturbance from some unseen planet revolving about the sun beyond the present boundaries of our system. If, after a lapse of years, the tables formed from a combination of numerous observations should still be inadequate to represent the motions of Uranus, the discrepancies may reveal the existence, nay even the mass and orbit of a body placed forever beyond the sphere of vision.[15]

But in the eighth edition (1848) Somerville was able to announce that John Adams and Urbain Leverrier had calculated the orbit of Neptune, resulting in the discovery of that planet, having been stimulated by her note:

> spend time with Airy and Adam [sic] the latter tells Mr. S. that a remark of mine in *Phys Sci* put it into his head to compute the orbit of Neptune, if I had possessed originality or genius I might have done it (a proof that originality in discovery is not given to women???)[16]

In 1838 Somerville was able to convince the Russian government to make simultaneous observations of the tides on every coast of their empire, and following the August 1835 return of Halley's comet, she published an extensive account of current ideas on the subject of comets.

Honours now began pouring in: honorary memberships to the Royal Astronomical Society, the Royal Academy of Dublin, the British Philosophical Institution and the Société de Physique et d'Histoire Naturelle of Geneva. More importantly, in 1835 Mary Somerville was awarded an annual pension of 200 pounds. Two years later her income was increased to 300 pounds.

In 1848 Mary Somerville published her most successful book, *Physical Geography*. The opening sentence announced: 'Physical

Geography is a description of the earth, the sea and the air, with their inhabitants animal and vegetable, of the distribution of these organized beings, and the causes of that distribution.' Relying on the new geology of Charles Lyell and Roderick Murchison, Somerville described the 'successive convulsions which have ultimately led to its present geographical arrangement, and to the actual distribution of land and water.'[17] But the text was very nearly destroyed. *Physical Geography* was almost ready to go to press when the first volume of Alexander von Humboldt's *Kosmos* appeared. Although Mary's would still be the first work of its kind in English, she decided to burn her manuscript. Her husband and Sir John Herschel, to whom the work was dedicated, convinced her to finish it. It went on to go through seven editions.

Physical Geography was purely descriptive, on occasion, imaginatively and poetically so. For the first time Somerville gave vent to some of her political views: she criticised slavery, and discussed class conflict and the inevitable inequality among people. She anticipated twentieth-century science historians, arguing against the 'great man' theory and stressing that most discoveries were the result of slow progress by many scientists: 'When society has arrived at a certain point of advancement, certain discoveries will naturally be made; the general mind is directed that way, and if one individual does not hit upon the discovery, another will.[18]

The Somervilles moved to Italy in the 1840s. More honours followed, among them election to the Italian Academy of Science (1856), the Italian Geographical Society (1870) and various other Italian scientific and literary societies; and election to the American Geographical and Statistical Society (1857) and the American Philosophical Society (1869). In the balloting of this last society, Somerville ranked second behind American astronomer Maria Mitchell and just ahead of the naturalists Elizabeth Agassiz and Charles Darwin. She also received the Victoria Gold Medal of the Royal Geographical Society, the Victor Emmanuel Gold Medal and the first gold medal of the Geographical Society of Florence. Somerville College, one of the first colleges for women at Oxford, was named after her.

Although her books were popular, Mary Somerville was not a populariser of science. Rather she was an expositor, describing and explaining the current state of science in terms understandable to the well-educated reader. She emphasised experimental findings and used precise scientific vocabulary. She presented both sides of controversial issues; but once an idea was discredited, it disappeared from subsequent editions.

Perhaps the one exception to this thoroughness was her complete avoidance of the evolutionary theories of Charles Darwin. She knew and admired Darwin, and in *Physical Geography* often referred to his travels and his work as a naturalist. She approved the choice of H.W. Bates, a staunch evolutionist, to revise the 1870 edition of *Physical Geography* provided that 'no Darwinism' would be interjected.[19] It is possible that Mary Somerville was convinced that Darwin was wrong; it is certain that she feared public censure. After the publication of *Mechanism of the Heavens* she had been denounced as a godless woman in the House of Commons, and her acceptance of the geological antiquity of the earth in *Physical Geography* had resulted in denunciations both in the Commons and from the pulpit of York Cathedral.

Her last book, *On Molecular and Microscopic Science* was published in 1869 when Mary Somerville was 89 years old. She had considered revising *Physical Sciences*, but decided instead to write a completely new work on recent discoveries made with the improved microscope. The book opened with a section on atomic theory and the solar spectrum, followed by a catalogue of plants. The second volume covered animals, from protozoa to molluscs, including discussions of internal structure, methods of reproduction and habitats. It was outdated and the least well-written of her books. The reviewers were kind, but it was a financial failure, and her revised edition was never published.

Mary Somerville died in 1872. She spent her last days reworking a mathematical paper on quaternions begun 40 years earlier. Her friend Frances Power Cobbe requested that she be buried in Westminster Abbey. But after the arrangements had been made the Astronomer Royal, out of 'jealousy, either scientific or masculine', refused to make the necessary formal request 'on the ground that *he* had never read Mrs Somerville's books!'[20] Her scientific library was donated to newly-founded Girton College for Women at Cambridge.

Mary Somerville did not begin serious scientific work until she was middle-aged and she always regretted not having concentrated on mathematics. It is impossible to know what this brilliant woman might have accomplished with early encouragement and training. When her eldest daughter died at the age of 10 she blamed herself, at least in part, for having pushed the child intellectually. Yet in old age she wrote: 'Age has not abated my zeal for the emancipation of my sex from the unreasonable prejudice too prevalent in Great Britain against a literary and scientific education for women' (1873, p. 345).

Mary Somerville was the last of the great amateur scientists. By the end of her life, the various sciences had become too complex to be understood in their entirety by a single individual. She was one of the fortunate women scientists. As Charles Lyell wrote to his future wife Mary Horner in 1831 (I, 325): 'Had our friend Mrs Somerville been married to La Place, or some mathematician, we should never have heard of her work. She would have merged it in her husband's, and passed it off as his.'

Epilogue

In Paris in 1898 Marie Curie discovered that radioactivity was an intrinsic property of the atom. It was a discovery that would change the world. Within a decade major advances had revolutionised mathematics, physics, astronomy, biology, and other sciences. William Whewell's term 'scientist' was becoming outdated: soon there would be nuclear physicists, geneticists, molecular biologists, and computer engineers. Never again would important discoveries be made by amateurs. Science had become a profession in every sense of the word, and its structure and that of the scientific establishment was changed irrevocably.

From the earliest times women contributed to the development of scientific knowledge, yet most of the women in this book remain unknown – even to historians of science – and most of those recorded here were women of privilege; as such, they represent only the surface of the history of women in science. Thousands of other women scientists have undoubtedly been forgotten forever.

At the end of the nineteenth century, for the first time in history, it became possible for a woman to join the scientific establishment. Yet the words of Henrietta Bolton, written in *Popular Science Monthly* in 1898 (p. 511), apply not only to thousands of years of history, but they are also still true today:

> As a general rule the scientific woman must be strong enough to stand alone, able to bear the often unjust sarcasm and dislike of men who are jealous of seeing what they consider their own field invaded.

Notes

Prologue

1. Late in her life, to the consternation of Henry More, Anne Conway's philosophical study led her to Quakerism, both because of the similarities between Quaker doctrine and the *Kabbala* and because of the Quaker belief in the equality of women. By 1677 Conway and van Helmont had both converted to Quakerism. The religious leaders George Fox, George Keith and William Penn were frequent visitors to Ragley Hall, and over a four-year period Anne collaborated with van Helmont and Keith on a treatise entitled *Two Hundred Queries . . . Concerning the Doctrine of the Revolution of Humane Souls* (1684).

2. *Essays upon Several Subjects in Prose and Verse* (London, 1710), p. 123; quoted in Lovejoy, pp. 190–1.

3. Unfortunately, historians of mathematics have gone to extremes to play down Elizabeth's intellectual achievements. For example E.T. Bell wrote: 'One theory to account for this remarkable young woman's unusual appetite ascribes her hunger for knowledge to a disappointment in love' (p. 47). There is no evidence for such a bizarre supposition. Queen Christine (1626–89), on the other hand, did enjoy collecting scientific and mathematical manuscripts and the scientists to go with them. She employed Descartes as her teacher in 1649. Due to the press of state affairs, the Queen demanded her lessons at five a.m., but the freezing winter mornings proved too great a strain on Descartes' health and he died in Stockholm in 1650.

Chapter 1 Goddesses and Gatherers

1. Childe, 1964, p. 66.

2. Washburn and Lancaster, p. 297.

3. In parts of Africa women continued as small-scale farmers until European-imposed land reforms deprived them of their rights (see Boserup, p. 60).

4. Cited in Boccacio, ch. 42.

Chapter 2   *Women and Science in the Ancient World*

1. Quoted in Hurd-Mead, 1933, p. 18.

2. Cited in Diogenes, 8, 8. Themistoclea is sometimes referred to as Aristocleia or Theiocleia.

3. See Osen, p. 15.

4. Osen (p. 16) suggests that Pythagoras wanted to lecture openly and freely disseminate knowledge, but that conservative elements within the Order fought to keep the doctrines secret. It was not until the mid-fifth century BC when there was a split among the Pythagoreans into religious and scientific factions that their scientific views became widely known.

5. There was at least one outstanding defect in this model: as the earth moved around the central fire during the 24-hour day, the fixed stars should change their positions relative to one another (the phenomenon called stellar parallax) unless the stars were infinitely far away. Yet no parallax effect was observed and the geometry of the musical scale necessitated that the distance to the fixed stars be finite. Later Pythagoreans rescued the cosmology by placing the earth, rather than a fire, at the centre of the universe and having the earth rotate daily on its axis.

6. Little is known of these daughters of Theano and Pythagoras. Damo or Arignote may have been responsible for teaching the Pythagorean doctrines to other women. Myia, another disciple of Pythagoras, has also been called his daughter.

7. This scenario is common in ancient history. Perhaps biting off one's tongue, if only symbolically, was one of the few means women had of expressing defiance of authority.

8. Spartan women held an advantage because they produced warriors – the society's most important commodity. Pomeroy (p. 36) suggests that only in Sparta were female children as well nourished as males. To my knowledge, the possibility of a relationship between childhood nourishment and female intellectual development in ancient times has never been examined.

9. Menagius (*Historia Mulierum Philosopharum* [Amsterdam: 1692], p. 3) found 65 women philosophers mentioned in the writings of the ancients; Athenaeus in his *Deipnosophistae* (c. AD 200) mentioned several Greek women mathematicians (cited in Mozans, p. 137).

10. Plutarch, 'Pericles', pp. 132–3.

11. Mozans, p. 198.

12. Quoted ibid., p. 8.

13. Cited ibid., p. 8.

14. When Artemisia's husband, King Mausolus, died in 355 BC, she built him a tomb, the Mausoleum, in her capital city of Halicarnassus. It became the Seventh Wonder of the ancient world. The widow-queen was also a superb

military leader who conquered neighbouring Rhodes after its naval attack on her city. An earlier Artemisia, Queen of Halicarnassus and Cos (c. 480 BC), participated in Xerxes' expedition against the Greeks. The Athenians were so indignant at a woman leading in battle against them that they offered a financial reward for her capture.

15. Quoted in Jex-Blake, p. 11.

16. Quoted in McMaster, p. 202.

17. Quoted in Jex-Blake, p. 11.

18. Cited in Hurd-Mead, 1933, p. 291. Elephantis and Lais were both common names and there is confusion as to whether they lived in the third century BC or in the time of Soranus. Lais was the name of at least three prominent Greek courtesans. There was an Elephantis who wrote obscene poetry admired by the Emperor Tiberius, perhaps the same Elephantis whom Galen cites as having written on cosmetics (see translator's footnote, Pliny, 28,81). The beautiful woman scholar lecturing from behind a screen is a story that reappears in many cultures from ancient times until well into the Renaissance.

19. Scribonius Largus, *De Compositione Medicamentorum Liber* (1529), cited in Hurd-Mead, 1933, p. 293.

20. Cited in Needham, 1959, p. 65.

21. Quoted in Mozans, p. 270.

22. James Ricci (p. 12), translator of Aetios, says that Aspasia may have been a beautiful Phoenician woman doctor, mistress of Cyrus the Younger and Artaxerxes, kings of Persia. She is also confused with the much earlier Athenian, Aspasia of Miletus. In the most blatant type of historical rewriting (which will be encountered again with Trotula during the Middle Ages), 'Aspasia' is said to have been a man – 'Aspasios' – or the title of a lost text on women's diseases written by a man.

23. Hurd-Mead, 1933, p. 398.

Chapter 3   From the Alexandrians to the Arabs

1. Maria is referred to in the literature by a variety of names and epithets including Mary or Maria Prophetissa, 'Maria the Sage', or Miriam. It is unclear whether Maria the Jewess and Mary the Copt were one and the same. 'The Letter of the Crown and the Nature of the Creation by Mary the Copt of Egypt', a translation from the Greek found in a volume of Arab alchemical manuscripts, describes a number of chemical processes, including the manufacture of coloured glass.

2. Quoted in Taylor, 1945, p. 190.

3. M. Berthelot, *Collection des anciens alchimists Grecs* (Paris, 1888), III, 196; quoted in Stephen Mason, p. 67.

4. She has been confused with Queen Cleopatra who may also have been interested in alchemy. It is possible that her work was deliberately ascribed to

the infamous queen.

5. F. Sherwood Taylor (trans.); quoted in Burland, p. 24.

6. Elbert Hubbard's portrait of Hypatia was fanciful and sarcastic. Following the *Chronicle* of John of Nikiu, a Coptic bishop who rewrote history to fit his Christian prejudices, Hubbard asserted that Hypatia hypnotised her students with satanic wiles (see Parsons, p. 379). Other writers identified her as an alchemist. Charles Kingsley, the popular nineteenth-century novelist, also fictitiously portrayed the life of Hypatia. Kingsley had her killed at the age of 25 instead of 45, and imagined her as a fanatical neoplatonist caught up in political intrigue. Hypatia never married and for centuries historians haggled over the question of her chastity.

Richardson's *The Star Lovers* exemplifies the treatment accorded women scientists in histories, on those occasions when they are discussed at all. Although he includes a chapter on women astronomers, he ignores some of the most important ones and generally ridicules those he does mention. Much of the chapter is devoted to the moon craters named after women astronomers! Heading the list is Hypatia: 'A learned woman who died defending the Christians [sic].' She is followed by Catherina: 'an extremely learned young woman of noble family who died in AD 307 defending the Christians' (p. 173).

7. McCabe, p. 271.

8. Quoted in Marrou, p. 134.

9. The Athenian school was later taken over by Asclepigenia's daughter, Asclepigenia the Younger. This eastern branch of neoplatonism also included other women such as Sosipatra, wife of the prefect Cappadocia. It has commonly been assumed that Hypatia was a neoplatonist in the tradition of Plotinus; but Rist presents evidence that the philosophy of Plotinus did not become well established in Alexandria until late in the fifth century, and that neither Hypatia nor Synesius were particularly interested in his doctrines.

10. Quoted in McCabe, p. 269.

11. Edward Gibbon (II, 816) implied that Cyril was so jealous of Hypatia's influence and popularity that he 'prompted, or accepted, the sacrifice of a virgin, who professed the religion of the Greeks'. Rist (p. 223) suggests that the mob was maddened by Lenten fastings.

12. Hurd-Mead (1933, p. 585) has suggested that there were indeed important Arab women scientists, but their works were anonymous or falsely ascribed, or their names mutilated by historians. Burton noted that the story of Tawaddud was often omitted from the *Arabian Nights* because it would be 'extremely tiresome to most readers' (p. 189).

Chapter 4 Medicine and Alchemy

1. Cited in Castiglioni, p. 315.

2. Trotula, pp. 1–2. Dr Mason-Hohl's is the first modern English translation.

Its source was the 1547 Aldine Press (Venice) edition of *Passionibus Mulierum Curandorum*, included in Paulus Manutius's anthology *Medici Antiqui Omnes*. A study (see Benton) suggests that this work was in fact written by male physicians in the twelfth and thirteenth centuries and attributed to Trota, a twelfth-century medical scholar whose major treatise has been lost.

3. 'Le Dit de l'Herberie', quoted in Jusserand, p. 178. Chaucer referred to Trotula's treatise as included in a scholarly text read by the Wife of Bath's bookish spouse.

4. Victorius Faventinus, *Empirica* (Venice, 1554); quoted in Hurd-Mead, 1930, p. 359. The *Regimen Sanitatis Salernitanum*, which included parts of Trotula, went through 20 printed editions between 1450 and 1500.

5. Erotian, probably physician to Mark Antony or Nero, wrote a commentary on Hippocratic gynaeocology, printed in Strasbourg in 1552.

6. Hughes, p. 100.

7. Antonio Mazza, *Historium Epitome de Rebus Salernitanis* (Naples, 1681), p. 128; cited in Hurd-Mead, 1938, p. 127.

8. Hall and Hall, p. 121. In 1322, Jacoba Felicie was tried in a Paris court for practising medicine illegally. Although witnesses testified that she had cured them for substantially less money than the respected male doctors whose treatments had failed, the court ruled that medicine was a science that could only be learned from books and Felicie was prohibited from practising (see Hughes; also Power).

9. Münster (p. 139) attributes the works of Mercuriade to Costanza Calenda.

10. Michele Medici, *Compendio storico della scuola anatomica di Bologna* (Bologna, 1857), p. 30; quoted in Hughes, p. 87.

11. Eirenaeus Orandus, *Nicholas Flammel. His Exposition of the Hieroglyphical Figures* (London, 1624); quoted in F.S. Taylor, pp. 166–70. Flammel's account was a best-seller, and often reprinted from the fifteenth to the seventeenth centuries.

12. Doberer, p. 77.

13. Quoted ibid., p. 79.

Chapter 5 'The Sybil of the Rhine'

1. Hall and Hall, p. 78.

2. Héloise (1101–64), educated by her lover, the scholastic Abelard, was the most famous French medical abbess. Hroswitha of Gandersheim (935–1000) was known for her scholarly and artistic works and for her medicine. It is a familiar story: the nineteenth-century Austrian historian, Joseph Aschbach, succeeded for a time in eliminating Hroswitha from history. He thought the writings ascribed to her were too knowledgeable, and the Latin too refined, to be the work of a woman. (See Haight.)

3. Hildegard's scholarly writings have not been translated into English. Vol 197 of *Patrologia Latina* (ed. J.P. Migne [Paris, 1855]), includes *Liber Scivias* (cols. 383–738), *Liber Divinorum Operum* (cols. 741–1038) and *Physica* (cols. 1117–352), along with some of Hildegard's strictly religious writings and her correspondence. The only printed edition of *Liber Vitae Meritorum* is in Vol. 8 of *Analecta Sacra* (ed. J.B. Pitra [Monte Cassino, 1882]). *Causae et Curae* was published separately (ed. Paul Kaiser [Leipzig: Teubner, 1903]). The translations quoted in this chapter appear as excerpts in Steele, and in Singer (1928). Other sources of information on Hildegard's writings include Eckenstein, Singer (1955), Pagel and Thorndike, Vol. 2, pp. 124–54. Two of Hildegard's assistants, the Benedictine monks Godefrid and Theodor, wrote her biography between 1180 and 1191. Theodor claimed to have made use of her autobiography for his account. There is no other reference to such a work, although some of Hildegard's writings do contain autobiographical information. The Acts of Inquisition, drafted to establish her claim to sainthood, likewise contain details of her life. The biography and the Acts are included in Migne, Vol. 197, cols. 91–140. The epithet 'Sibil of the Rhine' also appears in Migne, vol. 197. (See Eckenstein, p. 277).

4. B.L. Grant, p. 558.

5. The Wiesbaden illuminated manuscript, completed at Bingen about 1180, is the most important extant copy. *Scivias* was first printed by J. Faber Stapulensis of Paris in 1513.

6. Steele, p. 82. To Hildegard's consternation, Richarda left Rupertsberg anyway, taking a number of nuns with her. Heinrich was soon deposed and died in exile.

7. This use of German and the style of *Physica* and *Causae et Curae* led Singer to assert that the treatises had been erroneously ascribed to Hildegard: other scholars disagree. The works are referred to by her biographers and in the Acts of Inquisition. A scholar who was also a famous healer could be expected to turn her attention to medical writing and, as Thorndike pointed out, 'it would be natural to employ vernacular proper names for homely herbs and local fish and birds and common ailments, while in works of an astronomical and theological character'like her other visions there would be little reason for departing from the Latin' (Vol. II, p. 128). As with his opinions concerning Trotula, Singer's arguments may reveal more about his own prejudices than about Hildegard's work.

8. The Lucca manuscript of *Liber Divinorum Operum* (c. 1200) is considered to be the most authentic.

9. Hildegard's 77 poems with music, *Symphonia Armonie Celestium Revelationum (The Symphony of Heavenly Relations)*, have recently come to the attention of classical musicians who now regard them as among the best and most unique of mediaeval songs. Thus Hildegard has been rediscovered, but as a composer rather than a scientist.

10. Hildegard has occasionally been credited with expounding a new

heliocentric gravitational theory (see Mozans, p. 169). But this seems unlikely. Her ideas concerning gravity were basically Aristotelian: gravity was the force causing everything to move toward its proper place, thus, stones fell to the ground because they were made of the element earth.

11. Hildegard may have recognised that the stars were not always fixed in the heavens and were of unequal magnitude, giving off pulsations of light as they moved. She compared this to the way blood flowed in the veins causing them to pulsate. But this too may be an over-zealous interpretation (see Davis, p. 133). It is possible that by 'moving stars' she meant the planets.

12. Singer (1928), p. 67.

13. She has been credited – probably erroneously – with foreshadowing a number of important discoveries including the circulation and chemistry of the blood, the causes of auto-intoxication, the origin of nerve action in the brain, and the idea of a living contagion.

14. Sarton, Vol. 2, Pt. 1, p. 310. He also called Hildegard 'the most original medical writer of Latindom in the twelfth century' (p. 70).

15. See Singer (1928).

Chapter 6   The Rise of the Scientific Lady

1. Quoted in Borer, p. 19.

2. Bernard de Fontenelle, *Week's Conversation on the Plurality of Worlds*, trans. William Gardiner (London, 1737), p. 16; quoted in Merchant, p. 272.

3. Behn, 'An Essay on Translation and Translated Prose', p. 7. Aphra Behn, widowed at the age of 26, first began writing plays to avoid the threat of debtor's prison. There have been a number of other English translations of Fontenelle, including one in 1808 by Elizabeth Gunning.

4. Cited in Meyer, pp. 49–51.

5. Quoted in Reynolds, p. 32.

6. Martin, I,2. Martin also wrote *A Plain and Familiar Introduction to the Newtonian Experimental Philosophy . . . Designed for the use of Such Gentlemen and Ladies As would acquire A Competent Knowledge of this Science, without Mathematical Learning; And more especially those who have, or may attend the Author's Course Of Lectures and Experiments On these Subjects*, 5th edn (London, 1765). John Newberry created a best-seller with *The Newtonian System of Philosophy Adapted to the Capacities of Young Gentlemen and Ladies ... BEING the Substance of Six Lectures Read to the Lilliputian Society, by Tom Telescope ...* (1766). Other Newtonian works included Robert Heath's *Truth Triumphant: or, Fluxions for the Ladies* (1752) and Richard Steele's 3-volume encyclopaedia, *The Ladies Library* (1714). Charles Leadbetter's *Astronomy: or, The True System of the Planets Demonstrated* (1727) was dedicated to Mrs Catherine Edwin, who had 'great Learning and Skill in the Mathematical Sciences, especially in the Celestial One' (quoted in Meyer, p. 78). This work, full of astronomical tables and

mathematical calculations, was more technical than most books directed at the scientific lady of this period. Jasper Charlton's popular *The Ladies Astronomy and Chronology* (1735) was written as much to advertise and sell his 'assimilo' as to teach science – the instrument, used to demonstrate the stars and planets, comets, eclipses, tides and the Ptolemaic and Copernican systems, was a necessary adjunct to his text. (See Meyer, p. 80).

7. Virginia Woolf described William Cavendish as a 'princely nobleman, who had led the King's forces to disaster with indomitable courage but little skill' (p. 101).

8. The Duchess wrote that it was 'against nature for a woman to spell right' (quoted in D. Grant, pp. 112–13). Grammar and the rules of poetry she considered silly encumbrances.

9. 'Memoirs of Margaret, Duchess of Newcastle: A true Relation of my Birth, Breeding, and Life', included in the same volume with 'The Life of the thrice Noble, High and Puissant Prince William Cavendishe … written by the thrice Noble, Illustrious, and Excellent Princess Margaret Duchess of Newcastle, His 2D. Wife' (1916, p. 209). (The Duchess's title pages always included a similar encomium.) The 1667 biography of her husband was Margaret's one work of lasting value. It is a laudatory account of the Duke's finances, military adventures and purported wisdom. The Duchess's other non-scientific works include: a book of speeches, *Orations of Divers Sorts accommodated to Divers Places* (1662, 1668); *Poems, or, Several Fancies in Verse: with the Animal Parliament, in Prose* (1668); and a number of plays, 21 of which were published in 1662 and another five in 1668. Several of these, including *The Female Academy*, treat the learned lady in a positive way. Lacking any redeeming dramatic value, none of her plays was ever produced.

10. 'To the Reader', *Philosophical and Physical Opinions* (London, 1655); quoted in Reynolds, p. 48.

11. Kargon, p. 73. *Nature's Pictures* (1656 and 1671) was a collection of silly romances. Her husband wrote a preface for this volume praising Margaret as cleverer than Homer, beyond Aristotle, more modern than Hippocrates and more eloquent than Cicero; her writing, he said, put Virgil and Horace to shame.

12. Quoted in Reynolds, p. 49. In *Philosophical and Physical Opinions* (1655) William Cavendish defended his wife in his 'Epistle to justifie the Lady Newcastle, and Truth against falsehood, laying those false and malicious aspersions to her, that she was not Author of her Books'.

13. Nicolson, p. 237.

14. Evelyn, p. 271, n. 3. In his novel, *Peveril of the Peak*, Sir Walter Scott makes Charles II say of the Duchess: 'Her Grace is an entire raree-show in her own person – a universal masquerade – indeed a sort of private Bedlam hospital' (p. 281).

15. The Duchess's feminism often surfaced unexpectedly in her writing. For example, a woman should not

desire children for her own sake, for first her name is lost as to her particular in her marrying, for she quits her own, and is named as her husband; also her family, for neither name nor estate goes to her family.... Also she hazards her life by bringing them into the world, and hath the greatest share of trouble in bringing them up. (1664, pp. 183–4).

16. Thomas Wright's comedy *The Female Vertuosos* (1693) featured Mrs Lovewit who conducted laboratory experiments to extract the quintessence of wit from all the plays ever written to sell by the drop to poets; Lady Meanwell who, discovering that rain came from clouds, approached the Lord Mayor with a scheme for blowing away the clouds to keep the streets of London clean and dry; and Catchat who used her telescope to watch the men on the moon making eyes at her. (Cited in Reynolds, p. 383.) Susanna Centlivre's very successful play *The Basset-table* (1705) portrayed her heroine Valeria as too absorbed in dissecting her pet animals to notice her fiance's lovemaking. (Ironically, the prefaces to Centlivre's plays bespoke a strong feminist stance; see Mahl and Koon, pp. 209–22.)

Chapter 7   From Alchemy and Herbs

1. 2nd edn (Lyon, 1680), p. xxxii; translated in Bishop and De Loach, p. 449; see also Houlihan and Wotiz, p. 362. The Electress Anna, a member of the Danish Royal Family, was also experimenting with alchemy. She built a laboratory on her estate at Annaberg that the German alchemist Kunckel described as the 'largest and finest he had ever seen' (Holmyard, p. 139). Among the German alchemists of the eighteenth century was Susanne Katharina von Klettenberg (d. 1775) of Frankfurt. Her home was equipped with a laboratory where she worked with her friend, the young scientist and author Goethe. He left a record of their attempts to extract the atmospheric panacea 'air salt'. Mary Anne South Atwood (1817–1910) was the anonymous author of one of the last alchemical works. A feminist and progressive thinker, Atwood was interested both in science and psychic phenomena. *A Suggestive Inquiry into 'The Hermetic Mystery'* (London 1850) was a scholarly compilation of ancient and medieval philosophical alchemy, based on the works in her father's library of rare volumes. After about 100 copies of the book had been sold, Atwood withdrew as many copies as she could and proceeded to burn them, afraid that she had stumbled on a great and dangerous secret and had revealed too much. Nevertheless, in her later years she revised *A Suggestive Inquiry*.

2. Cited in Hurd-Mead, 1938, pp. 352–3, and Chaff *et al.*, p. 14, n. 42.

3. Cited in Guthrie, pp. 150–67. In 1739 Joanna Stevens received from the English Parliament the sum of 5000 pounds to reveal her remedies for bladder-stone. The prescriptions consisted of a powder made of egg-shells and smoked garden snails, a decoction of herbs and soap, and pills made of these components

and held together with honey. It proved ineffective. (See Partington, p. 121.)

Mrs Hutton, a botanist and pharmacist of Shropshire, discovered that wild foxglove of the genus *Digitalis* was useful for the treatment of heart disease. She experimented until she found the proper preparation and dosage, and was soon receiving patients from throughout the country. In 1785 she sold her recipe to Dr William Withering who is usually credited with its discovery.

4. Cited in Robb, 1893, pp. 76–80; Goodell, pp. 46, 51; Hurd-Mead, 1938, pp. 420–2. The second edition of *Observations diverses sur la stérilité, perte de fruict, fécondité, accouchements et maladies des femmes, et des enfants nouveaux naiz; amplement traittés et heureusement practiquées, par Louyse Bourgeois dite Boursier, sage-femme de la reine* appeared in 1617 with the addition of a long list of clinical cases, an account of her education, and instructions for her daughter who was in training as a midwife. (This last section was published separately on 1626. A sixth edition in 1634 included 'A Collection of the Secrets of Louyse Bourgeois'.) The treatise went through many revised editions over the next 100 years and was translated into German, Dutch, English and Latin. When the Duchess of Orleans died of puerperal fever Bourgeois, as her midwife, came under severe attack. In retaliation she launched a 28-page counter-attack on male physicians: 'Apologie contre le rapport des Médecins'.

Several renowned midwives of the Hôtel Dieu followed Bourgeois's lead. Mme Angélique Marguérite le Boursier du Coudray (1712–1789) introduced the use of a mannikin for teaching delivery methods. Her textbook, first published in 1759, went through five editions. In 1767, despite vehement opposition from male surgeons, she was awarded an annual salary by Louis XV to teach obstetrics at hospitals throughout France.

5. Cited in Loomis, p. 523.

6. Cited in Robb, 1894, pp. 5–8. Siegemundin's book was very popular. It went through six editions and was translated into Dutch.

7. For a complete list of d'Arconville's published medical works, see Hurd-Mead 1938, p. 492.

8 Elizabeth Nihell, who had studied midwifery at the Hôtel Dieu and practised with her husband in London's Haymarket, published a vehement diatribe in 1760 against the use of forceps and other instruments, and against the obstetrician William Smellie in particular. (Smellie invented a type of forceps and led the movement which replaced midwives with male obstetricians.) But other English midwives adopted the use of forceps. Margaret Stephen, midwife to Queen Charlotte, wife of George III, wrote *The Domestic Midwife* (1795) and taught anatomy and the use of instruments. *The Pupil of Nature; or Candid Advice to the Fair Sex* (1797) on obstetrics and gynaecology was printed and sold by its author Martha Mears, who occasionally used forceps, but generally opposed intervention. Her advice, translated into German in 1804, was firmly grounded in hygiene and common sense. (Cited in Hurd-Mead, 1938 pp. 472–3.) The most important seven-

teenth-century English text, *The Midwives Book* (1671) by Jane Sharp, was being reprinted as late as 1725. Sarah Stone, who had studied with her mother and in London under the patronage of the Duchess of York, wrote a standard text, *The Complete Practice of Midwifery* (1737). Elizabeth Lawrence Bury (1644-1720) was a feminist scholar and physician whose writings included 'Critical Observations in Anatomy, Medicine, Mathematics, Musick, Philosophy, Rhetorick'. (See Ballard, pp. 423-8.)

9. Florence Nightingale, founder of the nursing profession, also had a profound effect on the role of women in medicine. She was vehemently opposed to women doctors. Ironically, Nightingale's true love was mathematics. She was perhaps the most brilliant private pupil of the great London mathematician, James Sylvester.

Chapter 8 The New Naturalists

1. 1840, pp. iv-v; published anonymously and subsequently attributed to Elizabeth Fitton. The quote is from Edgeworth (1795), pp. 66-7.

2. *Letters on the Elements of Botany, addressed to a lady*, trans. Thomas Martyn (London: John White, 1807), p. 19; quoted in Rudolph, p. 92.

3. J.-J. Rousseau, *Emilius; or, an Essay on Education*, trans. Mr Nugent, 2 vols. (London: J. Nourse & P. Vaillant, 1763), p. 229; quoted in Rudolph, p. 93.

4. Preface; quoted in Allen, 1976, p. 48.

5. A contemporary of Wakefield, Maria Elizabeth Jackson published her earliest works anonymously: *Botanical Dialogues, between Hortensia and her four children, Charles, Harriet, Juliette and Henry. Designed for the use of schools. By a lady* (London: J. Johnson, 1797) and *Botanical Lectures. By a lady. Altered from 'Botanical dialogues for the use of schools,' and adapted to the use of persons of all ages, by the same author* (London: J. Johnson, 1804). Under her own name Jackson published a children's book, *Sketches of the Physiology of Vegetable Life* (London: John Hatchard, 1811), and several editions of *The Florists' Manual* and *The Pictorial Flora* (1840) on British botany.

6. Cited in Allen, 1978, pp. 247-9. Allen (1980) attempted to trace the women members of the Botanical Society of London. This is one of the first sociological studies of the history of women in science. He points out that a number of women attended the meetings of the Society and contributed to it without becoming members. Katherine Sophia Baily (later Lady Kane) of Dublin, author of an *Irish Flora*, was the first woman admitted to the Botanical Society of Edinburgh, shortly after its founding in 1836. Elsewhere in Europe, women were also becoming botanists. Josephine Kablick (b. 1787) of Hohenelbe in Bohemia collected fossils and plants for schools, museums and societies throughout Europe. Amalie Konkordie Dietrich (1821-1891) was a German botanist and zoologist. After becoming an expert on the alpine flora of Europe, she spent twelve years collecting in Australia and the Tonga Islands. In 1873 she was appointed curator of the Hamburg Botanical Museum.

7. Madeleine Frances Basseport (1701-80) became the salaried painter for the French Royal Gardens in 1735 and Geneviève de Nangis Regnault was responsible for the 500 hand-coloured etchings in François Regnault's *La Botanique* (1774). (See Blunt, pp. 153-4.) At the age of 72, Mary Granville Delany (1700-88), the translator of Hudson's *Flora Anglico*, took up 'paper-mosaics'. Her *Flora* consisted of 10 volumes of these botanically accurate coloured paper flowers, along with 47 pages of text: the work was sub-titled a 'Catalogue of Plants copyed from Nature in Paper Mosaick, finished in the year 1778, and disposed in alphabetical order, according to the Generic and Specific names of Linnaeus'. (Cited in Johnson, pp. xxxviii-xlii.) In her letters and autobiography Mrs Delany referred to herself as 'Aspasia'. She collaborated with Margaret Cavendish Bentinck, the Duchess of Portland, who had established what was perhaps the largest natural history collection in all of Europe. Spending vast sums of money, she hired eminent naturalists to collect for her. Mary Delany, Mary Montagu, and the Duchess were all members of the Bluestocking Society.

The *Botanical Magazine* employed a succession of women artists and illustrators. Miss Drake (fl. 1818-47) illustrated the *Botanical Register* and Lindley's *Sertum Orchidaceum* (1837-42). Mrs Withers (fl. 1827-64), as well as becoming a famous teacher, was 'Flower Painter in Ordinary to Queen Adelaide' (wife of William IV) and illustrated the *Pomological Magazine*, Maund's *Botanist* and much of the *Illustrated Bouquet* (1857-63). Anne Pratt (1806-93) published some 15 botanical works: *The Flowering Plants and Ferns of Great Britain* (1855) was her most popular book. Elizabeth Twining (1805-89) produced botanically accurate drawings for her *Illustrations of Natural Orders* (1849-55). The founder of Bedford College in London, she was the author and illustrator of several botanical works. Only one county flora was compiled by women, the *Flora of Leicestershire* (1848) by the Kirby sisters. (Cited in Allen, p. 250; see also Blunt, pp. 186, 214, 236-7.)

8. Quoted in Allen, 1976, p. 127.

9. Cited in Mozans, pp. 238-40.

10. C.P. Lounsbury, who worked with his wife in South Africa, was an entomologist employed by the British government. In September 1898 Ormerod wrote to him: 'How fortunate you are in having such a skilled colleague; it must be a real comfort to you to have an entomological *alter ego*, and yet such a charming companion.

Chapter 9   The Women Astronomers

1. Queen Sophia, great-grandmother of the Electress Sophia of Hanover, was the Brahes' patron. After the death of her husband, Frederick II of Denmark and Norway, in 1588, Sophia retired from public life, devoting herself to astronomy, chemistry and other sciences. Galileo's eldest daughter, Polissena Galilei (1601-34), lived with her younger sister, at the Franciscan convent at

Arcetri where, at the age of 13, she took the veil as Sister Maria Celeste. From her 120 surviving letters it is clear that she followed her father's scientific discoveries carefully, reminding him in one letter of his promise to send her a small telescope (see Olney). The women of the Harvard College Observatory, including Anna Palmer Draper, Williamina Fleming, Antonia Maury, Annie Cannon and Henrietta Leavitt, revolutionised astronomy in the early twentieth century with their immense studies of the photographic spectra of stars.

2. *Acta Eruditorum* (Leipzig, 1712), pp. 78-9; translated in Mozans, p. 174. Another German astronomer, a Viennese baroness, Elisabeth von Matt (d. 1814), equipped her small observatory with excellent instruments. Her many observations were first published anonymously and later under her own name (see Davis, p. 214.)

3. *Journal de Savans*, III, 304 (Amsterdam, 1687); translated in Mozans, p. 171.

4. Jérôme Lalande, *Bibliographie Astronomique* (Paris, 1803), pp. 676-87; translated in Rizzo, p. 8.

5. Ibid.; translated in Mozans, pp. 181-2.

6. Osen, p. 79.

7. Quoted in Lubbock, p. 45.

8. Ibid., p. 216.

9. Ibid., p. 168.

10. Over the years William Herschel, with Caroline's tireless assistance, discovered the gaseous nature of the sun's surface, two satellites of Saturn, the planet Uranus and two of its satellites; the periods of rotation for a ring of Saturn and for several satellites, and many planetary nebulae and variable stars (stars whose luminosity varies periodically). He studied the Milky Way and other galaxies, the evolution of nebulae, and developed a system for their classification. He discovered infra-red radiation and that the sun's heat and light were independent phenomena.

11. South, p. 411.

12. Quoted in Herschel, 1876, p. 227. In February 1862 the Royal Astronomical Society bestowed honorary membership on a third woman, Anne Sheepshanks (1789-1876), a patron of astronomy who lived with her astronomer brother. Elizabeth Brown was largely responsible for the founding of the British Astronomical Association. She became director of the Association's solar section and established her own private observatory. Mary Ann Hervey Fallows assisted her husband at the newly-founded Royal Observatory at the Cape of Good Hope.

13. Translated in Herschel, 1876, p. 346.

Chapter 10   The Philosophers of the Scientific Revolution

1. Quoted in Frederic Ritter, *François Viète, Inventeur de l'algebre moderne*

(Paris, 1895), p. 20; translated in Mozans, p. 363.

2. 10th letter from Italy; quoted in 'Some account of Maria Agnesi', in Agnesi, pp. xiii–xiv. Following this intellectual display, Maria's younger sister Maria Teresa entertained the gathering with her original compositions for voice and harpsichord. Apparently Maria Agnesi was a somnambulist, often retiring for the night with a mathematical problem on her desk and rising the next morning to find that she had solved it in her sleep.

3. L'Hôpital's wife was said to have done much of the work for his treatise published in Paris in 1696.

4. The English mathematician John Colson undertook the study of Italian late in life in order to translate *Analytical Institutions*. It was published posthumously in 1801. Colson had also begun an English popularisation of the book:

> in order to render it more easy and useful to the Ladies of this country, (if indeed they can be prevailed upon by his [Colson's] persuasion and encouragement, to show to the world, as they easily might, that they are not to be excelled by any foreign Ladies whatever, in any valuable accomplishment). (John Hellins, 'Editor's Advertisement', in Agnesi, p. vi)

5. Translated in Beard (1931), p. 442. In an ironic twist, Laura Bassi arranged for Voltaire's admission to the Bologna Academy of Science in 1774. He of course could not return the favour.

6. Quoted in Perl (1978), p. 53.

7. Translated in Edwards (1970), p. 268.

8. Voltaire's friend, the salonist Mme du Deffand, hated Emilie du Châtelet with a vengeance – although the two women kept up the appearance of intimacy. Deffand wrote a scathing portrait of the marquise after her death, describing her character as insufferably vain, and her scholarship as mere pomposity. (See Lewis and Smith, p. 116.) The memoirs of Voltaire's secretary and valet, Longchamp, were also highly critical of the marquise. Many historians have accepted these self-serving accounts at face value.

9. Translated in Edwards (1970), p. 4.

10. Mme de Richelieu also numbered among Maupertuis's pupils. Anna Barbara Reinhardt of Winterthur in Switzerland was known for having improved upon the solution to one of Maupertuis's difficult problems. According to Johann Bernoulli, Reinhardt was a better mathematician than Mme du Châtelet. (Cited in Mozans, p. 154.)

11. Cited in Wade (1947), p. 114. Some historians have objected to this interpretation on the grounds that at the time Emilie du Châtelet was completely enamoured of Leibniz, but this claim is unfounded. Like Voltaire, Châtelet was fundamentally a Newtonian.

12. Ira Wade (1947, pp. 119–20) inferred from the extant section that Chapter 1 dealt with the composition of light, Chapter 2 with refraction and Chapter 3 with reflection.

13. Cited in René Taton, 'Emilie du Châtelet', in Gillespie, III, 215–17.

14. Cited in Edwards (1970), pp. 133–4. Leonhard Euler wrote *Letters to a German Princess* on physics and astronomy for Frederick the Great's niece, the Princess of Anhalt-Dessau. (See Bell (1937), p. 152.)

15. The London edition was published in 1741. A revised edition of *Institutions* appeared in Amsterdam a year later and was translated into Italian in 1743.

16. Quoted in Edwards (1970), p. 264. Emilie du Châtelet also authored a number of non-scientific works. Three chapters of her study on grammar, *Grammaire raisonnée*, have survived among Voltaire's papers in the Leningrad library. Also included there is her translation and elucidation of a part of Bernard de Mandeville's moral philosophy, *Fable of the Bees*. Her 1735 preface to this work included a feminist plea for the participation of women in literary activities. (See Wade (1941), p. 26 and (1969), p. 347.) Her five-volume attack on the Bible, *Examen de la Genèse*, circulated in manuscript. Châtelet's *Discours sur le bonheur* was an immediate best-seller when it was published in pamphet form in 1744. Candidly autobiographical, the work opened with a discussion of gambling which Emilie insisted was one of three pleasures available to women in their old age. (The other two were gluttony and study – see Edwards (1970), pp. 223–9.) Châtelet's translations included the poetry of Catullus, a classic translation of *Oedipus Rex*, and a lost translation of Virgil's *Aeneid*.

17. *Lettres de la Marquise du Châtelet*, ed. Eugène Asse (Paris, 1878), p. 487; translated in Parton, p. 562.

18. Translated in Edwards (1970), p. 1.

Chapter 11   The Nineteenth-Century Mathematicians

1. Bucciarelli and Dworsky, p. 22.

2. Translated ibid., p. 25.

3. Cited ibid., p. 27.

4. Ibid., p. 30.

5. Translated ibid., p. 61.

6. Translated ibid., pp. 63–4.

7. Ibid., p. 78.

8. H. Stupuy's 1879 edition of *Sophie Germain, Oeuvres philosophiques* (Paris) aroused new interest in the female mathematician. As a result, her memoir on elasticity was recovered from Prony's estate and published in 1880 (Paris: Gauthier-Villars); cited in Bucciarelli and Dworsky, p. 141.

9. S. Germain, 'Memoire sur la courbure des surfaces', and 'Note sure la manière dont se composent les valeurs de y et z dans l'équation $4(x^p - 1)/(x - 1) = y^2 + pz^2 \ldots$' *Jour. für die reine und angewandte Mathematik*, 7 (1831), 1–29, 201–4; cited in Bucciarelli and Dworsky, p. 143. The paper on surface curvature may have been inspired by an 1827 publication by Gauss that

Germain obtained by chance in 1829. In a letter to Gauss in that year, she complained openly for the first time about her lack of access to publications and her isolation from the scientific community (cited ibid., pp. 112–15).

10. J. Lherbette (ed.) (Paris: Lachevardière, 1833); cited ibid., p. 125.

11. Quoted in Elwin p. 219.

12. Quoted in Moseley, p. 182.

13. Quoted in Moore, p. 157.

14. Somerville Papers: 15, 30; November 1844; quoted ibid., p. 215–6.

15. 14 August, 1845; quoted ibid., pp. 163–4.

16. 1844; quoted ibid., p. 213.

17. Quoted in Mayne, pp. 477–8.

18. Quoted in Leffler, pp. 173–4. Julia Lermontova's 'Recollections of Sóphia Kovalévksy' were written at the request of Anna Charlotte Leffler and are incorporated into her biography of Sóphia as quotations from 'Sonya's anonymous friend'. Julia was exceptionally well-educated, her parents having brought in specialised teachers from Moscow to tutor their children in each subject. Her family encouraged her interest in chemistry and her attempts to study at Moscow University. But they objected to her plans for studying abroad. It was Sóphia who convinced Julia's parents to let her come to Heidelberg. Later she worked in the private organic chemistry laboratory of A.M. Bulterov until, with the death of her parents, she had to take over management of the family estate. Zhanna Evreinova eventually obtained permission to study law in Leipzig. She returned to Russia as its first woman lawyer in 1873 and later became a well-known feminist. After being denied entry to the Swedish universities, Anna Leffler received the equivalent of a university education from her brothers. In 1888, after divorcing her first husband, she married an Italian mathematician and became the Duchess of Cajanello. She published Kovalévsky's *Recollections* along with her own admittedly romanticised memoir of Sóphia. It was a very successful book and was translated into several languages. Ellis Carter, in his review of the 1895 English edition, described Sóphia as exemplifying the tragic fate that awaits the woman unfortunate enough to be born with a 'male mind'.

19. L.A. Vorontsova, *Sofia Kovalevskaia* (Moscow: 1957), p. 147; quoted in B. Stillman (1974), p. 287.

20. Cited in Kennedy, pp. 200–1.

21. Quoted in Leffler, p. 204.

22. Translated in Kennedy, pp. 225–6. During her first year at Stockholm Sóphia was a private docent, rather than a regular faculty member, and so was paid by her students individually. Given their choice of lectures in French or German, they chose German. By her second year she was lecturing in Swedish. Classes at the university were open to auditors of both sexes although there is no evidence that she ever had a woman student.

23. Translated in B. Stillman (1974), p. 289.

24. Translated in Kennedy, p. 237.

25. Leffler, p. 231.

Chapter 12.   The Popularisation and Professionalisation of Science

1. *La Pedagogia, lo Stato e la Famiglia*, pp. 84ff; translated in O'Faolain and Martines, pp. 251-2.

2. Quoted in Smith, p. 68. Marcet's most successful book was not on science at all: *Conversations on Political Economy* first appeared in 1816 and was reprinted frequently. She also wrote numerous children's books on a variety of subjects.

3. Quoted in Lonsdale, p. 49.

4. Buckland Papers, DRO 138M/F244, Devon Record Office; quoted in Morrell and Thackray, p. 150.

5. Babbage to Daubeny, 28 April 1832; quoted ibid., p. 151.

6. Quoted in Lonsdale, p. 47. Although most of the reports were descriptions of birds and fish, there were a few papers which officials apparently feared would be offensive to ladies: 'The Wild Cattle of Chillingham Park,' 'Pouched Rats', 'Reproduction of the Actiniae' and 'Peculiarities of the Reproductive Economy of Marsupials'. When Richard Owen spoke on marsupials, 'Mrs Buckland and lots of ladies, mostly Quakeresses, were there, and [he] modified the reproductive part . . . as delicately as possible' (I, 126). Owen was married to Caroline Clift, the daughter of the curator of the College of Surgeons. A self-educated woman whose speciality was comparative anatomy, she regularly assisted her husband with his research in zoology and paleontology and herself attended sessions of the BAAS. Their scientific and intellectual circles included Jeanette de Villepreux Power who carried out extensive research on molluscs and Lady Hastings, a paleontologist who prepared a joint memoir with Owen for the Oxford Meeting of the BAAS.

Caroline Fox went on to become a champion of women's education. She was deeply interested in science and regularly attended scientific lectures and the meetings of the BAAS. Her journal is full of anecdotes concerning the major English scientists of the nineteenth century.

7. 28 November 1840; quoted in Morrell and Thackray, p. 148.

8. Quoted in Toth and Toth, p. 25.

9. 19 February 1832, Somerville Collection; quoted in Patterson (1969), p. 319. Towards the end of the nineteenth century when Martha Somerville, the feminist journalist Frances Power Cobbe and publisher John Murray edited and appended Somerville's *Personal Recollections*, anti-feminist sentiment was back in fashion. Since they wanted the book to be a financial success, they focused on Mary's domestic and maternal qualities, eliminating passages that might appear too outspoken or 'unladylike'. (Ibid., p. 337).

10. *Philosophical Transactions*, 126 (1826), 132-9; cited in Richeson, p. 9. Somerville's 1836 paper was also published in the *Edinburgh Philosophical Journal*, 22 (1837), 180-3.

11. Somerville Collection; quoted in Patterson (1969), p. 318.

12. Cited in S.F. Mason, p. 442.

13. Quoted in Mitchell, p. 570.

14. The only critical review appeared in *The Athenaeum*, No. 221 (1832). Somerville's introductory essay came under attack for bottling up 'the spirit of La Place ... in an octavo' (p. 43). Years later the same journal praised her admirable summary of the 'Mécanique Céleste' (No. 2154 (1869), p. 202). For his part, John Murray refused to share in the profits from *Mechanism of the Heavens*. In the coming years he and his son would publish all of Mary's books, supply her with scientific works, and occasionally lend her money. (See Patterson (1969), pp. 321-2.)

15. p. 60; quoted in Patterson (1969), p. 323. The simultaneous calculation of Neptune's orbit by Adams and Leverrier erupted into one of history's great battles over priority of discovery.

16. Somerville collection; quoted in ibid., p. 323.

17. (London: John Murray, 1848), p. 2; quoted in ibid., p. 326.

18. Quoted in Toth and Toth, p. 29. Edward Sabine's wife Elizabeth translated von Humboldt's *Kosmos* and other scientific works, including Gauss's 1839 treatise on terrestrial magnetism, for a series subsidised by the BAAS. She also helped her husband develop his system of terrestrial magnetism. (See Somerville (1873), pp. 138-9.) Caroline Fox called the Sabines the 'married magnetists' (p. 147). Their contemporary, Janet Taylor, wrote several works on navigation and became known as 'The Mrs Somerville of the marine world'. (Quoted in Toth and Toth, p. 27).

19. Somerville Collection; quoted in Patterson (1969), p. 336.

20. Cobbe, p. 385.

Bibliography

Agnesi, Maria Gaetana, *Analytical Institutions*, trans. John Colson, ed. John Hellins. London: Taylor & Wilks, 1801.

Allen, D.E., *The Naturalist in Britain: A Social History*, London: Allen Lane, 1976.

Allen, D.E., 'The First Woman Pteridologist', *British Pteriodological Society Bulletin*, 1 (1978), 247-9.

Allen, D.E., 'The Botanical Family of Samuel Butler', *Journal of the Society for the Bibliography of Natural History*, 9 (1979), 133-6.

Allen, D.E. 'The Women Members of the Botanical Society of London, 1836-1856', *British Journal for the History of Science*, 13 (1980), 240-54.

Allen, D.E. and Lousley, Dorothy W., 'Some Letters to Margaret Stovin (1756?-1846), Botanist of Chesterfield', *The Naturalist*, 104 (1979) 155-63.

Anderson, Louisa Garrett, *Elizabeth Garrett Anderson, 1836-1917*. London: Faber & Faber, 1939.

Appleby, Valerie, 'Ladies with Hammers', *New Scientist*, 84 (1979), 714-15.

Aristotle, *De Partibus Animalium I* and *De Generatione Animalium*, trans. D.M. Balme. Oxford: Clarendon, 1972.

Armstrong, Eva V., 'Jane Marcet and Her "Conversations on Chemistry" ', *Journal of Chemical Education*, 15 (1938), 53-7.

Ashton, Helen and Davies, Katharine, *I Had a Sister: A Study of Mary Lamb, Dorothy Wordsworth, Caroline Herschel, Cassandra Austen*. London: Lovat Dickson, 1937; rpt. Folcraft, Pa.: Folcraft, 1975.

Atwood, Mary Anne South, *Hermetic Philosophy and Alchemy: A Suggestive Inquiry into 'The Hermetic Mystery' with a Dissertation on the More Celebrated of the Alchemical Philosophers*, rev. edn. New York: Julian Press, 1960.

Babbage, Charles, 'Selections from *Passages from the Life of a Philosopher*,' London, 1864; rpt. in *Charles Babbage and His Calculating Engines: Selected Writings by Charles Babbage and Others*, ed. Philip Morrison and Emily Morrison. London: Constable, 1961; New York: Dover, 1961.

Ballard, George, *Memoirs of Several Ladies of Great Britain, who have been*

Celebrated for their Writings or Skill in the Learned Languages Arts and Sciences. Oxford: Jackson, 1752.

Barber, W.H. 'Mme du Châtelet and Leibnizianism: The Genesis of the *Institutions de Physique*', in *The Age of the Enlightenment: Studies presented to Theodore Besterman*, ed. W.H. Barber, *et al.* Edinburgh: Oliver & Boyd, 1967, pp. 200–22.

Bayon, H.P. 'Trotula and the Ladies of Salerno: A Contribution to the Knowledge of the Transition between Ancient and Mediaeval Physick', *Proceedings of the Royal Society of Medicine*, 33 (1940), 471–5.

Beard, Mary R., *On Understanding Women.* New York: Longmans, Green & Co., 1931; London: Greenwood Press, new edn., [n.d.].

Beard, Mary R., *Women as a Force in History: A Study in Traditions and Realities.* New York: Macmillan, 1946.

Behn, Aphra, *Histories, Novels, and Translations.* London: 1700, Vol. II.

Bell, E.T. *Men of Mathematics.* London: Gollancz; New York: Simon & Schuster, 1937.

Bell, Susan G. (ed.), *Women from the Greeks to the French Revolution: An Historical Anthology.* Belmont, Ca: Wadsworth, 1973.

Benton, John, 'Trotula, Women's Problems, and the Professionalisation of Medicine in the Middle Ages', *Bulletin of the History of Medicine*, 59 (1985) 30–53.

Bishop, Lloyd O. and De Loach, Will S., 'Marie Meurdrac – First Lady of Chemistry?', *Journal of Chemical Education*, 47 (1970), 448–9.

Blunt, Wilfrid, *The Art of Botanical Illustration*, 2nd edn. London: Collins, 1951.

Boccaccio, Giovanni, *Concerning Famous Women*, trans. Guido A. Guarino. New Brunswick: Rutgers University Press, 1963; London: George Allen & Unwin, 1964.

Boileau-Despréaux, Nicolas, 'Satire X. On Women', in *The Satires*, trans. Hayward Porter. Glasgow: James Lehose, 1904, pp. 77–101.

Bolton, Henrietta I., 'Women in Science', *Popular Science Monthly*, 53 (1898), 506–11.

Borer, Mary Cathcart, *Women Who Made History.* London: Frederick Warne, 1963.

Boserup, Ester, *Woman's Role in Economic Development*; London: George Allen & Unwin; New York: St Martin's Press, 1970.

Bowden, Bertram Vivian (ed.), *Faster than Thought: A Symposium on Digital Computing Machines.* New York: Pitman, 1953.

Brittain, Vera, *The Women at Oxford: A Fragment of History.* London: George Harrap; New York: Macmillan, 1960.

Brunton, Lauder, 'Some Women in Medicine', *Canadian Medical Association Journal*, 48 (1943), 60–5.

Bryan, Margaret, *A Compendious System of Astronomy, in a Course of Familiar Lectures . . . Also Trigonometrical and Celestial Problems, with a*

Key to the Ephemeris, and a Vocabulary of the Terms of Science used in the Lectures . . . . London, 1797.

Bryan, Margaret, *Lectures on Natural Philosophy . . . With an Appendix: Containing a Great Number and Variety of Astronomical and Geographical Problems; and some Useful Tables, and a Comprehensive Vocabulary.* London: Thomas Duvison, 1806.

Bucciarelli, Louis L. and Dworsky, Nancy, *Sophie Germain: An Essay on the History of the Theory of Elasticity.* Dordrecht, Holland: D. Reidel, 1980.

Buckland, Francis, T. (ed.), 'Memoir of the Very Rev. William Buckland, D.D., F.R.S., Dean of Westminster', in *Geology and Mineralogy*, by William Buckland. 4th edn. London: Bell & Daldy, 1869.

Buckler, Georgina, *Anna Comnena. A Study.* 1929; rpt. London: Clarendon, 1968.

Burland, C.A., *The Arts of the Alchemists.* London: Weidenfeld & Nicolson, 1967; New York: Macmillan, 1968.

Burney [d'Arblay], Fanny, *Diary and Letters*, Vol. III. London: Macmillan, 1905.

Burton, Richard F., 'Abu Al-Husn and his Slave-girl Tawaddud', in *A Plain and Literal Translation of the Arabian Nights' Entertainments* . . . Vol. V. Burton Club, 1900, pp. 189–245.

Cajori, Florian, *A History of Mathematics*, 3rd edn. New York: Chelsea, 1980.

Carter, Ellis Warren, 'Sophie Kovalevsky', *Fortnightly Review*, NS 62 (1895), 767–83.

Castiglioni, Arturo, *A History of Medicine*, ed. and trans. E.B. Krumbhaar, 2nd edn. New York: Knopf, 1947; London: Routledge & Kegan Paul, 1948.

Cavendish, Margaret [Lady Newcastle], *Poems, and Fancies.* 1653; rpt. Menston, England: Scolar, 1972.

Cavendish, Margaret, *Plays.* London: Martyn, Allestry & Dicas, 1662.

Cavendish, Margaret, *Philosophical and Physical Opinions.* London: William Wilson, 1663.

Cavendish, Margaret, *CXI Sociable Letters.* 1664; rpt. Menston, England: Scolar, 1969

Cavendish, Margaret, 'Observations upon Experimental Philosophy: To which is added, the Description of a New Blazing World*, 2nd edn. London: Maxwell, 1668a.

Cavendish, Margaret, *Grounds of Natural Philosophy.* London: Maxwell, 1668b.

Cavendish, Margaret, *Nature's Pictures Drawn by Fancies Pencil to the Life*, 2nd edn. London: Maxwell, 1671.

Cavendish, Margaret, *The Life of the (1st) Duke of Newcastle and Other Writings*, ed. Ernest Rhys. London: J.M. Dent, 1916

Centlivre, Susanna, *The Basset-Table: A Comedy*, in *The Dramatic Works.* London: John Pearson, 1872, I, 199–258.

Chaff, Sandra L. *et al.* (eds), *Women in Medicine: A Bibliography of the Literature on Women Physicians.* Metuchen, N.J.: Scarecrow, 1977;

London: Bailey Bros., 1978.

Childe, V. Gordon, *Man Makes Himself*, London: C.A. Watts, 1948; 3rd edn. New York: New American Library, 1951.

Childe, V. Gordon, *What Happened in History*, Harmondsworth: Penguin, [n.d.]; 3rd edn. Baltimore: Penguin, 1964.

Clarke, Agnes, M., *The Herschels and Modern Astronomy*. New York: Macmillan, 1895.

Cobbe, Frances Power, *Life, as Told by Herself*, posthumous edn. London: Swan Sonnenschein, 1904.

Comnena, Princess Anna, *The Alexiad*, trans. E.R.A. Sewter. Harmondsworth: Penguin, 1969.

Conway, Anne, *The Principles of the Most Ancient and Modern Philosophy. Concerning God, Christ, and the Creature; that is, concerning Spirit, and Matter in General.* London, 1692.

Couture-Cherki, Monique, 'Women in Physics', in *Ideology of/in the Natural Sciences, The Radicalisation of Science*, Vol I., ed. Hilary Rose and Steven Rose. London: Macmillan, 1976, pp. 65-75.

Crellin, John K., 'Mrs Marcet's "Conversations on Chemistry",' *Journal of Chemical Education*, 56 (1979), 459-60.

Dashkov, Princess, *The Memoirs*, trans. and ed. Kyril Fitzlyon. London: John Calder, 1958.

Davis, Herman S., 'Women Astronomers (400 A.D.-1750)', *Popular Astronomy*, 6 (1898), 129-38.

Debus, Allen G. (ed.), *World Who's Who in Science: A Biographical Dictionary of Notable Scientists from Antiquity to the Present.* Chicago: Marquis, 1968.

Descartes, René, *Philosophical Letters*, trans. and ed. Anthony Kenny. London: Clarendon, 1970.

Diogenes Laertius, *Lives and Opinions of Eminent Philosophers*, trans. R.D. Hicks. London: Heinemann, 1925; Cambridge, Mass.: Harvard University Press, 1965.

Doberer, K.K., *The Goldmakers: 10,000 Years of Alchemy*, trans. E.W. Dicks. London: Nicolson & Watson, 1948.

Durant, W. and Durant, A., *The Age of Voltaire.* New York: Simon & Schuster, 1965; London: Angus & Robertson, 1966.

Duveen, Denis I., 'Madame Lavoisier 1758-1836', *Chymia*, 4 (1953), 13-29.

Eckenstein, Lina, *Woman under Monasticism.* Cambridge, 1896; rpt. New York: Russell & Russell, 1963.

Edgeworth, Maria, *Letters for Literary Ladies.* London, 1795; rpt. New York: Garland, 1974.

Edgeworth, Maria, *The Life and Letters.* Boston: Houghton Mifflin, 1895.

Edwards, Harold M., *Fermat's Last Theorem.* New York: Springer-Verlag, 1977.

Edwards, Samuel, *The Divine Mistress.* New York: David McKay, 1970; London: Cassell, 1971.

Elwin, Malcom, *Lord Byron's Family: Annabella, Ada and Augusta 1816-1824*, ed. Peter Thomson. London: John Murray, 1975.

Engbring, Gertrude M., 'Saint Hildegard, Twelfth-Century Physician', *Bulletin of the History of Medicine*, 8 (1940), 770-84.

Evelyn, John, *Diary*, ed. Austin Dobson. London: Macmillan, 1906, Vol. II.

Federmann, Reinhard, *The Royal Art of Alchemy*, trans. Richard H. Weber. Philadelphia: Chilton, 1969.

Fee, Elizabeth, 'Is Feminism a Threat to Scientific Objectivity?', *International Journal of Women's Studies*, 4 (1981), 378-92.

Forbes, R.J., *Short History of the Art of Distillation*. Leiden: Brill, 1948.

Fox, Caroline, *Memories of Old Friends. Being Extracts from the Journals and Letters of Caroline Fox, of Penjerrick, Cornwall, from 1835 to 1871*, ed. Horace N. Pym. Philadelphia: J.B. Lippincott, 1882.

Fuller [Ossoli], Margaret, *Woman of the Nineteenth Century, and Kindred Papers Relating to the Sphere, Condition, and Duties of Woman*, new edn., ed. Arthur B. Fuller. 1874; rpt. New York: Greenwood, 1968.

Gade, John Allyne, *The Life and Times of Tycho Brahe*. Princeton: Princeton University Press, 1947.

Gibbon, Edward, *The Decline and Fall of the Roman Empire*, 3 vols. New York: Modern Library [n.d.].

Gillespie, Charles Couston (ed.), *Dictionary of Scientific Biography*, 14 vols. New York: Scribner, 1970-80.

Glasgow, Maude, 'Women Physicians', *Journal of the American Medical Women's Association*, 9 (1954), 24-5.

von Goethe, J.W., *Poetry and Truth: From My Own Life*, trans. Minna Steele Smith. 1908; rpt. London: G. Bell & Sons, 1911, Vol. I.

Goldsmith, Oliver, 'An Enquiry into the Present State of Polite Learning', in *Collected Works*, ed. Arthur Friedman. Oxford: Clarendon, 1966, I, 253-341.

de Goncourt, Edmond and de Goncourt, Jules, 'The Soul of Woman', in *The Woman of the Eighteenth Century*, trans. Jacques LeClercq and Ralph Roeder. New York: Minton, Balch, 1927, pp. 267-96.

Goodell, William, *A Sketch of the Life and Writings of Louyse Bourgeois*. Philadelphia: Collins, 1876.

Goodwater, Leanna, *Women in Antiquity: An Annotated Bibliography*. London: Bailey Bros.; Metuchen, N.J.: Scarecrow, 1976.

Grant, Barbara L., 'Five Liturgical Songs by Hildegard von Bingen (1098-1179)', *Signs*, 5 (1980), 557-67.

Grant, Douglas, *Margaret the First: A Biography of Margaret Cavendish, Duchess of Newcastle, 1623-1673*. Toronto: University of Toronto Press, 1957.

Griffin, Susan, *Woman and Nature: The Roaring Inside Her*. New York: Harper & Row, 1978; London: The Women's Press, 1984.

Guthrie, Leonard, 'The Lady Sedley's Receipt Book, 1686, and Other Sevententh-Century Receipt Books', *Proceedings of the Royal Society of*

Medicine, 6 (1913), Section of the History of Medicine, 150-70.

Haber, Louis, *Women Pioneers of Science*, rev. edn. New York: Harcourt, Brace & Jovanovich, 1979.

Hacker, Carlotta, *The Indomitable Lady Doctors*. Toronto: Clarke Irwin, 1974.

Haight, Anne Lyon (ed.), *Hroswitha of Gandersheim: Her Life, Times, and Works, and a Comprehensive Bibliography*. New York: The Hroswitha Club, 1965.

Hale, Sarah Josepha, *Woman's Record: Or Sketches of All Distinguished Women from the Creation to A.D. 1854*. New York: Harper, 1860.

Hall, A. Rupert and Hall, Marie Boas, *A Brief History of Science*. New York: New American Library, 1964.

Hamel, Frank, *An Eighteenth-Century Marquise: A Study of Emilie du Châtelet and her Times*. New York: James Pott, 1911.

Hamilton, Edith, *Mythology*. London: Frederick Muller; New York: New American Library, 1940.

Hamilton, George L., 'Trotula', *Modern Philology*, 4 (1906), 377-80.

Haywood, Eliza, *The Female Spectator*, 5th edn., 4 vols. London: Gardner, 1755.

Heath, Thomas L., *Diophantus of Alexandria: A Study on the History of Greek Algebra*. New York: Dover, 1964; London: Constable, 1965.

Herschel, Caroline, 'An Account of a New Comet', *Philosophical Transactions*, 77 (1787), 1-4.

Herschel, Caroline, 'Account of the Discovery of a Comet', *Philosophical Transactions*, 84 (1794), 1.

Herschel, Caroline, 'An Account of the Discovery of a New Comet', *Philosophical Transactions*, 86 (1796), 131-4.

Herschel, Caroline, *Memoir and Correspondence*, ed. Mary Herschel. New York: Appleton, 1876.

Hollingdale, J.H. 'Charles Babbage and Lady Lovelace – Two 19th-Century Mathematicians', *Bulletin of the Institute of Mathematics and its Applications*, 2 (1966), 2-15.

Holmyard, E.J., 'An Alchemical Tract Ascribed to Mary the Copt. The Letter of the Crown and the Nature of the Creation by Mary the Copt of Egypt', *Archivio di Storia della Scienza*, 8 (1927), 161-7.

Holmyard, E.J. , *Alchemy*. 1957; rpt. Harmondsworth: Penguin, 1968.

Homer, *The Iliad*, trans. Richmond Lattimore. London: Routledge & Kegan Paul; Chicago: University of Chicago Press, 1951.

Homer, *The Odyssey*, trans. Robert Fitzgerald. Garden City: Doubleday, 1961; London: Heinemann, 1962.

Hopkins, Arthur John, 'A Modern Theory of Alchemy,' *Isis*, 7 (1925), 58-76.

Hopkins, Arthur John, 'A Study of the Kerotakis Process as Given by Zosimus and Later Alchemical Writers', *Isis*, 29 (1938), 326-54.

Hoskin, M.A., *William Herschel and the Construction of the Heavens*. London: Oldbourne, 1964.

Hoskin, Michael and Warner, Brian, 'Caroline Herschel's Comet Sweepers', *Journal for the History of Astronomy*, 12 (1981), 27–34.

Houlihan, Sherida and Wotiz, John H., 'Women in Chemistry Before 1900', *Journal of Chemical Education*, 52 (1975), 362–4.

Hubbard, Elbert, *Great Teachers*, Vol. 10 of *Little Journeys to the Homes of the Great*. Cleveland: World Publishing, 1928.

Hughes, Muriel Joy, *Women Healers in Medieval Life and Literature*. Oxford: Oxford University Press, 1943; rpt. Freeport, N.Y.: Books for Libraries Press, 1968.

Hume, Ruth Fox, *Great Women of Medicine*. New York: Random House, 1964.

Hurd-Mead, Kate C., 'Trotula', *Isis*, 14 (1930), pp. 349–67.

Hurd-Mead, Kate C., 'An Introduction to the History of Women in Medicine', *Annals of Medical History*, NS 5 (1933).

Hurd-Mead, Kate C., *A History of Women in Medicine. from the Earliest Times to the Beginning of the Nineteenth Century*. Haddam, Ct.: Haddam Press, 1938.

Iacobacci, Rora F., 'Women in Mathematics', *The Arithmetic Teacher*, 17 (1970), 316–24.

Iltis [Merchant], Carolyn, 'Madame du Châtelet's Metaphysics and Mechanics', *Studies in History and Philosophy of Science*, 8 (1977), 29–48.

Jex-Blake, Sophia, *Medical Women: A Thesis and a History*, 2nd edn. Edinburgh, 1886; rpt. New York: Source Book Press, 1970.

Johnson, R. Brimley (ed.), *Mrs Delany: At Court and Among the Wits Being the Record of a Great Lady of Genius in the Art of Living*. London: Stanley Paul, 1925.

Jones, Thomas P., *New Conversations on Chemistry . . . On the Foundation of Mrs. Marcet's 'Conversations on Chemistry'*. Philadelphia: Grigg & Elliot, 1846.

Jusserand, J.J., *English Wayfaring Life in the Middle Ages*, trans. Lucy Toulmin Smith, 8th edn. London: T. Fisher Unwin, 1891.

Kargon, Robert Hugh, *Atomism in England from Hariot to Newton*. Oxford: Clarendon, 1966.

à Kempis, Sister Mary Thomas, 'The Walking Polyglot', *Scripta Mathematica*, 6 (1939), 211–17

Kennedy, Don H., *Little Sparrow: A Portrait of Sophia Kovalévsky*. Athens: Ohio University Press, 1983.

Kingsley, Charles, *Hypatia: Or New Foes with an Old Face*. 1853; rpt. New York: Hurst, 1910.

Kovalévsky, Sonya, *Her Recollections of Childhood*, trans. Isabel F. Hapgood. New York: Century, 1895.

Kovalévsky, Sonya, *Vera Barantzova*. London: Ward & Downey, 1895.

Kramer, Edna E., *The Nature and Growth of Modern Mathematics*. New York: Hawthorn, 1970.

Lancaster, C.S., 'Women, Horticulture, and Society in Sub-Saharan Africa', *American Anthropologist*, 78 (1976), 539–64.

Lancaster, Jane Beckman, *Primate Behavior and the Emergence of Human Culture*. New York: Holt, Rhinehart & Winston, 1975.

Lee, Elizabeth, 'Jane Marcet', *DNB* (1917).

Leffler, Anna Carlotta, '*Biography* of Sonya Kovalévsky', in *Her Recollections of Childhood*, trans. A.M. Clive Bayley. New York: Century, 1895.

Leibniz, Gottfried Wilhelm, 'The Controversy Between Leibniz and Clarke, 1715-16', in *Philosophical Papers and Letters*, trans. and ed. Leroy E. Loemker, 2nd edn. Dordrecht: D. Reidel, 1970, pp. 675-721.

Lerner, Gerda, 'Placing Women in History: A 1975 Perspective', in *Liberating Women's History: Theoretical and Critical Essays*, ed. Berenice A. Carroll. Urbana: University of Illinois Press, 1976.

Lesko, Barbara S., *The Remarkable Women of Ancient Egypt*. Berkeley: B.C. Scribe, 1978.

Levey, Martin, 'Babylonian Chemistry: A Study of Arabic and Second Millenium B.C. Perfumery', *Osiris*, 12 (1956), 376-89.

Levey, Martin, *Chemistry and Chemical Technology in Ancient Mesopotamia*. Amsterdam: Elsevier, 1959.

Lewis, W.S. and Smith, Warren Hunting, (eds.), *Horace Walpole's Correspondence with Madame du Deffand*. New Haven: Yale University Press, 1939; Oxford: Oxford University Press, 1940, Vol. VI.

Leybourn, Thomas, *The Mathematical Questions Proposed in the Ladies' Diary, and their Original Answers, together with some New Solutions ...* 1704 to 1816, 4 vols. London: Mawman, 1817.

Lindsay, Jack, *The Origins of Alchemy in Graeco-Roman Egypt*. London: Frederick Muller; New York: Barnes & Noble, 1970.

Lonsdale, Kathleen, 'Women in Science: Reminiscences and Reflections', *Impact of Science on Society*, 20 (1970), 45-59.

Loomis, Metta May, 'The Contributions Which Women Have Made to Medical Literature', *New York Medical Journal*, 100 (1914), 522-4.

Lovejoy, Arthur O., *The Great Chain of Being: A Study of the History of an Idea*. Oxford: Oxford University Press, 1933; rpt. Cambridge, Mass., Harvard University Press, 1966.

Lovelace, Ada Augusta (trans.) ' "Sketch of the Analytical Engine Invented by Charles Babbage" by L.F. Menabrea with Notes upon the Memoir by the Translator', in *Charles Babbage and His Calculating Engines*, ed. Philip Morrison and Emily Morrison. New York: Dover; London: Constable, 1961, 225-97.

Lubbock, Constance A. (ed.), *The Herschel Chronicle: The Life-Story of William Herschel and His Sister Caroline Herschel*. Cambridge: Cambridge University Press; New York: Macmillan, 1933.

Lyell, Charles, *Life: Letters and Journals*, 2 vols., ed. Mrs Lyell. London: John Murray, 1881.

Mahl, Mary R. and Koon, Helen (eds.), *The Female Spectator: English Women Writers before 1800*. Bloomington: Indiana University Press, 1977.

Manly, John M. and Rickert, Edith, *The Text of the Canterbury Tales*, Vol. III. Cambridge: Cambridge University Press; Chicago: University of Chicago Press, 1940.

[Marcet, Jane], *Conversations on Chemistry; in which the Elements of that Science are Familiarly Explained and Illustrated by Experiments*, revised by Thomas Cooper from the 5th London edn. Philadelphia: M. Carey & Sons, 1818.

[Marcet, Jane], *Conversations on Natural Philosophy in which the Elements of that Science are Familiarly Explained*, ed. Thomas P. Jones. Philadelphia: Grigg & Elliot, 1836.

[Marcet, Jane], *Conversations on Botany*, 9th edn. London: Longman, Orme, Brown, Green & Longmans, 1840.

[Marcet, Jane], *Conversations on Natural Philosophy in which the Elements of that Science are Familiarly Explained, and adapted to the Comprehension of Young Pupils*, ed. J.L. Blake. Boston: Gould, Kendall & Lincoln, 1847.

Marks, Geoffrey and Beatty, William K., *Women in White: Their Roles as Doctors through the Ages*. New York: Scribner's, 1972.

Marrou, H.I., 'Synesius of Cyrene and Alexandrian Neoplatonism', in *The Conflict between Paganism and Christianity in the Fourth Century*, ed. Arnaldo Momigliano. London: Oxford University Press, 1963, pp. 126–50.

Martin, Benjamin, *The Young Gentleman and Lady's Philosophy*, 2nd ed., 2 vols. London: W. Owen, 1772.

Martin, M. Kay and Voorhies, Barbara, *Female of the Species*. New York: Columbia University Press, 1975.

Mason, Otis T., *Woman's Share in Primitive Culture*. London, 1895; rpt. New York: Appleton, 1924.

Mason, Stephen F., *A History of the Sciences*, rev. edn. New York: Collier, 1962.

Mayne, Ethel Colburn, *The Life and Letters of Anne Isabella, Lady Noel Byron*. New York: Scribner's, 1929.

McCabe, Joseph, 'Hypatia', *Critic*, 43 (1903), 267–72.

McLeod, Enid, *The Order of the Rose: The Life and Ideas of Christine de Pizan*. London: Chatto & Windus; Totowa, N.J.: Rowman & Littlefield, 1976.

McMaster, Gilbert, 'The First Woman Practitioner of Midwifery and the Care of Infants in Athens, 300 BC.', *American Medicine*, 18 (1912), 202–5.

'A Medico-Literary Causerie: The Evolution of the Medical Woman', *Practitioner*, NS 3 (1896), 288–92, 407–12.

Merchant, Carolyn, *The Death of Nature: Women, Ecology, and the Scientific Revolution*. San Francisco: Harper & Row, 1980; London: Wildwood, 1982.

Meyer, Gerald Dennis, *The Scientific Lady in England 1650–1760: An Account of her Rise, with emphasis on the Major Roles of the Telescope and Microscope*. Berkeley: University of California Press, 1955.

Mill, John Stuart, *The Subjection of Women*. 1869; rpt. London: Dent, 1965.

Miller, James, *Humours of Oxford*, 2nd edn. London: J. Watts, 1730.

Mintz, Samuel I., 'The Duchess of Newcastle's Visit to the Royal Society', *Journal of English and Germanic Philology*, 51 (1952), 168-76.

Mitchell, Maria, 'Maria Somerville', *The Atlantic Monthly*, 5 (1860), 568-71.

Molière, Jean-Baptiste, *The Learned Ladies*, trans. Richard Wilbur. New York: Harcourt, Brace & Jovanovich, 1978.

Montagu, Lady Mary Wortley, *The Letters and Works*, ed. Lord Wharncliffe and W. Moy Thomas, 3rd edn., 2 vols. 1861; rpt. London: George Bell, 1886 (I), 1908 (II).

Moore, Doris Langley, *Ada Countess of Lovelace: Byron's Legitimate Daughter*. London: John Murray, New York: Harper & Row, 1977.

Morrell, Jack and Thackray, Arnold, *Gentlemen of Science: Early Years of the British Association for the Advancement of Science*. Oxford: Clarendon, 1981.

Moseley, Maboth, *Irascible Genius: The Life of Charles Babbage*. London, 1964; rpt. Chicago: Henry Regnery, 1970.

Mozans, H.J. [John Augustine Zahm], *Woman in Science*. 1913; rpt. Cambridge, Mass.: MIT Press, 1974.

Münster, L., 'Women Doctors in Mediaeval Italy', *Ciba Symposium* 10 (1962), 136-40.

Needham, Joseph, *Science and Civilization in China*, 5 vols. Cambridge: Cambridge University Press, 1954-80.

Needham, Joseph, *A History of Embryology*. Cambridge: Cambridge University Press; New York: Abelard-Schuman, 1959.

Neugebauer, O., 'The Early History of the Astrolabe', *Isis*, 40 (1949), 240-56.

Nicolson, Marjorie Hope (ed.), *Conway Letters: The Correspondence of Anne, Viscountess of Conway, Henry More, and their Friends: 1642-1684*. Oxford: Oxford University Press; New Haven: Yale University Press, 1930.

North, Marianne, *Recollections of a Happy Life*. 2 vols., ed. Catherine Symonds. London: Macmillan, 1892.

Obit. of Sir Charles Lyell, *Nature*, 11 (1875), 341-2.

O'Faolain, Julia and Martines, Lauro (eds.), *Not in God's Image: Women in History from the Greeks to the Victorians*. New York: Harper & Row, 1973; London: Virago, 1979.

Ogilvie, Marilyn Bailey, 'Caroline Herschel's Contributions to Astronomy', *Annals of Science*, 32 (1975), 149-61.

[Olney, Mary Allen], *The Private Life of Galileo: Compiled Principally From his Correspondence and that of his eldest daughter, Sister Maria Celeste*. Boston: Nichols & Noyes, 1870.

Ormerod, Eleanor, *Autobiography and Correspondence*, ed. Robert Wallace. London: John Murray, 1904.

Osen, Lynn M., *Women in Mathematics*. Cambridge, Mass.: MIT Press, 1974.

Owen, Richard, *The Life of Richard Owen by his Grandson*, 2 vols. London:

John Murray, 1894.

Packard, Francis R., History of the School of Salernum. New York: Paul B. Hoeber, 1922.

Pagel, Walter, 'Hildegard of Bingen', in Dictionary of Scientific Biography, ed. Charles C. Gillespie. New York: Scribner, 1970; Vol. VI, pp. 396-8.

Parish, H.J., A History of Immunization. Edinburgh: E. & S. Livingston, 1965.

Parsons, Edward Alexander, The Alexandrian Library: Glory of the Hellenic World: Its Rise, Antiquities, and Destructions. Amsterdam: Elsevier, 1952.

Partington, James R., A History of Chemistry, vol. I, pt. I, vol. III. London: Macmillan, 1970, 1962.

Parton, James, Life of Voltaire. London: Sampson Low, Marston, Searle & Rivington, 1881, vol. I.

Patterson, Elizabeth C., 'Mary Somerville', British Journal for the History of Science, 4 (1969), 311-39.

Patterson, Elizabeth C., 'The Case of Mary Somerville: An Aspect of Nineteenth-Century Science', Proceedings of the American Philosophical Society, 118 (1974), 269-75.

Pepys, Samuel, The Diaries, ed. Henry B. Wheatley. New York: The Collegiate Society, 1905, Vols. XII and XIV.

Perl, Teri, Math Equals: Biographies of Women Mathematicians + Related Activities. Menlo Park, Ca: Addison-Wesley, 1978.

Perl, Teri, 'The Ladies' Diary or Woman's Almanack, 1704-1841', Historia Mathematica, 6 (1979), 36-53.

Perry, Henry ten Eyck, The First Duchess of Newcastle and Her Husband as Figures in Literary History, Harvard Studies in English, Vol IV. 1918; rpt. New York: Johnson Reprint, 1968.

Pfeiffer, Ida, A Lady's Second Journey Round the World: From London to the Cape of Good Hope, Borneo, Java, Sumatra, Celebes, Ceram, the Moluccas, etc., California, Panama, Peru, Ecuador, and the United States. New York: Harper, 1856.

Pfeiffer, Ida, A Woman's Journey Round the World: From Vienna to Brazil, Chile, Tahiti, China, Hindostan, Persia and Asia Minor, 6th edn. London: Ward Lock, 1856.

Pfeiffer, John E., The Emergence of Man. New York: Harper & Row, 1969.

Pierce, Elizabeth, 'Caroline Herschel: Tale of a Comet', Ms., January 1974, pp. 16-17.

Plato, Symposium, trans. Walter Hamilton, Harmondsworth: Penguin, 1951; trans. Benjamin Jowett, 2nd edn. Indianapolis: Bobbs-Merrill, 1956.

Pliny, Natural History, trans. W.H.S. Jones, vols. 6-8. London: Heinemann; Cambridge, Mass: Harvard University Press, 1951-63.

Plutarch, 'Pompey', in Lives of Illustrious Men, vol. 3, trans. Dryden and Clough. Philadelphia: Winston, 1900.

Plutarch, 'Pericles', in Twelve Lives, trans. John Dryden. Cleveland: Fine Editions, 1950.

Polwhele, Richard, *The Unsex'd Females: A Poem*. London, 1798; rpt. New York: Garland, 1974.

Pomeroy, Sarah B., *Goddesses, Whores, Wives, and Slaves: Women in Classical Antiquity*. New York: Schocken, 1975; London: Robert Hale, 1976.

Power, Eileen, 'Some Women Practitioners of Medicine in the Middle Ages', *Proceedings of the Royal Society of Medicine*, 15 (1921); Section of the History of Medicine, pp. 20–3..

Price, Derek J., 'Precision Instruments to 1500', in *From the Renaissance to the Industrial Revolution c. 1500–c. 1750*. Vol. III of *A History of Technology*, ed. Charles Singer et al. Oxford: Clarendon, 1957, pp. 582–619.

Read, John, *Humour and Humanism in Chemistry*. London: G. Bell, 1947.

Reid, Robert, *Microbes and Men*. London: BBC Publications, 1974; New York: Saturday Review Press, 1975.

Reiter, Rayna A. (ed.), *Toward an Anthropology of Women*. New York: Monthly Review, 1975.

de Renzi, Salvatore, *Collectio Salernitana*, 5 vols. Naples: 1852–59.

Reynolds, Myra, *The Learned Lady in England: 1650–1760*. Boston: Houghton Mifflin, 1920.

Ricci, James V. (trans. and annot.), *Aetios of Amida: The Gynaecology and Obstetrics of the VIth Century, A.D.* Philadelphia: Blakiston, 1950.

Richardson, Robert S., *The Star Lovers*. New York: Macmillan, 1967.

Richeson, A.W., 'Mary Somerville', *Scripta Mathematica*, 8 (1941), 5–13.

Rist, J.M., 'Hypatia', *Phoenix*, 19 (1965), 214–25.

Rizzo, P.V., 'Early Daughters of Urania', *Sky & Telescope*, 14 (1954), 7–10.

Robb, Hunter, 'Remarks on the Writings of Louyse Bourgeois', *Johns Hopkins Hospital Bulletin*, 4 (1893), 75–81.

Robb, Hunter, 'The Works of Justine Siegemundin, the Midwife,' *Johns Hopkins Hospital Bulletin*, 5 (1894), 4–13.

Rudolf, Emanuel D., 'How it Developed that Botany Was the Science Thought Most Suitable for Victorian Young Ladies', *Children's Literature*, 2 (1973), 92–7.

Russell, M.P., 'James Barry – 1792 (?) –1865, Inspector-General of Army Hospitals', *Edinburgh Medical Journal*, 50 (1943), 558–67.

Sanderson, Marie, 'Mary Somerville: Her Work in Physical Geography', *The Geographical Review*, 64 (1974), 410–20; rpt. in *Woman's Role in Changing the Face of the Earth: Selected Readings for a Course*. ed. Marie Hartman. 1976, pp. 56–61.

Sarton, George, *Introduction to the History of Science*, 3 vols. London: Baillière, Tindall & Cox; Baltimore: Williams & Wilkins, 1927–48.

Scott, Sir Walter, *Peveril of the Peak*, rev. edn. Philadelphia: Porter & Coates [n.d], Vol. II.

Sewter, E.R.A. (trans.), *The Chronographia of Michael Psellus*. New Haven: Yale University Press, 1953.

Shapiro, Max S. and Hendricks, Rhoda A. (eds.), *Mythologies of the World: A*

Concise Enclycopedia. Garden City: Doubleday, 1979.

Sharistanian, Janet et al., 'The (Dr Aletta H. Jacobs) Gerritsen Collection, the University of Kansas', Feminist Studies, 3, Nos. 3/4 (1976), 200–6.

Sidgwick, J.B., William Herschel: Explorer of the Heavens. London: Faber & Faber, 1953.

Singer, Charles, From Magic to Science: Essays on the Scientific Twilight. 1928; rpt. New York: Dover, 1958.

Singer, Charles, 'The Scientific Views and Visions of Saint Hildegard (1098–1180)' in Studies in the History and Method of Science, ed. Charles Singer, 2nd edn. London: William Dawson, 1955; Vol. I, pp. 1–55.

Singer, Charles and Singer, Dorothea, 'The Origin of the Medical School of Salerno: The First European University. An Attempted Reconstruction', in Essays on the History of Medicine Presented to Karl Sudhoff, ed. Charles Singer and Henry E. Sigerist. London: Oxford University Press, 1924, pp. 121–38.

Smith, Edgar Fahs, Old Chemistries. New York: McGraw Hill, 1927.

Socrates Scholasticus, 'The Murder of Hypatia', in A Treasury of Early Christianity, ed. Anne Fremantle. New York: Viking, 1953, pp. 379–80.

Somerville, Mary, Mechanism of the Heavens. London: John Murray, 1831.

Somerville, Mary, Mechanism of the Heavens, revd., The Athenaeum, 21 January 1832 (#221), pp. 43–4.

Somerville, Mary, On the Connexion of the Physical Sciences, London: John Murray, 1834.

Somerville, Mary, On the Connexion of the Physical Sciences, revd., The Athenaeum, 15 March 1834 (#333), pp. 202–3

Somerville, Mary, 'Astronomy - The Comet'. Quarterly Review, 55 (1835), 195–233.

Somerville, Mary, On Molecular and Microscopic Science, 2 vols. London: John Murray, 1869.

Somerville, Mary, On Molecular and Microscopic Science, revd., The Athenaeum, 6 February 1869 (#2154), pp. 202–3.

Somerville, Mary, Personal Recollections, From Early Life to Old Age: With Selections from her Correspondence, ed. Martha Somerville. London: John Murray, 1873.

Somerville, Mary, Personal Recollections, revd., Nature, 9 (1874), 417–18.

Somerville, Mary, The Connexion of the Physical Sciences. 10th edn., ed. Arabella B. Buckley. London: John Murray, 1877.

Soranus, Gynaecology, trans. Owsei Tempkin. Oxford: Oxford University Press; Baltimore: Johns Hopkins Press, 1956.

South, James, 'An Address Delivered at the Annual General Meeting of the Astronomical Society of London, on February 8, 1828, on Presenting the Honorary Medal to Miss Caroline Herschel', Memoirs of the Astronomical Society of London, 3 (1829), 409–12.

Spender, Dale. Women of Ideas and What Men Have Done to Them: From

Aphra Behn to Adrienne Rich. London: Routledge & Kegan Paul, 1982.

Steele, Francesca Maria, *The Life and Visions of St Hildegarde*. London: Heath, Cranton & Ousely, 1914.

Stillman, Beatrice, 'Sófya Kovalévskaya: Growing up in the Sixties', *Russian Literature Triquarterly*, 9 (1974), 276–302.

Stillman, Beatrice, 'Introduction' to *A Russian Childhood* by Sófya Kovalévskaya, ed. and trans. Beatrice Stillman. New York: Springer-Verlag, 1978.

Stillman, John Maxson, *The Story of Alchemy and Early Chemistry*. 1924; rpt. New York: Dover, 1960.

Stuard, Susan Mosher, 'Dame Trot', *Signs*, 1 (1975), 537–42.

Sudhoff, Karl, 'Salerno: A Mediaeval Health Resort and Medical School on the Tyrrhenian Sea', trans. John C. Hemmeter and Fielding H. Garrison, in *Essays on the History of Medicine*, ed. Fielding H. Garrison. New York: Medical Life Press, 1926, pp. 227–47.

Synesius of Cyrene, *The Letters*, trans. Augustine FitzGerald. London: Oxford University Press, 1926.

Tanner, Nancy and Adriene Zihlman, 'Women in Evolution: Part I. Innovation and Selection in Human Origins', *Signs*, 1 (1976), 585–608.

Taton, René (ed.), *Ancient and Medieval Science: From the Beginnings to 1450*. Vol. I of *History of Science*, trans. A.J. Pomerans. New York: Basic Books, 1963; London: Thames & Hudson, 1964.

Taylor, F. Sherwood, 'A Survey of Greek Alchemy', *Journal of Hellenic Studies*, 50 (1930), 109–39.

Taylor, F. Sherwood, 'The Evolution of the Still', *Annals of Science*, 5 (1945), 185–202.

Taylor, F. Sherwood, *The Alchemists: Founders of Modern Chemistry*. New York: Schuman, 1949; London: Heinemann, 1952.

Taylor, Henry Osborn, *The Mediaeval Mind: A History of the Development of Thought and Emotion in the Middle Ages*, Vol. I. London: Macmillan, 1911.

Tee, Garry J., 'Sof'ya Vasil'yevna Kovalévskaya', *Mathematical Chronicle*, 5 (1977), 113–39.

Thorndike, Lynn, *A History of Magic and Experimental Science*, Vols. 1–4. New York: Columbia University Press, 1923–34.

Toth, Bruce and Toth, Emily, 'Mary Who?', *Johns Hopkins Magazine*, January 1978, pp. 25–9.

Trotula of Salerno, *The Diseases of Women*, trans. Elizabeth Mason-Hohl. Los Angeles: Ward Ritchie, 1940.

Valléry-Radot, René, *The Life of Pasteur*, trans. Mrs R. L. Devonshire. Garden City: Doubleday, 1926.

Wade, Ira O., *Voltaire and Madame du Châtelet: An Essay on the Intellectual Activity at Cirey*. Oxford: Oxford University Press; Princeton, N.J.: Princeton University Press, 1941.

Wade, Ira O., *Studies on Voltaire: With some Unpublished Papers of Mme. du Châtelet*, Princeton, N.J.: Princeton University Press, 1947.

Wade, Ira. O., *The Intellectual Development of Voltaire*, Princeton, N.J.: Princeton University Press, 1969.

Wakefield, Priscilla, *An Introduction to Botany, in a Series of Familiar Letters, with Illustrative Engravings*, 3rd Amer. edn. Philadelphia: Solomon W. Conrad, 1818.

Wallis, Ruth and Wallis, Peter,' Female Philomaths', *Historia Mathematica*, 7 (1980), 57–64.

Walters, Robert L., 'Chemistry at Cirey', *Studies on Voltaire and the Eighteenth Century*, 58 (1967), 1807–27.

Ward, Adolphus William, *The Electress Sophia and the Hanoverian Succession*, 2nd edn. London: Longmans, Green & Co., 1909.

Washburn, S.L. and Lancaster, C.S., 'The Evolution of Hunting', in *Man the Hunter*, ed. Richard B. Lee and Irven DeVore. Chicago: Aldine, 1968, pp. 293–303.

Weiser, Marjorie P.K. and Arbeiter, Jean S., *Womanlist*. New York: Atheneum, 1981.

Welt, Ida, 'The Jewish Woman in Science', *Hebrew Standard*, 50 (1907), 4.

Whewell, William, 'On the Connexion of the Physical Sciences. By Mrs Somerville', *Quarterly Review*, 51 (1834), 54–68.

Wilson, Dorothy Clarke, *Lone Woman: The Story of Elizabeth Blackwell, First Woman Doctor*. London: Hodder & Stoghton; Boston: Little, Brown, 1970.

Woolf, Virginia, 'The Duchess of Newcastle', in *The Common Reader*. London: Hogarth Press, 1925, pp. 98–109.

Wystrach, V.P., 'Anna Blackburne (1726–1793) – a Neglected Patroness of Natural History', *Journal of the Society for the Bibliography of Natural History*, 8 (1977), 148–68.

Young, Arthur, *Travels in France and Italy During the years 1787, 1788 and 1789*. 1917; rpt. London: J.M. Dent, 1927.

Index